I THINK
I'M OUTTA HERE

•••••••••••••••

CARROLL O'CONNOR

I Think I'm Outta Here

·············

A Memoir of All My Families

POCKET BOOKS

New York   London   Toronto   Sydney   Tokyo   Singapore

POCKET BOOKS, a division of Simon & Schuster Inc.
1230 Avenue of the Americas, New York, NY 10020

ISBN: 0-671-01758-6

First Pocket Books hardcover printing March 1998

10   9   8   7   6   5   4   3   2   1

To Nancy

I THINK
I'M OUTTA HERE

·············

PROLOGUE

· · · · · · ·

San Francisco, October 1, 1997

Looking out of my window in the Clift Hotel in San Francisco, I made up my mind about the meaning of the title of this memoir. What it meant when I first thought of it was nothing in particular, merely an interim working title, and I chose it knowing that for anyone of seventy-three "out of here" would sooner or later have to mean something. I would cull out a meaning in due course. And now I had it: it meant out of the theatre. And I refer not to any particular old barracks with seats inside and a sign outside that spells theater with "er" at the end,[1] but to the art and professional activity known as theatre with "re" at the end.

My play *A Certain Labor Day* had opened in San Francisco a week before, and the man the *San Francisco Chronicle* pays to kill

---

[1] Both spellings being in loose uses, let's hold them to useful uses.

1

CARROLL O'CONNOR

new plays killed it: he hated it—hated the sets, the direction, the acting, the plot, in brief, the very thought of it. The plot, I should explain, was not what he was told it was going to be. In the arts section of his own paper, in a cover article with a full-page photo of me, he had read a week before opening that the play was autobiographical, with emphasis on my son's drug problem. The play, about an old New York labor union official, had nothing to do with me or my son. How to explain that misleading article? I don't know. Evidently the *Chronicle* is as unreliable in its feature writers as it is in its reviewers. The reviewer was unable to recover from his confusion, wrote that the play was not what it was supposed to be, and panned it. The people he sways, evidently most of his readers, declined to buy tickets and the play died.

What also died was my interest in theatre. I hope and trust that no one will greatly care, because my purpose in reporting the death is not to cause widespread mourning, but just to acknowledge my own folly in trying to make a mark in theatre, which I think belongs in a memoir, and to say that now at last the folly is exorcised. I think I'm out of here. I will no longer try to remain in Theatre Row, that wonderfully charming street where lunatics behind trees, unrestrained, protected from reprisal, throw bricks. I have become sweatingly brick-shy. Is this paranoia? Yes, classic paranoia, but it comforts me. I leave the wonderfully charming Theatre Row to the lucky ones who have prevailed, and are somehow evading, surviving and quietly abiding the brick shower.

My surrender was almost pleasant at the Theater on the Square on Post Street just off Union Square. Seven hundred seats and a stage do not a theater make, and I felt great relief in hurrying away from this structural imposter. A former Elks hall, positioned in the middle of a small hotel and reached by stairs and elevators to the second floor, it was conceived without regard to the science of acoustics, for what need had carousing

2

Elks of modulated sound? Subsequent tenants, theater managers (though merely space sellers of the SDN type),[2] had left it as it was, a speech trap. The space is not air-conditioned and therefore all but airless, unless lobby windows are opened to wailing sirens and clarion car horns. In unseasonably warm weather, which it was our bad luck to encounter, the space is unbearably muggy and close. Outside the theater there is no marquee, merely a narrow cloth banner dangling vertically and invisibly over the sidewalk, and on the sidewalk itself is a small sandwich board announcing play and players. This place, however, is no place for play and players. Only one fool, I myself, was responsible for bringing them to this venue at this humid time of year— to this city wherein lurks the worst bushwhacker of art, posturing as a critic, that ever a fiendish editor foisted upon a heedless town.

The radio stations and a couple of suburban papers gave us rave notices, but the *Chronicle* thug beat me bowlegged. He arrogantly reported as fact that the standing, cheering ovation at the final curtain was merely an appreciation of the old TV favorite Carroll O'Connor, not of his current work. The man, failing to follow the action of the play, the characters and their story, described it all like someone who had seen it through a curtain of beads. The review bewildered our small audiences, who came in spite of it; and it stunned my actors, who referred to it as a crazed attack.[3] Still, a call to the box office at this hour of three P.M. ascertained that we would have forty-six playgoers in the seats at eight P.M. that night. I looked out at the city from a very expensive hotel suite and saw not the legendary bay but urban concrete—the backs and sides of buildings. I knew I was going to leave my money, but not my heart, in San Francisco.

Luck rules life, high life or low life, easy or hard. I decided that

---

[2]Shrug and Do Nothing.
[3]They began, on their own, to give out handbills in Union Square and neighboring hotels.

when one is lucky at something, as I have been at acting, one ought not turn and intrude into strange dominions. Given talent and ability or even genius, luck is of the essence, and one ought not expect to have it in running a small shuttle airline, or a restaurant, or a couple of stage productions.[4] Indeed the lucky actor ought not go into a business of any sort (though he had best assist a businesslike wife); he should content himself with acting for someone else, with being some gross impresario's fool. I go further and advise any man in any walk of life that if good luck blesses his endeavor, he should not try to transfer it; it does not travel. What then accounts for the many men who have moved swiftly from one great capitalistic success to a variety of others? Do not presume genius: these fellows did not brilliantly extend their luck. They got their extras because other people's luck reached out and drew them blindly in. Thus, willy-nilly, a man's own luck may be doubled and redoubled. He may be only a simple fellow, a clown perhaps, yet unconsciously he may be taken in hand, bloated to billionaire, success icon, and *Time* cover image—allowed briefly to enjoy the gaze of the world, and to be eclipsed by another ersatz eminence.

Returning to the death of my theatrical interest in theatre, I myself don't mourn it because it was taking up a lot of room in my head and yielding no return. Age shrinks ponder-space, and I have to reserve what's left for things of clamoring importance. Time presses. A promised novel[5] is in the computer, and so is this memoir, in which, on other pages, I will further consider the piteous fate of drama in today's careless press. My howl over the demented assault in San Francisco might have been left for inclusion in this later segment, but I said to myself *Put it up front. It's a vengeful and ignoble outburst and reveals what you're really like,*

---

[4]Follies of mine.
[5]Promised before my vow to lie low. Do I plunge into another folly in spite of myself? We'll see.

you queer memoirist—a fellow who, disregarding one enviable tri-
umph, aspires to others, and lashes out at whoever refuses to praise
him. Better expose yourself at the start, reveal that your triumphant self
stands on feet of clay; readers are going to glean it anyway, they always
do.

Thus exposed, I feel I can begin, relying on sympathy and
understanding, and trusting that in my misshapen mental condition I am not entirely alone.

1

·······

 ome time during the fifties I read an actor's autobiography,
Errol Flynn's, and loved it; it was full of fun, an unblushing
confession of marvelous outrages, and I envied it because it was
the kind of story I wasn't able to write about myself. What could I
tell that would be even half so entertaining? What, for instance,
about sex and love, topics large in the Flynn book and requisite
to success in all biographies of no consequence. Boy and man I
had been the typical American innocent of the thirties and
forties (an innocence annihilated by the fifties), suffering a few
semi-arid attachments and the one long wet blundering affair. I
could reveal nothing that would nowadays excite more than a
shrug. I married once—so did my wife—in 1951, and the
marriage was still happy and promising, untroubled by supple-
mental relationships or disagreeable surprises. I often wondered
whether Nancy and I did not strike some of our mobile friends as
quietly repressed. My life had not been dull, but it was a chain of
events that did not glitter even for me. I was thinking about all
this because of Jimmy Cagney. Jimmy's was the next actor's
autobiography I read, and it differed from Flynn's as a glow in

the hearth from a fire in the rafters. Jimmy wrote about a life that was hard and professionally painful, yet not without fun. I thought that if I could arrive somewhere in that neighborhood I might do a book some time; not now, later, probably when I retired. One day over lunch—this was in 1977—Jimmy told me that I ought to start a book, and noting my reluctance he told me that he himself had never wished to write one. He looked wistfully at his collection of Charles Russell sculptures (which I love even more than the miniatures of Donatello), and said "I know I'm unimportant, but a couple of hacks who think anything is important if it turns up a buck were going to write about me, so in self-defense I had to do it myself." He was a keenly intelligent man who had made a very modest estimate of the actor's contribution to life and art.

By the most improbable chance, on the very next morning my mail included a letter from a man who wanted to write my life story. I knew the man slightly; he was a Hollywood writer, a distinction not meant to be geographical but which I leave to a later consideration, and he formally apprised me, in a kind of raw puerile English, of his intention to write his book whether I approved or not. I couldn't remember when anything bothered me more. Writers of unauthorized biographies have the decency of burglars, and here was a burglar coming straight at me with a brazen warning that if I did not let him in through the door he would break in wherever he could. A prospective victim of burglary should really be entitled to legal protection, but your life story, if you are well known, is lawfully subject to seizure, distortion, and sale by any browsing hack who finds himself without provender in television. You can't protect yourself from him. You may bring suit against him only after he has robbed and assaulted you, and then the law will want to be shown your damages, the proof in cash terms, or any other terms, of the harm done you—not an easy thing to show.

I got in touch with a publisher right away and made a writing deal for myself, and then placed an ad in *The Hollywood Reporter* and in *Variety*, the two show business trade papers. The ad reprinted became a news story in *The Los Angeles Times, The New York Times* and a number of other widely read papers.

Carroll O'Connor Fights With a Biographer
by Aljean Harmetz
Special to the New York Times

Los Angeles—The letter appeared as a full-page advertisement in the Hollywood trade papers on Feb. 24.

"From Carroll O'Connor to His Friends and Colleagues of The Bizness, 1951–1977 in Dublin, London, Paris, Rome, New York and Mostly Hollywood;

"Dollings All,

A furtive fellow may come among you hunting bits of information for a biography of me. I do not approve. I have seen his other unauthorized biographies and they are wretched; they have provoked some unwilling subjects, his father included, to furious legal reprisal.

"He does not invite a collaboration—an 'as-told-to' joint authorship—because that would require sharing the proceeds from the book, and the mind of the poacher runneth not to the even split. He knows I would not work with him anyway.

"If he approaches you, show him your backs, my loves! Show him not, I beg you, the way to my property! The still-forming vines of my life are hardly burgeoning, God knows. What fruit may come, let me with mine own hand offer when I judge it worthy, but expose not my pale buds to the ignorant teeth of the fox.

"Or to put it succinctly, I am writing my own book, so tell the bum nothing.

"Your imperiled pal, Carroll." . . .

The writer in question—Arthur Marx, son of Groucho Marx—quotes George Bernard Shaw in rebuttal. "Shaw

9

said, 'Nobody is good enough or bad enough to tell the truth about himself.' That's why I won't write an as-told-to book. O'Connor is a public figure, and I'm a legitimate writer. He may think my books are wretched, but they've been very well reviewed. Even The New York Times said 'Life With Groucho' was great."

Mr. O'Connor's letter "hasn't deterred me at all. It's made me more determined," says Mr. Marx, who has also written "television scripts, four Bob Hope movies and a play, 'The Impossible Years,' which ran for two years on Broadway."

Although Mr. Marx started out by "admiring and respecting O'Connor" and still insists he has "no hard feelings," he thinks the whole incident "makes O'Connor look like an ass. A fellow who claims to be liberal should not be trying censorship."

To Mr. O'Connor, the question is not censorship but privacy. He stopped giving interviews even to legitimate publications several years ago "because The National Inquirer distorted them and then republished them." He winces even now at the memory of a "maudlin, tasteless, revolting piece of writing they served up on the adoption of my son."

He questions whether the false stories, doctored photographs and pictures of homosexuals and heterosexuals fornicating in certain publications deserve protection. "I don't think the action of a printing press on newsprint makes something The Press. There is a violence to personal freedom these people do on a daily basis."

Both Mr. Marx and Mr. O'Connor have, at least fleetingly, thought of suing the other. "There are lies in his ad," says Mr. Marx. "I've never been sued. He said I had."

"There are laws in New York and California," says Mr. O'Connor, "giving you remedy if people use your name or image to hawk a product. My lawyers don't think anyone has tried to use those laws quite this way."

In the meantime, both men are working on their Carroll O'Connor books. Mr. Marx will neither confirm nor deny that W. W. Norton—which published his last book, on Samuel Goldwyn—is his publisher. And Mr. O'Connor has started writing his autobiography—without outside help—for Simon & Schuster.

Note that my trade ad mentioned no name but my own. How a man of common sense could come bounding onto the public stage, eager to fit his foot to the ugly shoe I had fashioned and then stick the ensemble into his mouth, is hard to imagine. But then everything nowadays is hard to imagine.

"Above all, keep it light!"

That was my wife's warning on hearing that I was going to write an autobiography. I had just hung up the phone in the bedroom after agreeing to the deal.

"You're not at your best" Nancy told me, "when you get too serious. You've been too serious on a couple of those talk shows. You disappoint people; they expect you to be entertaining."

"I know" I said, leaving the bedroom.

"Just keep it light!" she trilled.

"I'm not getting the book out today" I called back.

"Play down the politics and the anger. People much prefer to know about all the fun you've had." I was on the stairs. Her words were at my heels. "But of course when it comes to my advice you seldom listen!"

I pressed an intercom button near the kitchen door and said "I always listen. I seldom reply."

Silence. She was postponing her response. She was aware that corroded wires in the kitchen speaker made everybody sound ridiculous. She did not want to sound ridiculous.

I got the car out and headed for CBS, a twenty-minute drive

from Brentwood by way of Sunset Boulevard through Beverly Hills, and then along Beverly Boulevard to the corner of Fairfax Avenue. Because the day was Monday, I was driving a Rolls-Royce. And of course I must explain this odd offering of intelligence.

I was not due till eleven on Mondays. I wanted to pass the Bel Air Gate as a certain television executive, who was not due till eleven on any day, was himself driving out onto Sunset. I hoped my arrival at the gate would be timely. This executive had roared at my agent, who was demanding a revision of my contract, "Don't tell me the son-of-a-bitch needs more money. I see him driving to work every day in a goddam Rolls-Royce!" That was not so. He may have seen me in the car once. But I was thereafter determined that he should see me in it a lot.

Luck ran in my favor that very morning. He and I stopped abreast at a red light. His passenger window slid down and he, looking directly at me, taking no notice of the car, called out "Doing anything new?"

I shrugged. "Maybe a book about me."

"Sensational! Who's going to write it for you?"

"Well—," I began.

"Spill it all on tape. Your press agent'll find somebody to pull it together. Say hello home—"

He sped away, and I was amused to note that he was driving a luxurious foreign car that certainly cost him more than mine cost me—because I had acquired the Rolls-Royce at cost. Bill Harrah, the late gentleman gambler, who was also an importer of foreign cars, had offered the car to me at cost. That was in 1972 when I was making a nightclub appearance at Harrah's Hotel-Casino in Reno. I did not need the car, but Bill's generosity, and my own lust for a saving on anything, swept me away. During the next four years, to the morning of my literary decision, the car had traveled fewer miles than Nancy's car usually travels in a year.

The executive's advice sounded frivolous, but it was well

meant. He was a man who got things done and moved on energetically to other things, a man who succeeded not by merit but by force. I admire and envy such men. I am inclined to be dilatory, and if I had not enjoyed extraordinary luck in life and love I might have been living with my mother at that very moment, doing nothing. In evidence of this tendency I offer the fact that six years later my book was not finished, nor even well begun. Still I refused to consider giving the job to another writer. There was no public clamor for my story; it was not commercially promising, and besides, I did not believe that a good writer would be willing to "ghost" for an actor. Why not inch along with it myself, as the sluggish spirit moved me? For all I knew a rogue was still plotting entry somewhere, but at least I had fired a round of shot into the dark and maybe it would prove discouraging.

I suddenly wanted to begin my book. I recall a surge of enthusiasm, but it soon subsided. How was I to begin? Who was I, anyway? Did I know? I asked myself that question until I got tired of it and one day the question was asked of me by a pretty blond woman who, with her friend, a pretty brunette, was looking at me across a luncheon table.

"Do you know who you are?"

I was thinking about a response but the brunette preempted me: she said "Of course he does—he knows exactly who he is." I smiled at her and looked back at the blonde, who shrugged; she would have preferred the answer from me. I was not acquainted with these ladies. They had won me in a raffle. Or rather their winning tickets had entitled them to a lunch with me at my Beverly Hills restaurant. I said to the brunette: "Funny you should think I know exactly who I am. If I knew, I could start writing about it."

"An autobiography!" said the brunette.

The blonde shook her head and said very seriously "You can't tell who you are in an autobiography. Who you are—that's not to write about, it's just for you to know."

"And he knows!" said the brunette. "He knows exactly. I know he knows."

She knew I knew? What did she mean by that? Where did she? . . . What? Who was she? My face is a sphere on which little, least of all apprehension, may hide, and the brunette hastened to put me at ease. "Of course I have no personal knowledge" she said, "only psychic." I relaxed. Nothing psychic ever alarms me.

"Exactly what is a book?" interposed the blonde. She did not wait for the answer I was trying to form. She said "A book is just a bunch of events from when you were born up to whenever. But the past can't tell anybody who you are because the past is not who you are."

I said "Well the past, after all, is your life." Trying to make more of the commonplace, I asked the ladies whether they knew anything about the Great Depression of the thirties. They laughed and said they did not, and how could they? They were born, both of them, during the Second World War, nearer the end of it than the beginning.

Hastily I said "It's obvious of course that you couldn't have lived before the war. I just thought you might have heard or read—"

"I know it was a real poor time" the brunette said in a voice suddenly sad. "Were you a poor kid?"

"No" I assured her, "I was well off, but there was something about that time, growing up in it—"

"Who you are" said the blonde, "has nothing to do with any of that; it's about right now, today, and no other day matters."

"Not even yesterday?"

"Right now only. We are who we are, moment to moment, and every moment's different and things are always different."

"You don't mean all things" I said.

"All things."

"Inanimate things? Objects?"

14

"Objects too. Objects are only what we see them as. So objects change as we change, all the time."

This kind of talk was not unfamiliar. It was, during that decade of the seventies, the kind of talk one often heard at trendy but goofy parties in the Hollywood Hills. The sense of it was that nothing and no one retained form, and there could be no valid standards, no definitions, no qualitative judgments—nothing that people could be fully agreed upon. Whatever you happened to be was wonderful. Whatever you happened to know was more than enough. And if you had been conned into believing this by some self-realization guru you could fancy yourself a savant regardless of the debris or vacuity of your past; you could feel whole and worthy right now.

The brunette said "My friend is right, change is always going on, and people and things get better all the time. I'm an optimist" she added with a giggle. The blonde smiled tolerantly to imply, I think, that her friend's comprehension was characteristically in arrears. "The word 'better' " she softly advised, "is not really useful." And that was about all there was to that, but the point of the story is that the encounter put me off stride. Three brooding analysts could not have unbalanced me, but one blithe young woman could. Why? Because I take women very seriously, far more seriously than most men take them, or than I take most men. If a woman disapproves of what I'm doing, I worry, regardless of whether or not her reason makes complete sense to me. Woman's intuition may be an ancient cliché, but I believe in it, respect it, and sometimes panic in the face of it.

I stopped working on the book. Two years later a letter came from the offices of Simon & Schuster in New York: "Your editor has passed on. I am your new editor. Can I help in any way? When may we expect to see something?" I replied "I don't know. Shall I return the advance?" A brief answer came from New York: "No, just stay in touch." In the summer of 1983, I happened to be in New York and contacted S & S again, not to report that I had any stuff to show them, just to say I had not forgotten the deal. Alas! they had. No one there had ever heard of it.

I had a lot of notes with me, a briefcase full, in a kind of chronological disorder, and I thought I would just start somewhere, anywhere, maybe Dublin—because I got married there, finished college there, went into the theatre there. More than half my life has been in the theatre, one form of it or another, but getting into it obliged me to get myself out of some other things. I am not sure even now that I made the best choice in spite of the exceptional rewards of show business. Choice: that is what I would write about. Choice and of course discovery and the development of points of view. I would doubtless drift far, for better or worse, from both Flynn and Cagney.

I certainly had drifted far from the expectations of Simon & Schuster, who, when they read my first seventy-five trial pages, decided that they had no need of the rest. Incidentally, they had found traces of my deal. Mr. Korda in a letter to my manager, Lionel Larner, explained that the difference between the public perception of me and what I evidently was, was too large to be promotable. I didn't know what that precisely meant, but I couldn't doubt that a man like Korda must have something there, so I put the briefcase aside and forgot about it. A couple of years later a lawyer at Simon & Schuster, a charming young woman, reviewing the moribund deal, had an afterthought, and it was this: I owed them $6,000; it was the first installment of a $25,000 advance. They had bought for $6,000 something they found they didn't like, an irremediable mistake that occurs hourly in the movie business at far greater costs to the buyer. She asked if I intended to give back the money. I laughed. She started laughing. We laughed a lot and said a cordial, almost a fond good-bye. That was the end of the affair.

I soon got my first chance, however, to write something about myself.

In that same year, 1983, and again in 1984, I failed on Broadway. Not because audiences did not like the plays or me, but because the man on the *Times* hated both. He wrote more modishly than the *Chronicle*'s crude fellow, but like the latter he conceived it his duty to run strangers out of town. Of course complaining about reviews from your seat in the rubbish barrel gets you nothing but laughs, and now when I am asked "What happened to you on Broadway?" I merely say "I appeared in two flops." Press agents for those two unlucky shows had asked me for a biographical sketch. I wrote one and they used some of it in the theater program *Playbill* for the play *Brothers* and the play *Home Front.* Here is that sketch for the convenience of the hurried reader, say a talk show host who wants to know something about me but not much.

ABOUT CARROLL O'CONNOR

He has won five Emmy Awards[1] and the Peabody Award for television acting. He attended the University of Montana, but earned his degree in history and English at University College Dublin (UCD), the main branch of Ireland's National University.

While still a UCD undergraduate he began acting professionally in a company formed by the Irish playwright Lennox Robinson. The company played the Edinburgh Festival of Drama in 1951, and later performed on BBC television in London. This was O'Connor's first appearance in the medium that, twenty years afterward, made him known throughout the world.

He joined in 1951 the internationally famous Dublin Gate Theatre Company, and in 1953 another Irish company formed by the actor-manager Cyril Cusack. In 1955

---

[1] Four were for comedy acting. The TV Academy later gave me a fifth Emmy for dramatic acting in *In the Heat of the Night.*

he returned to the University of Montana to obtain an M.A.

O'Connor appeared on the New York stage and in London and Paris in a renowned production of James Joyce's *Ulysses,* adapted and directed by Burgess Meredith. He acted in a number of important television dramas in New York and was invited to Hollywood in 1960 by Warner Brothers. Up to 1971 he acted in twenty-six motion pictures, the best known being *A Fever in the Blood, Lonely Are the Brave, Cleopatra, Hawaii, Point Blank, Waterhole Number Three, In Harm's Way* and *Kelly's Heroes.* One of his several TV movies was his own adaptation of *The Last Hurrah* for Hallmark. He is of course best known for the television series *All in the Family.*

The O'Connors have a son Hugh, born in Rome in 1962 while *Cleopatra* was being filmed, and Italy is the home-from-home they love best. They live in the Brentwood section of Los Angeles in a house built in 1926 for the opera singer Amelita Galli-Curci.

2

· · · · · · ·

N ow why did I mention Galli-Curci? Not out of pretentious-
ness (though that flaw is not strange to me), because the name of
the great diva would not impress the impressionable today, and
her house, situated in a neighborhood of sidewalks and pleasant
homes near the UCLA campus, is not a famous place like
Pickfair.[1] What then compelled me?

I was contemplating my first Broadway play and I was at my
mother's house, the house where I grew up in Forest Hills,
browsing through a cabinet of sheet music published during the
twenties and thirties. I had a recollection—of my father operating
the Victrola and announcing the performing artists, whose names
were on the old 78-rpm record labels, and I fancied I again heard
his voice pronouncing with pleasure the names Martinelli, Caru-
so, Galli-Curci, and informing us about the legendary soprano:
"No one ever sang 'Caro nome' like that! She was peerless!"

---

[1]The sumptuous home built by the actors Mary Pickford and Douglas Fairbanks in
Beverly Hills.

Recently a friend gave me a few of those new computer re-recordings on compact discs, and by chance one of them was of "little Amelita" singing famous soprano arias. I unwrapped it and played it and heard Galli-Curci again, this time through the latest audio technology as she really sounded, or very close to it. And indeed she was, and remains, the most wonderful of them all.

About things like that my father was always right. I heard myself saying audibly (I am given to involuntary murmurings): "He was always right."

My mother was in the room and she said "What was that?"

"Nothing."

"You said he was always right. Who?"

"My father" I replied.

She laughed. "Easy now . . ."

"I know" I said, "I know. I suppose he was always wrong, really."

"That's more like it."

"But he was always right too."

"You'll have to explain that to me sometime."

"Okay" I said, "sometime."

Whether or not my father lived a life of correctitude is another matter, and I will come to it, but my bringing Galli-Curci into the program note brought my father, in my fancy, to Broadway with me. He loved Broadway. He would have loved to see me there. He is long gone. He died in 1967. My mother died the first of January 1994 and, as I write, the house with the sunporch that served as a music room stands vacant.[2] She used to play the piano in that room, and he the violin, on Sundays after church, and I grew up hearing not only classical music but the world repertoire of popular theatre music from Herbert, Romberg and Kern to Porter, Gershwin and Rodgers. They both sang very well.

---

[2]My brother Bob sold it later and our mother's grandchildren got the money.

A happy pair and most unhappy. A merry house and very sad. A man who was always right and always wrong.

I saw the light of day in Manhattan.

They brought me newborn from St. Ann's Maternity Hospital in East 67th Street to an apartment in the borough of the Bronx at 168th Street and the Grand Concourse—then considered a fine neighborhood—and we lived there until I was about four. My recollections of the place are of two misdeeds and the punishments I got for them. The first was defiantly climbing a gate into the forbidden premises of a nearby synagogue, being ejected and chased and finally walloped on the behind by a girl known as a maid—our maid. The second was torturing this girl with matches until she retaliated by dangling me by the ankles down a dumbwaiter shaft. The poor girl got fired when I calmly squealed on her. Her scare tactic had not troubled me in the least, but I knew that a report of it would evoke panic in my mother, which was always interesting to watch.

When my brother Hugh was born in 1929 we moved to a larger apartment in Elmhurst in the borough of Queens. I was five, and too young to be admitted to public school, but my mother demonstrated to the principal of P.S. 89 that I had learned to read and write at home to something of an adult level, that is, of at least the sixth grade, which meant that I could with comprehension read any New York newspaper—and I did so for the principal. She judged me instantly to be a genius, admitted me to the first grade without detention in kindergarten, and thence quickly on to the second grade where everybody might be more comfortable with me. Thereafter I became impossible to teach, and nobody was comfortable with me.

The ability to read at five and four and three is not today considered prodigious. We now know that, given wise instruction, any child can learn. The wise instruction I got was from Minnie, our nanny, who discovered that when I was immersed in books I became tranquil. She dunked me daily into *The World Book,* a multivolume encyclopedia for children of the seventh or eighth level, a premature gift from my father's brother John, president of the Grolier Society, publishers. Minnie read with me, and taught me to write with pencil and paper, and set me to copying text.

I once conducted a casual survey to find whether something between my ears had not gone awry as I passed from age four to eight. My friends could recall many wonderful events, and this disturbed me because, of my years in Elmhurst, I could recall so little. I do recall doing my very first acting at that time, my first character work, not for a school play but for the entertainment of my Elmhurst neighbors. We were living on Britton Avenue, and round the corner on Forley Street there were some houses with open porches where men sat in their undershirts on summer evenings drinking Prohibition near beer and yelling across narrow driveways in good-natured argument whether or not Schmeling would take Sharkey, Hoover would win a second term, Lindy's baby had been kidnapped by the mob. I used to sit on the running boards of parked cars and listen to the ribald language, the funny accents, the raucous laughter, and wait to be offered a treat by any of the women, all of whom seemed constantly to be making and serving cake. In return I was obliged to entertain the ladies with an imitation of one or another of the men, some of whom were foreign born; and my performances always got howling approval.

One night, or very early morning, one of those open porches where I gave my award-winning skits was blown away by an explosive missile of some sort, well pitched, everyone agreed, from a moving car. I had been awakened by the sound and so had neighbors several blocks from it. The house itself, when we all went to look at it, appeared undamaged; it just looked oddly unfinished without its porch.

"Who did that?" I asked my father.

"Some gentlemen in the spirits business" he said. There was a weariness in his voice.

"Racketeers!" Minnie said. She pressed her lips together, closed her eyes and shook her head. A boy standing beside me said "Racketeers is what the lousy bohunks call us Italians."

"Isn't it the mercy of God they didn't harm any of the people in there?" said Minnie.

"I would say they didn't intend to harm anybody" my father said.

"Then why did they do it?" I asked.

"To show that they could" he said, "for reasons that shouldn't interest us."

I overheard the superintendent of our building saying "That's what the wops bring to this country—bombs and bump-offs."

I asked Minnie what "wops" meant, but she kept silent. When I asked her what "bohunks" were, she nodded at the superintendent. She was wrong. I learned that the super was a Swede, and that the appropriately insulting name for him was "squarehead."

Incidentally, recalling Elmhurst, my mother once happily gave an Elmhurst picture of me to a tabloid whose reporters told her they were going to do a "nice piece" on me. She wasn't aware that "nice" copy, truthful copy, is not what a tabloid is after— that the tabloid's stock in trade is malice, and that the editor judges the value of it by the likelihood of its causing a victim momentary anger, or an hour or so of insanity, or lifelong sadness. The pictures Mama supplied were of me in an Eton suit receiving my first holy communion in 1931—another of my few clear memories of Elmhurst[3]—and in the uniform of a midshipman eleven years later. The photos were innocuous but the story, true to the tabloid character, was a merry smear, likening me personally to Archie Bunker even as a kid: i.e., reporting that I was a precocious racist.

* * *

---

[3]The church of St. Bartholomew.

We moved again in 1933 when my father and mother bought their first and only house in Forest Hills, and there I finished the eight years of my elementary schooling. Of the education imparted to me during that time, next to nothing took hold. I recall from "music appreciation" that *The Tales of Hoffman* was written by Offenbach. Further information about Hoffman and Offenbach I identify with adulthood. Whatever the subject class, I spent the time making phantasmagoric drawings in a copy-book, watching the clock on the wall, engaging my classmates in distracting talk and infuriating the teacher. To my mother's despair my monthly report cards usually rated both my work and my conduct at the C-level, rarely higher, sometimes lower. My brother Hugh's later performance in school was in all respects better, as might be anticipated in a second child who has seen his parents alarmed by the foibles of the first. (I am merely repeating someone else's analysis; it sounds reasonable.) I doubt though whether school days yield reliable forecasts of later life. I recall in one family a brood of four or five who were high achievers in adolescence, grew up, and went on to fulfill every high expectation; and another whose school records, like mine, recorded nothing but perversity but who got along remarkably well in later years. Both my younger brothers, Hugh and Robert, became physicians and I, of course, wandered into a business where the undisciplined are welcome.

Forest Hills was in those days real suburbia. It was beautiful. There lived the rich, the near-rich, the well-to-do, and the comfortable. "This is a premium neighborhood" I had heard a real estate sales agent say to my father.

"What's the premium?" my father asked.

"No Jews" said the agent.

A lie. In fact there were proportionally as many Jews in Forest Hills as anywhere else. When my father, in my presence, related this to Jules Kahn, his law partner, Kahn's burst of laughter actually expelled his cigar. "Your face and name" he howled at my father, "made him think you'd be happy to hear that!"

I asked why, and my father explained: "We Irish Catholics are widely assumed to be unfriendly to Jews."

"Why?" I asked again. "Because you are!" laughed Kahn. "Jules is clowning" my father said. But he did not say that Jules was dissembling. Obviously the real estate agent thought that anti-Jewishness was popular enough to be a winning sales pitch. My father's sour reaction to him was undetectable, though of course I sensed it, but at age nine I didn't question his apparently passive attitude to bigotry. I recalled it to him years later and he replied that he was never a reformer—he could not have reeducated the man. He said "Rather than warn him about dangerous waters, I preferred to let him swim confidently toward the falls." I told this to someone who said "Your old man was copping out." Maybe. I didn't think so. You have to be afraid of something to cop out, and I don't think my father was ever afraid of anything at all. He was simply above ethnic and religious preconceptions—never emotional about prejudice but always quietly mocking. "It's all low brow" was the comment I remember best. He was right. I have never known a hater with a reliable intelligence.

Ruminating in later years on how nations have come under the control of haters and fools, I began to understood that it was only the brilliant foresight of the men who made the Constitution that compelled this country to progress within God-given laws of humanity. Only that insistent clutch of intellectuals, not the ordinary mob of "good" people we praise so fulsomely, prevented the most evil traditions of Europe from flourishing three centuries ago on these helpless shores, already defiled by slavery. And yet even so, the ordinary good people have retained their private benighted beliefs. America's ethnic prejudices and hatreds, and the reactive hatreds they have engendered, have sickened the life of the country.

My old neighborhood Forest Hills today is nothing more than the attenuated city, crowded, traffic clogged and boring; but then it was the fair and spacious place to be, if one could swing it, and my father felt he could. He had a legal practice; he was a criminal lawyer, a trial lawyer. In later years I had occasion to meet one or two of the high-living incorrigibles who paid him large fees to keep them untrammeled. He was also in business: he had an interest in a popular adult school that prepared candidates for various civil service examinations. He had plenty of money.

My mother was an earner too. Wonderful to recall, she was holding down a second job. She used to leave her school at three in the afternoon and go by subway to the World Building on Park Row; there she kept records and accounts and prepared tax returns for her father.[4] Often at six-thirty she met my father midtown and they went home together, driving in their new Chevrolet over the East River by way of the Queensboro Bridge and out along Queens Boulevard through Sunnyside and the other little residential neighborhoods of Woodside, Winfield and Rego Park. In the early thirties the land between these neighborhoods was undeveloped, covered by shrubs and thickets and patches of woods, though one saw here and there a farmhouse and a working farm. A public school teacher when she married, my mother helped put my father through New York University law school and continued working in the school system for thirty years until retirement.

She had taught right through her first pregnancy, though a maternity leave was mandatory, since it was then an unarguable proposition that school children were upset by the sight of pregnancy, and teachers were obliged to withdraw for a year and a half at the first blush of frontal swelling. It was also unarguable that teachers might not be above holding the school system liable for parturient mishaps. But my mother never stopped teaching.

---

[4]John C. O'Connor, for whom I was named, owned and edited the weekly *Irish Advocate,* which he founded in 1893.

"I was small" she explained to me in later years, "so I took a chance." Whether or not anyone was deceived by her smallness, her supervisors never questioned her. Why should they? She was not merely a training-school teacher, she was a Hunter College graduate and it was not easy to find young women of her merit who would work in Forsyth Street on the Lower East Side. She finished the school year in June 1924, produced me in August and returned to teaching in September.

For kids there was a bonanza of open fields within and around Forest Hills, flat fields for ball playing in summer and hilly for sledding in winter. Baseball was the passion of our neighborhood gang, and in season our team played on weekends against teams from Rego Park, Richmond Hill, Elmhurst and Corona. We played against ourselves on weekdays.

I was not a first-class player but good enough to be expected to play regularly. We were also devoted followers of the professional game and had our favorites—mine was Brooklyn. We did not often go to see the pros at Ebbet's Field, the Polo Grounds and Yankee Stadium; we ourselves were playing whenever we had free time, and besides, a radio account broadcast by a superb announcer like Red Barber or Mel Allen cost us nothing and seemed as exciting as the witnessed event. I thought of becoming a sports announcer.

I knew the roster of every team in the National League and most in the American, and the batting and pitching averages of the players, and I understood game strategy. I might have been able to announce a game even then; I was glib enough. I also wanted to be a sports writer like Dan Parker of the *Mirror* and was a joyful and ceaseless reader, especially of books and periodicals not required nor even recommended at school. I also wanted to be a writer of stories and novels. I wanted to make a career out of everything that gave me pleasure, and imagined a future me who was an amalgam of Red Barber, Dan Parker, James Farrell and Ring Lardner. Why I did not want to be an actor too makes me wonder, because nothing, not even baseball, gave me greater pleasure than the movies. I suppose a movie career seemed too utterly unattainable: the movies were a realm of miracles where only someone himself miraculous might enter.

The Depression was not apparent in Forest Hills. The poor didn't live there, and the poor who worked there were not visible, coming by trolley and jalopy from ragged regions elsewhere and disappearing into their jobs. You had to go to Manhattan to see soup-and-bread lines. I saw them in Union Square while walking with my father one cold pre-Christmas afternoon in 1934. But as I remember that gray decade[5] there were many residents of Forest Hills, idled by the times, who were reclusively getting poor—men who had gone out of business, or had been let out of management jobs, who were now and then seen puttering in their gardens or ambling aimlessly about the neighborhood, or who were seen not at all, having finally sold their handsome homes and moved to cheaper areas. Living in protected circumstances I was aware only tangentially of the grimness of the time. I recall a classroom, a teacher filling in a form and we fifth-termers responding aloud to questions about our families, hearing the word "unemployed" again and again, observing the teacher noting it impassively. The word embarrassed no child, so many were saying it, so many fathers were losing jobs even in this ostensibly secure community. Naturally, none of us comprehended it. But our elders at home did not comprehend it either.

In 1936 the economy tumbled into a deep slough. For years afterward the professional thinkers were at pains to explain the misfortune as merely another one of those "panics" (we had weathered a number of them, though none nearly so enervating), just another aberration, non-endemic, the fault of individuals of heedless ambition, lapsed integrity, faint heart in the face

---

[5]A name I gave the thirties in a musical record album in 1972.

of peril—nothing to blame "the American system" for. The truth, which I was yet many years from learning, was that there was no system to blame; a system had never existed in this country—if we take "system" to mean a rationally developed plan by which dynamic elements interact with each other to some logical purpose. It was a lack of system that had made the thirties Depression as inevitable as all others previously suffered. The few—the prosperous powerful few—had never been willing to hear of a system; their own delightfully privileged status required a doctrine of unrestrained operations. The nonprivileged had long suspected that the consequence to themselves was the recurring blight of poverty, but they resisted the notion of a system with a ferocity hardly exceeded by the privileged. The Archie Bunkers were willing to put up with cyclical demolition so long as they could hope that someday luck might hoist them too from rags to riches.

Under the persuasive leadership of Franklin Roosevelt they did accept a modest system for about ten years—four of them war years when the need for government supervision and control was unarguable, but for the long run they would have none of it. As soon as the Second World War was over they realigned themselves politically with the privileged, and energetically, righteously and patriotically began to pull the rug out from under themselves. They are wildly at it to this day. Mencken was dead right when he wrote that America, instead of producing an interesting proletariat, had produced two dull bourgeoisies, an upper and a lower.

Still, in the thirties men like Archie were looking at each other and saying "What's the answer? Has Roosevelt got the answer? Who's got the answer?" I remember angry arguments. I heard the barber, an Italian, say "We got thirty percent unemployed. Hilter's got the answer; he's got everybody in Germany working." The customer in the barber chair laughed and said "What's he got them working on, tanks and planes?"

"No" replied the barber, "people in Germany are working on

highways and railroads and buildings and stadiums—in mines and steel mills—everybody works. Why can't everybody work here?"

The man in the chair, in a hard cold voice, said "You're a dumb guinea—know that?" Mr. Grillo the barber ordered the man out. The man cursed him. The barber cursed the man, and then, white-faced, said that he would have to postpone my haircut—come back another time. He closed his shop and sat down alone, and I saw, glancing back through the window, that he was trembling. I was sad. He was the father of a friend of mine. He was ordinarily a soft-spoken man, a gentlemanly man, whom I had often heard telling customers what he thought was wrong with the world and the country and how things might be changed for the better. And I heard many customers agreeing with him. I had never heard anybody call him "dumb"—and worse, a "guinea," an unaccountable variation of "wop," which was said to be an acronym for "without papers."

Defamatory argot was as prevalent in Forest Hills as in Elmhurst. Germans were "heinies" or "krauts." "Bohunks," for Bohemians, was also applied to Slovaks; and "hunkies" identified a variety of eastern Europeans from the Baltic to the Danube, but particularly Hungarians. "Hunky," I imagine, was the forerunner of "honky," a later black appellation for the white brethren generally. Jews were "yids," which was unobjectionable coming from other Jews, "yid" being a true Jewish noun, but impermissible coming from a goy, the Jewish name for "the others." A Jew might also be called a "sheeny" or a "kike," but not safely to his face, unless he happened to be alone and his tormentor was with friends. The Irish were not much affected: "mick" caused them to smile more than glower—unless an antagonist thought about putting "dumb" or "thick" in front of it.

In Forest Hills in the thirties the local public schools were like private schools. Situated in beautifully built and landscaped locales, they were exceedingly well staffed, well equipped and well maintained. The kids, few of whom were poor, were even more privileged than private school kids; the quality of their instruction was higher, commensurate with higher levels of teacher preparation and pay in the city school system. Public School 101 in Forest Hills Gardens, my school, must have seemed to parents and teachers the most desirable elementary school in New York. The Gardens neighborhood itself was especially desirable; it was developed to the taste of our upper middle class in precious imitation of an English village, and at the center of it was situated the Forest Hills Inn, a pleasant apartment-hotel in Station Square. The station belonged to the Long Island Railroad, then a respectable and efficient enterprise that boarded passengers and whisked them to Penn Station in Manhattan in twenty minutes. No mode of travel has in the past sixty years improved on that. Christmas was celebrated in Station Square by the raising of a forty-foot lighted spruce tree in front of the Inn, and hardly a Christmas went by without a big fall of snow to turn the Square into a picture for a postcard.

I remember a lot of churchgoing and many churches of all creeds. I remember three synagogues. The Jewish population in the area grew a little because of the arrival after 1935 of a handful of refugees from Germany. I heard gentile snarls about being "overrun by Jews," but I saw organized open anti-Jewish demonstrations only at Rockaway Park. A rabble calling itself America First sent speakers who set up platforms where Rockaway residential streets met the beach; they exhorted small crowds to "fight the Jews, who want to push our country into a war to save England." There were much bigger Nazi meetings in the cities, but I saw them only on news film in movie theaters. One in particular was memorable; the German-American Bund, which was the American Nazi party, held a rally in East 86th Street that turned into a riot involving five thousand people inside and outside the Yorkville Casino, a big two-bar dance hall where various immigrant societies whooped it up on weekends.

The American Nazis of course vilified President Roosevelt, and they were joined in their hatred by crypto Nazis, like the Silver Shirts and the Coughlinite America Firsters, because they believed FDR to be either a Jew or a tool of the Jews who wanted us to fight Hitler for the sole reason of saving Jews.

In those days, Scott Fitzgerald's "very rich," a small minority, lived farther out on Long Island in Nassau and Suffolk Counties. My father and grandfather, my mother's father, drove us out to Westbury one Sunday because John C. wanted to see a polo match between select teams of rich Americans and rich Argentinos and Chilenos. He particularly wanted to see and say hello to a scion of the Bernardo O'Higgins family, born in the Argentine of Irish immigrants known to my grandfather; the elders became miners and beef barons. The South Americans utterly routed our gentlemen—Winston Guest, Jock Whitney, among others—by the catastrophic score (for polo) of eleven goals to one. My grandfather's meeting with the young O'Higgins was brief; he spoke no Spanish, but was able, and gratified, to learn that the horses from the south were of Irish origin. I remember asking my grandfather how people managed to become very rich, and he said they were only a minority, but they did it while the great majority were looking the other way. They got control of resources and built industries. "The majority prefer to draw wages and amuse themselves." My grandfather, a Republican who had run for Congress in Manhattan and lost in a Democratic district, had a higher respect for the minority than the majority.

To this my father added that the rich meanwhile observed that in order to stay rich and get richer they had to run the government. They dedicated themselves to plotting and scheming—creating a government that would devote itself to the well-being of private industry, act as the business agent for commercial enterprise, invent policies domestic and foreign that promised profit to profit makers, and oppose taxation to pay for publicly owned, public interest, nonprofit enterprise. I said that the rich theory of distribution sounded pretty good to me, hoping to please John C., and my father said yes but it didn't work that way: it created panics and depressions. A familiar argument began between the New Deal man and the conservative man. My grandfather, being rich, shared the view of the rich that if private enterprise thrives, so will its dependents, the ordinary people and the poor, except of course a certain fragment of the poor known as the chronic poor.

"Ah, the chronic poor!" exclaimed my father in a mock lament. "The rich man looks at the chronic poor and recalls the words of the Lord, who said of them that they will always be with us, which the rich man understands to mean that he needn't worry about them."

My grandfather laughed and didn't argue the point. "You're right about that, anyway" he said.

I was allowed to comment that poor men were also in politics. "Yes" said John C., "for somebody told them that running things was great fun, and once they got into public office they wouldn't be poor for long. They gave up their innocent pursuits the following day."

One or two rich men, I discovered later in life, had supported nonconservative, or liberal or "leftist" government. Rich leftists had indeed existed,[6] but were considered eccentric by both rich and poor and were not influential. Poor men, however, have frequently and numerously supported "rightist" government, but it would be inaccurate to say that they too, the right-wing poor, have been harmlessly eccentric. No, they have done great harm to themselves. The right-wing poor are dumbbells, like the

---

[6]For instance Corliss Lamont, Henry Wallace.

television series character I played from 1971 to 1983; they will never be rich but have been led to believe that the rich will tow them along to safe harbor. They also have a feeling—something akin to being drunk—that in throwing their votes to the conservatives, they have joined a better class of people. Right wingers, the wolfish and the sheepish, the doctrinaire and the merely pretentious, have become comfortable with one another because of one powerful bond between them: a hatred of "welfare," the benevolence that government, through legislation, forces on them. The wolf-sheep allies detest paying for the careworn, the troubled, the unemployed, the unfranchised, the deprived and the migratory. They are encouraged doctrinally by a suspicious, ungenerous corporate press, including a bitter bunch of radio and TV carpers who would heckle a Mother Teresa. Keep in mind that all important American papers, periodicals, television networks and other communications systems are profit-making private corporate enterprises, and they evade all confrontations with social need by steering hard to starboard.

I put "leftist" in quotation marks above as there is no longer any trace of a left wing in this country, and looking back to the fifties and the twenties, the decades of our reckless thought purges, we never have had a socialist, communist or anarchist party that could get anybody elected to the lowliest public office in the land. Yet whenever the rich, through their vast media capabilities, have exhorted the rest of us to set upon the radicals, we have responded joyfully by assaulting the characters of all unorthodox persons, spying and informing on them, and denouncing them as unworthy to work and live among us. We are hard to cool down when the purge fever is upon us. We love it so!

3

•••••••

A war was coming, and at sixteen I did not want to be denied a war, presuming it would be as thrilling as the movies made it. Most of the boys in our crowd were of the same mind, and if we heard opposing thoughts from our parents we were the more confirmed in our own. Some credit for this is due the World War movies of the thirties, like *The Dawn Patrol* starring Errol Flynn, that made us long to fly fighter planes and shoot vicious-looking Germans out of the skies. The belligerents in the approaching war, French, Germans, Italians, Chinese, Japanese, were represented in America by tens of millions of immigrants, and their children and grandchildren had learned at their daddies' knees, both in the old country and the new, how to insult one another: the war of deadly weapons abroad had its counterpart in a war of nasty ethnic barbs at home. During the more than two years between the Anglo-French declarations of war on Germany and the Japanese attack on us, some of the teenage sons of immigrant tradesmen and artisans in Forest Hills were "rooting" for their fatherlands Germany and Italy; the rest of us rooted for Britain and the Commonwealth and the antifascist resistance in Europe.

Somehow we all remained pals, and all the comical partisan nonsense stopped when America went to war against the Axis and Japan.

Most exciting to me in those days were the pulp magazines about flying aces of the First World War, always available on the magazine racks for a dime. I never paid for mine. My friend Mr Greenberg allowed me to read them free in a booth in the luncheonette section of his store. Mr Greenberg, who ran what we called a candy store, was a man whose sayings and attitudes, right or wrong, I never forgot. War on foot was not much romanticized in fiction magazines because it was muddy, bloody and proximately deadly, and it seemed old-fashioned anyway. To the big military minds, this impending Second World War was going to be "fought and won in the air." Lindbergh predicted that the enormously superior air power of the Nazis would make short work of the British and the French. "Everybody thinks Lindy's right" I informed Mr Greenberg, who replied that what everybody thought was never right. As it turned out, the British were the Germans' equal in the air, but no one, including even the British, knew it at the time. And the war would finally be won, like all other wars, on the grisly ground through appalling human sacrifice.[1]

The male seers in my family thought that the big French army and the British expeditionary force were capable of stopping Hitler. I asked my grandfather: "And when they stop him the war will stop?" "Yes." "What about going all the way and beating him?"

Not necessary, was the answer to that, which I then referred to Mr Greenberg at the candy store—who was of the same mind. We were standing in front of his store beside the large news-stand. Mr Slatkin was there. Mr Grillo the barber was there.

---

[1]Studies after the war showed that allied air power killed a lot of Germans, but did not destroy the German military capability.

"If they stop him" said Mr Greenberg, "the war will stop, they'll all sit down again and hondle some more, Hitler will keep what he already got and promise everybody that the next person he attacks, it'll be Stalin—and maybe the Allies'll say yeah, and then they'll all go and knock off Uncle Joe."

Mr Slatkin, who always stood near the newsstand reading *The Jewish Daily Forward*, said "Hah!" He worked for the *Forward* and liked passersby to know that it was available right there at Greenberg's. He was well known for his interjections into any conversation that might be going on around him. He said his "Hah!" with contempt, but as he never took his eyes off the paper, no one was sure that his usually harsh comments were not about what he was reading. There was an often-told story about his saying "Bullshit!" into his paper when his real target was a policeman who was loudly maintaining that goldfish and birds ought to be licensed like dogs and cats.

Mr Grillo intervened: "That's what they oughta do now, smash Stalin, and we oughta help them."

"Should we?" I asked Mr Greenberg.

"Nah, we should mind our own business."

"Communism ain't our business?" repeated Mr Grillo in a suddenly fierce voice. "It ain't mine" Mr Greenberg coolly replied, and he lit a fresh Lucky Strike from the burning end of the one he was smoking. He stared calmly at the slightly quivering barber, and the latter, his face quite red, turned and strode away. Mr Slatkin grumbled *"Meshuggener"* into the *Forward;* "in fact I see two *meshuggeners."* Mr Greenberg directed a small razzberry at Mr Slatkin.

"So anyway" I said to Mr Greenberg, "we wouldn't have a chance to get into it, right?"

Surprised, he asked "You wanna get into it?" "Sure!" I said. But Mr Greenberg knew I was thinking about something exciting and glamorous and safe, and he looked at me and said in a weary voice "Don't be a jerk." He turned and went into his store, and I turned to follow him because I was worried about his losing respect for me. Mr Slatkin addressed me by staring into his paper: "Schools shouldn't close in the summer." I had once heard Mr Slatkin telling the inside of the *Forward* that schools should allow three-day weekends but no long vacations.

Germany invaded Poland in June 1939. Beck, the Polish leader, had assured Britain and France that he would crush the well-anticipated aggression within six or eight weeks. He thereupon lost thousands and thousands of horses and men in cavalry charges, and within the eight weeks of his prediction it was the Germans who had overwhelmed him.

For many months nothing else of military importance happened and our press during the fall and winter reported that the man in the street was calling it "the phony war," razzing the combatants, like a crowd at the Saint Nicholas Arena urging two wary pugs to mix it up. There were a few naval actions in which the British lost capital ships, but the clash of armies was deferred. At last in the spring of 1940 the world got the war it was waiting for. Big German armies suddenly moved by air, land and sea and occupied Holland and Denmark; they defeated Norway and France.

Looking at Europe in the prewar thirties, and the political movements that threatened peace, the adults closest to me were not prophetic or perceptive. My grandfather was one of those inclined to blame things on the English; that aside, he thought war solved no international problems. My father and my uncles (my mother's brothers) felt that Roosevelt would find some way to reconcile the warring powers, and that we probably would have no war in the Orient—because the Japanese would soon remove all cause by subduing the Chinese. In any event the Japanese, everybody agreed, were afraid of us. All predicted that, with the election year 1940 in view, Roosevelt was going to reiterate a policy of strict American neutrality everywhere. They were right: Roosevelt on the campaign trail promised the people that he would never send their boys to fight in a foreign war. My grandfather doubted him, recalling that in 1916 Wilson said the same thing; and Roosevelt's Republican opponent, a celebrated corporation lawyer named Wendell Willkie, warned that the President, far from keeping them out of a foreign war, was conspiring to get the boys into one. Willkie said that a vote for FDR was a vote to put them on the troop ships. I think my grandfather voted for Willkie.

At school one of my teachers instructed us that the French were a contemptible people, and that the British, though much finer human types, had been finished off at Dunkirk. Hitler would be in London by the end of the summer. Another teacher said that by the end of the summer the Italians would drive the British out of all of Africa; fascist Spain would drive the British out of Gibraltar; communist Russia would first invade Sweden and then the whole Balkan Peninsula including Greece.

By the end of the summer these terrible movements had not been accomplished nor even attempted. I was mystified. If teachers did not know what was going to happen, who did? A teacher now declared that he knew a couple of things he had not known when summer began: Hitler and Stalin were plotting a joint attack upon Brazil, and German flyers working for Colombia's airline were rigging passenger planes as bombers to bomb the Panama Canal. These projects evidently did not engage the thoughts of our enemies. The Canal was not as important logistically as people had imagined. We were a two-coast, two-navy country served by the biggest, fastest rail system in the world, much safer and more efficient than any canal.[2] Many years later when we turned the Canal over to Panama, the Congressional outrage that erupted, the phony security issue, and the campaign jingoism of candidate Ronald Reagan were no more than burlesque routines.

---

[2] We let it deteriorate after the war.

Were my teachers nitwits? Yes, a few. Most were intelligent men and women who religiously garnered information from the papers and the news-and-opinion journals of the day, but they were routinely misinformed. They relied on the press, and the press, true to form, not really knowing much, misled them.

France had built on her eastern frontier an "impregnable" mole-works of forts, inviting the Germans to flank it on the right and move upon Belgium as they had done in the First World War, but being ready this time to defeat them. The Germans moved as expected, but *Der Führer*, whom the American press and movies were busy characterizing as an imbecile, had prepared a surprise: he drove straight west into France, but through Luxembourg. The French and British, moving up to Belgium to meet him, were cut off; the British were driven backward to Dunkirk on the Channel, where Hitler treated them to an even bigger surprise. At his personal order,[3] the most powerful army the world had ever seen, the invincible Wehrmacht, halted and for three days watched a grand British retreat—celebrated as a victory in the movie *Mrs. Miniver*; a force of more than three hundred fifty thousand were heroically brought home by every ship and boat, civilian and military, on the east coast of England. The forty-five-thousand French and others who remained on the Belgian beach simply surrendered; they never forgot the tragic consequence for France, nor let the British forget it.

Everybody knew the Germans could have turned Dunkirk into the worst slaughter in history, but it was better to believe something else—better to believe that the British had foiled the Germans. Press and radio were saying so. Hitler's amazing decision was called an insane blunder (insanity being *Der Führer's* customary diagnosis) and therefore never seriously

[3]According to his tank general, Guderian.

investigated. Conjecture aside, in that month of June we saw news film of Hitler strolling in the Champs-Élysées.

It was well known that in Germany and the occupied countries Hitler was turning an ancient chronic sickness, Jew hating, into a national policy. What should be remembered as well is that this development did not trouble the America I knew because everybody here thought of the sickness as normal. Hitler had millions of admirers in America; he was promising to smash communism, "a creation of the Jews," and if he could accomplish that we were prepared to forgive him a few sins, confident that his sins were being overplayed anyway by a hysterical "left-liberal press."[4] Some American and French and British leaders deplored Hitler's racism and took note of his harassment of all dissenting religious opinion, but no one suggested opposing him with sanctions or force. President Roosevelt went so far as to ask Chamberlain, the British prime minister, to mention to the Führer at Munich the concern of our government over the fate of German Jews. That is all. Few in this world, besides the Jews, said more.

But then I had never heard that the fate of dissenting German Christians interested America's Christians. American Catholics seemed to be impressed by Hitler's vow to save the world from bolshevism. They interpreted the 1934 concordat between the Vatican and the Reich as papal approval of Nazism, though it was palpably a desperate attempt by the Pope to protect the German church[5] and its flock, who were also beginning to feel persecution. A pope of the Jews, had there been such a figure, would have attempted no less. Tragically the Jews had no one to negotiate for them. The best worldwide Jewry could do was raise a little bribe money during the war to save a few lives from the ovens.

---

[4]A leftist press never existed in America other than little papers like *The Worker* and *New Masses.*
[5]The church got nothing out of it.

Of Hitler my grandfather once said "Somebody would have bumped him off if the British hadn't declared war on him."

I referred this solution to Mr Greenberg. "The *zayde*[6] makes some sense" he said with a smile. And then he said "You know somethin?—I'd kill him myself. Just gimme a gun and show me the way in there. Why not? I'm tired of everything here. I might as well be doin' somethin' I like." It sounded crazy and funny, but I was sure he meant it, and I wondered how many other men in the world would be willing to try personally to put an end to Hitler. Years later I could still be fascinated by the remarks of my grandfather and Mr Greenberg—the possibility of the thing and the result. Probably no leader in history was the target of assassination more often than Hitler. The Germans themselves tried over and over to kill him during his dozen years of tenure; At his "table talks" with his coterie at Obersalzberg he brooded aloud about being murdered.[7] Assassins might have succeeded if war had not made the target unapproachable: the Führer was always at his military headquarters in East Prussia or some other well-guarded rendezvous. In 1939, with war in view, no public man in Britain and France would have suggested that the defeat of the Führer be left to a murderer. But what if they had left it so?—indeed postponed military action and relied on time and chance and a well-planned "hit"? Consider for a start what might have happened to Europe's Jews. Hitler's early idea was mass deportation. He told Mussolini that Madagascar might be a good place for them. His later plan, his "final solution," he put in train when he saw looming defeat on every front and began to crave a last victory in genocide. He told his coterie that if the Allies successfully invaded Europe, he would leave no Jew alive.

But suppose that in the first weeks of the war, after Hitler had overrun Poland, the democracies had tried once again to make

---

[6]Grandfather.
[7]He vaguely cited a dozen or more attempts.

peace with him, as Mr Greenberg had postulated, and as *Der Führer*, with apparently real hope, had invited them to do. Suppose the democracies had made the release of Jews a condition of the peace Hitler had asked for. They could have bought some time for the hit. They could have tried it. Why not? I wish we could say we tried.

4

· · · · · · ·

When the Japanese attacked our navy in Hawaii, I was sojourning profitlessly at Wake Forest College in the state of North Carolina,[1] at that time a small men's liberal arts college conjoined with a seminary for Baptist ministerial students; a curious whereabouts for the likes of me, but it will, I trust, be accounted for in the following correspondence of more than fifty years later.

WAKE FOREST
University Relations
March 24, 1997

Dear Mr. O'Connor:

When I came to work for Wake Forest twenty-five years ago, I read a thoughtful letter you had just written our students, who had asked you to speak on campus. You

---

[1]After the war, aided by R. J. Reynolds money, it became a big university at Winston-Salem.

wrote nostalgically of your year at Wake Forest . . . [mentioning] . . . a professor's daughter, Lib Jones, and . . . [also] . . . shooting pool at Shorty's. . . . The "new Shorty's" opened on the campus in Winston-Salem last month. It is a place dedicated to preserving the memories of student life at Wake Forest over all its decades . . . Marie Joyner, the 95-year-old widow of Shorty's founder, Millard "Shorty" Joyner, was with us for the dedication . . . and the professor's daughter you admired is now Lib Jones Brantley, my neighbor here on Faculty Drive. Her husband, Russell Brantley, '45, is director emeritus of our Communications office and wrote the official statement of dedication which hangs in Shorty's. We would love to have you come back to visit all of us at the "new" Wake Forest. Perhaps you could brush off your game of pool in the new Shorty's. This is the "Year of the Arts" at Wake Forest and a great time to see what has become of the school you knew in the town of Wake Forest.

    Robert D. Nells
    Assistant Vice President for
    University Relations

My reply to the students' letter that Mr Nells read twenty-five (now twenty-six) years ago was this:

August 22, 1972

H. Walter Townshend
7716 Reynolda Station
Wake Forest University
Winston-Salem, North Carolina

Dear Mr. Townshend,

    The kind of professional life I lead makes it impossible for me to do anything else. I have no free time. I do not want to tire us both with details of my disablement; suffice it to say that my home is quite beside the UCLA campus and I have had to decline invitations to speak even there. I cannot get down to Winston-Salem.

I am delighted that some of your colleagues remember me from the days (three wars ago) of the old magnolia campus at Wake Forest, though I was seen far less on campus than in Shorty Joyner's pool hall in the town. I came to Wake in a funny way. A close friend of mine in New York was planning to go there and I wanted to go where he went, so knowing nothing about the college I applied and was accepted. My friend then changed his mind, but my mother refused to let me follow suit a second time. Off I went in September 1941 to meet Shorty Joyner and to become a truly dangerous nine-ball player. I was a wretched student—utterly disinterested in the classroom learning situation—and when I resumed college in 1947 at the University of Montana, I could transfer only one semester's credit in English gleaned at Wake.

There were few girls at the old men's college, just the daughters of faculty, and with the most adorable of these, Elizabeth Jones, I naturally fell in love. This was futility. Between Miss Jones and any new admirer was a scrambling horde of old admirers, so my ardour was expressed merely in distant looks, of which Miss Jones was not aware.

My frustration caused me to explore the state. I was a frequent traveler (via thumb) to Raleigh, Durham and Greensboro, and though the goal was girls, I learned a great deal en routes about Carolina and its people. Believe it or not, one heard many, many whites even then expressing a certainty—yes, and an anxious wish—that the segregationist culture would soon wither away.

I knew only one violent Klan type and I knew a few brooding reactionaries who could sound sinister on occasion. I knew a number of racists of the bird-brained windbag type, but my larger impression of Carolinians (forgive me, but I am not fond of "Tarheels") was not at all of a hard people, but of a very sweet people—probably trapped and confused, as James Baldwin believes, in their own incomprehensible American History.

I last saw Wake in 1945. I was a merchant seaman then—a fireman on an oil tanker—and we were lying useless in Miami with a broken boiler when Truman dropped his persuaders on the Japanese. I quit my ship and found a fellow who was driving to New York, and when we came through Wake Forest we stopped at Mrs. Wootten's guesthouse on Route One. I was touched and surprised that so many people remembered me—and not only remembered me, but welcomed me back, welcomed me home, with love. Best wishes to you. Fond wishes to Wake.

Carroll O'Connor

P.S. If the campus paper would find interest in this letter, do pass it along.

The Seabord Railroad had a depot in Wake Forest, and on its sidings freight trains moving north to south and vice versa stopped to off-load. Passenger trains halted by day at the old platform to accommodate ordinary travelers, and the great express trains, the fabled streamliners that raced by night to Miami and New York carrying the privileged to their pleasures, merely slowed a little passing through. My mother and I stepped down from a slow-moving passenger train late in August 1941.

"You actually let her lead you by the ear, like a little boy, to Wake Forest?"

The questioner was Hugh McDougall, the friend who had changed his mind about the college. I rebuked him for his sarcasm, but I understood his amazement. I had been an obstreperous nuisance in all my high school years; it had taken three schools to graduate me, and I had battled my mother over everything she ever wanted to do for me except one—teach me to dance. Only at dances could I get my arms around girls without resistance. But I paid attention to her when she warned that if I did not get some good grades in my final high school year, no college would let me in. Being rejected by a college was a very alarming thought to boys of my background. I would be a laughingstock. I therefore got some good grades. Even so, my mother told me she would have to come down to Wake Forest with me to persuade the dean that three bad years and one good year deserved, in my case, serious consideration, for they proved that a genius was finally germinating. Somehow I knew how to sound plausibly like a genius, so Mama and I, a pair of city slickers, put one over on the kindly dean. I felt true remorse when, as the months wore on, he called me in once or twice and expressed his dismay that the germination had apparently aborted.

An ill-considered impulse of my own had brought me to a place wherein I no longer wished to be. I marshaled a few false-hearted pleas to return immediately to New York, one being a promise to clamor for entrance at the gate of every college in my home city, another being my fear of prostration in the unfamiliar heat. Mama was unmoved by my vows, and North Carolina was really much less hot than we thought a southern state would be—New York in August was worse—and I gave up whining. But I knew I would fail. I was temperamentally predestined to fail. My Ghost and my Divil were with me, or I should say in me (I'll explain these invisible lifelong companions in later pages), and the Ghost said "If you seriously tell your ma the truth, that you're simply unready and afraid, she might take you home."

But the Divil argued "Why would a brave young lad of seventeen tell his ma a pitiful thing like that?" The Ghost replied "To protect her, for it'll go hard with her when he fails." "It won't surprise her" laughed the Divil; "she's used to his failings." The remark was not funny, it was harsh. But it was true. I wish, even today, that I had been the kind of kid who gave some thought to making his mother happy.

Four months later, on the day after the country learned about Pearl Harbor, I was malingering at the Wake Forest rail depot listening to the philosophers who gathered there most afternoons or early evenings; the circle comprised, besides a telegrapher, a ticket agent, and a shipping clerk, a veterinarian, a warehouse owner, a car parts dealer, a man who had "a part-time county job" and usually someone like me, a stray student. Never women or girls. We gentlemen, notwithstanding our proclaimed enterprises, were essentially idlers. The elders played serious checkers now and then for twenty-five cents a game; they listened to a small radio, they read aloud items from the newspapers of different cities, they smoked lots of cigarettes, drank lots of cola, touched their straw hats to ladies traversing the raised rail crossing—stood and bowed to any lady crossing in a car. They were talking about the war the Japanese had just launched against us. They believed like nearly everybody else in America that the Japanese were a naturally inferior nation, and that their navy was as insubstantial as the products of their toy factories, which could be seen on the counters of American dime stores everywhere. The Japanese were denigrated as pilferers of Western ideas, nothing more. The gentlemen assured each other that our navy would blow theirs instantly out of the water. They did not at that moment know that Japanese aircraft had yesterday sunk the best part of our Pacific fleet. Someone said that in reprisal for the attack we would devastate Japan's shack cities. The telegraphy man offered the intelligence that Jap cities were not only shacks, but also grass huts, hardly worth the shells of our dreadnoughts, much more cheaply destroyed by matches. He may have been confusing the Japanese with the grass-hut natives in Tarzan movies. Our apprehension of all nonwhite peoples was largely imparted to us by the movies. In the Tarzan movies, for example, only the African natives were astonished and petrified at the sight of African animals. Similarly, Oriental men were depicted as funny looking, vicious little schemers, though some Oriental women were luscious little dolls, longing to be swept up into the burly white arms of Americans.

Some Americans, we later learned, showed signs of sophistication. For instance, W. R. Hearst, who knew that the Japanese possessed submarines, thought that one of these craft might surface in front of Marion Davies's home on the Santa Monica beach and try to hit him, W.R., with a burst of the deck gun. Why not? Was he not the most important man in America? He moved himself and Miss Davies to a grand secluded *schloss* in the forests of northern California.

I remained in Wake Forest until the spring of 1942, then left before the end of term, having wasted my freshman year. I busied myself at my grandfather's office running errands, and then got a job as a copyboy on *The New York Times.* In August, at eighteen, I decided to volunteer for the Naval Air Corps because it was romantically deadly, the darling service of all the most alluring girls for whose notice high peril was a low price to pay. But Naval Air rejected me. A recruiting officer who looked like my pal and colleague of later years, Robert Stack, told me that my current high school and college record indicated an inferior person, and that, to make matters worse, my upper and lower teeth did not meet in proper occlusion. While not disputing the question of my inferiority (I couldn't make a good case), I said I knew a fellow now flying for the navy who was inferior even to me. The officer told me he could not imagine this. On leaving him, I remarked snottily that I had not thought I would be asked to fly an airplane with my occlusion.

My mother was relieved by the navy's disinterest, but infuriated by its rejection of my teeth: "You've had the finest of dental care all your life, and your teeth are all there and they look wonderful!" Her sister, my Aunt Jo, suggested that my habitually careless appearance might have distressed the flawless navy men in lower Manhattan, and that I ought to fix myself up decently and try again—but in Philadelphia.

My mother told her to be still.

Americans were telling each other that they were ready to fight. Few felt that we had a good reason to fight a European war, but a war with Japan was a different case: it was a less disagreeable prospect, which is not to say that it was a popular wish, only that people could openly consider a Pacific war without fear of furious rebuttal. The Japanese had not, to that time, really deserved our hostility, but Americans disliked them—would not have liked so see Tammy or Barby bring one home.[2]

Americans felt in 1939 that England and France were wicked and degenerate and had brought the war on themselves. The argument then that Nazi Germany must sooner or later threaten America was likely to be dismissed as a warmongering fabrication. The antiwar grumblings I remember hearing everywhere identified our real enemies as Wall Street, the capitalists, the communists, "the interests," the Jews, or the dupes of any of the foregoing. Then, as now, the people in the street knew little about the workings of this world, and the newspapers saw to it that the little they knew was wrong.

Our press had criticized Germany in measured terms, but had freely condemned Japan. The public posture of our government invited us to regard the whole Pacific, China and Southeast Asia as areas of legitimate, if not superior, American interest. We did not understand—had never known—that our own Monroe

---

[2]Time, it seems, has not broadened us much.

Doctrine, designed originally to cut two ways, ruled us out of that hemisphere.

The policy of the United States in 1941 was to let Japanese leaders understand that if they wanted good relations with the United States they would have to clear out of China—to begin leaving immediately. Japanese leaders would have to commit political suicide—perhaps personal suicide as well. The Japanese presence in China was then more than four years in being, and represented the total commitment of Japan's military, economic and political endeavors. Imagine how we would have reacted to a Japanese demand that the United States withdraw from the Philippines and allow the Filipinos at last to govern themselves. The ironic story of how we, for commercial reasons, had aided, if not encouraged, Japan's invasion of China from the beginning is well known. Exports from the United States had furnished half of Japan's war effort. Our huge scrap iron sales were to evoke a grim joke among American draftees from the New York area: "It'll be bad enough to get plugged by the Japs, but to get plugged by the Second Avenue El is too much!" The president and Secretary Hull couched their commands in the most moral, and therefore (as everybody knows) the most unacceptable, terms.

Evidently President Roosevelt and his advisers never contemplated a practical live-and-let-live treaty with Japan. The absurd price we set for peace may have been a price the Japanese people were willing to pay, but their leaders, like all leaders, preferred not to offer their people choices. The Japanese response to our ultimatum was to attack us. This was described to the world as a "surprise," though it could hardly have surprised us, coming more than a year after General Marshall first warned Hawaiian commands to prepare for it.

The United States Merchant Marine Academy had set up a midshipman program, and I was accepted into it—I think because the Academy was short of applicants at the time. The program consisted of basic naval training and specific seamanship, small arms, gunnery, boat handling, and naval courtesy and discipline. This was to be followed by a five-month tour of sea duty on a working vessel plying the war zones, and finally another dose of schooling at the Academy at Kings Point, Long Island. Graduates of the program got licenses as third mates or third engineers (my option) and naval reserve commissions as ensigns.

For the basic training I was sent to a rather pretty station, formerly a small hotel of terra cotta stucco and red-tiled roof at the edge of the Gulf coast town of Pass Christian, Mississippi. I remember the town only as the place where the bus stopped on the way to New Orleans. I and all who had not gone "before the captain's mast"—a very quick little summary trial for malfeasances during the week, which resulted in confinement to the station—spent a couple of Sundays in Gulfport and Biloxi, but spent most weekends in New Orleans. The Old Quarter offered what it had always offered: uproarious merriment—bars, clubs, jazz bands, good restaurants for every purse; and in the genteel part of town tea dances at the Hotel Roosevelt attended by exceedingly beautiful girls from Tulane University. I had the time of my life, and wished that New Orleans might be my home port, in spite of rumors that the Germans were sinking ships just off the delta. My home port for a while was to be New York. Basic training over, I was ordered aboard a ship with a regular run between the Brooklyn Army Base and the ports of Swansea, Cardiff and Newport in England's Bristol Channel.

I should say here that before leaving Pass Christian for sea duty I was warned by officer instructors that my attitude needed improvement. Attitude to what? To anything of importance. I was still a bad student. My first ship out of New York was a large unusual freighter; it resembled the oil tankers of the day in that the stack and most of the living and working quarters were aft, and the bridge was mounted forward. She was named *S.S.*

Seatrain Lakehurst, and in peacetime had carried loaded freight trains from Caribbean fruit depots to rail terminals in New Jersey. Now her four long decks were ideal for shipping tanks, weapons-carriers, armored cars, trucks and jeeps, and appropriate army personnel to man them.

Everyone but me sailed her with taut nerves. I was not brave, just silly. There seemed little to be concerned about. The *Lakehurst* traveled in troop ship convoys protected by cruisers and destroyers and even on one crossing a battleship. And on her own she was faster than most submarines, having a twin-screw, high-pressure turbine plant that drove her to a speed of twenty-two knots. However, having no watertight compartments, she was uniquely vulnerable to any hole the enemy might make in her hull. She would have plunged swiftly. I sailed on the North Atlantic aboard the *Lakehurst* during the entire winter of 1943.

It was my failure to be concerned about studying, to complete a certain "sea project" (books of homework assignments), that decided the Merchant Marine Academy on my unfitness to continue officer training after my sea tour. There was also a question still pending about my attitude. Without intention, I was apparently condescending about any work at hand. I wish I could insist that I did the work well anyway. I can only say that I could have, but did not. The Academy, or at least one junior officer thereof, was assisted in the decision to bounce me by the chief engineer of the *Lakehurst,* a salty old Texan who reported that I was "useless as tits on a bull." He went a bit too far. Actually I had learned a lot about the engineering of a steamship, but I did not argue my case. I didn't care. For me, dreams always cast out disappointments. Dreams took precedence over duties. I cannot now recall what I dreamt about by day and by night (apart from sex), but generally it was of being what I wasn't, and what I wasn't ever likely to become—some kind of paragon admired by the world, probably a novelist/journalist. I wanted to be thought a serious fellow, but would not honestly try to be one. I shed the Academy uniform, and took and easily passed exams given by the Coast Guard for accreditation to sail in all steam engine rooms as an oiler or a fireman-watertender.

I joined the National Maritime Union and shipped out of the hiring hall as a civilian seaman. I sailed in engine rooms until 1944, as an oiler on ore ships to Trinidad and Cuba, and on several freighters to Italy, France and North Africa. An oiler, I should explain, stands watch below with an engineer, assists the engineer in a general way, and sees to the lubrication and efficient running of the engine, all pumps, generators and subsidiary machinery. Some oilers became engineer-officers. I myself was mulling, in an idle way, my chances of sitting for the third's exam, when I was asked to go, as acting refrigeration engineer, aboard a captured German passenger ship docked in Brooklyn. The job was to stand by in the engine room all day, keep a compressor working and maintain a prescribed temperature in the freezers. Easy enough: I had been an oiler on a refrigerator ship and knew what I was doing. And the job promised two weeks with good pay in New York—nights to myself.

I was collecting some of this pay over in Manhattan one evening at the North River offices of United States Lines, and remarked to the paymaster that his job seemed cushy. He challenged me to do it. I asked where and when. I was joking but the paymaster was not. There was a shortage of assistant pursers at that moment, and companies were willing to hire almost anyone not palpably mindless and train him on the job. The paymaster asked if I could be ready to take a train to Boston next day and become assistant purser on a passenger-freighter.

I took the train and never became an engineer. The rest of my seagoing experience was as assistant purser and purser making a number of voyages to France and Yugoslavia and Japan. And I was right. The job was, in fact, fairly cushy. A purser had his own office and his own cabin, worked at his own pace, and answered to no other officer but the captain. He was responsible for all the paperwork incident to the ship's business, crew lists, alien crew lists, cargo manifests. He ran the crew's store, prepared the crew's payroll, and paid out the cash at voyage end. I liked the job and did it well enough. I had been undisciplined, but learned to discipline myself. I even thought idly of making a career of the sea.

I had been very lucky during the war. Convoys I sailed in were attacked, ships were hit and sunk, but never one of mine. I saw foreign lands and met foreign people, and as a civilian in ordinary clothes, I got into closer touch with every experience than I might have done in uniform. America had not been quite a theater of war. Our coastal waters were preyed upon by German U-boats, and merchant ships were sunk in disastrous numbers, but our home territory was fairly safe. Our civilian population suffered only material inconveniences and restrictions, apart of course from severe emotional shocks to thousands of families who lost their young men. Americans had never made and enjoyed so much money—an excess of money. If the federal government had not exercised wide and firm control of prices, profit-takers would have inflated and destroyed the American economy and, cheerfully as always, destroyed themselves as well.

I shipped out of and into New York, Boston, Philadelphia, Norfolk, Miami, and San Francisco, among other ports, and they were all howling with a merriment wholly unknown during the prewar thirties. Distant peril gave urgency to fun and love; old restraints fell away, nightclubs and saloons were bursting with people making free. Booze was plentiful. The various elixirs that alone made Scotland important to Americans were supposedly out of stock, but were always miraculously produced for a gouger's price. Native distillations were more readily available. The whole population was showing a different side of itself: nobody seemed to give a damn about anything, not even about the war.

I never knew Humphrey Bogart, but he convinced me and every merchant seaman that what we were doing in the war was a heroic way to help win that war. That was the message of a movie starring Bogart called *Action in the North Atlantic;* it was about American sailors, civilian seamen, aboard freighters on the suicidal Murmansk run. No service seemed more dangerous, more glamorous, more desirable. Notwithstanding what the movie proclaimed, and I believed, the merchant seaman was not thought of as glamorous. The public didn't understand what he was doing or know who he was—he usually went ashore in civilian clothes. He was held in disfavor, if not contempt, by many members of the armed forces. The enemy was firing at him—firing at his armed cargo ship in and out of convoy—and he was firing back, but to be a civilian seaman was in the public's opinion to be anything but heroic. Our British allies took a different view, a very fond respectful view, of their "merchant navy."

But I did what I wanted to do, and if ever I worried about what anybody else thought of it, I can't recall the occasion. I signed on and off ten vessels of all kinds, and sailed the Atlantic, the Caribbean, the Mediterranean, and the Pacific. The men who sailed beside me, the ruined port towns we saw, the people we met—the war-weary people, the dead and the living, beaten in Italy and Japan, beaten but triumphant in France—gave me a gift of revelations that I was then too distracted to notice. But time and educated reflection let me remember and evaluate. My war years at sea were among the most influential of my life.

But in the fall of 1946 I returned from Le Havre to Jacksonville, Florida, settled affairs on my ship and went to New York, to my mother's house in Forest Hills. I was at loose ends. With the war over, deck officers had taken their opportunity to strike against all American-flag companies. I had no ship to go to. I relaxed at home. Days went by, then weeks, and I never again boarded a ship as a working seaman.

5

·······

In 1943 I met a girl in New York who came from the state of Montana. "Girls" is what we were permitted to call females under thirty-five in those days. So also did we call some over thirty-five; it all depended on attitude: if a female was inclined to be seriously motivated by some professional idea and was headed for a goal, she might be called a young woman, but goal or no goal, if she was a beauty, "girl" was the preferred specification. Loretto was a girl. In August of that year when I the man became nineteen, Loretto the girl became twenty-three. We fell in love and remained in love—but with lengthy separations—for the next four years.

In 1947, the war being over, we got together again with marriage in mind; we lived for a time at my mother's house in Forest Hills, and then for a time with Loretto's family in the tiny northern Montana town of Chinook. In New York I was working for my mother's sister Pearl, who was running the *Advocate*, the Irish weekly paper her father, my grandfather, had founded in 1893. I was editing the paper, and my qualifications for the job were slim in character and two in number. First, I had worked on the paper as a summer job when I was a high school kid, writing stories, taking pictures, running errands, and helping my grandfather make up the hot-type pages on press nights; and second, I had worked on *The New York Times* where, as a copyboy in the sports department, I was kept on the run with shouts like "Get this copy upstairs in a hurry!" "Get on that phone and take a paragraph on the Lawrenceville-Choate game!" "Get up to makeup, Spiker is yelling for you!" The last order meant to join the assistant sports editor at the "stone," the steel table on which the hot-type forms were laid out. It was from Spiker I learned, for what it was worth, to make up a *Times* page. It wasn't worth anything.

My grandfather had died, and Aunt Pearl needed my help for a while. There was very little money in this, and Loretto couldn't see where it was leading anyway. Neither could I. She went back to Chinook, and I soon followed her. Her mother Lillian and her grandmother ran a general store, and I helped them in the hardware department. They were rich people in terms of land and commercial holdings; they drew their largest income from ranches out on the prairies and commercial spaces in the town, but they were the kind of people who liked to keep personally busy at one small enterprise or another. They knew that as Loretto's husband—if ever I maneuvered my way to that situation, and they earnestly hoped I would be diverted—I could bumble around their various premises indefinitely, helping them with this and that for small pay; and they would have accepted me politely, because they were fond of me, but they knew well that their restless only child would not long tolerate a third-rate social situation in this windblown town on the Milk River.

Loretto's mother thought our parting was the most truly loving thing we ever did for one another. She, Mrs Glenn German, my darling Lillian, was quite right. I call her darling because she and I loved each other, and no one ever took a truer interest in my future than she. Lillian persuaded me to remain in

Montana and enroll in the state university at Missoula. She phoned an old friend, Professor Arthur Shallenburger, and asked him to tuck and squeeze me through the cracks in the registration process for the summer quarter of 1948, with a view toward a degree in English and journalism. The professor did Lillian the favor and I resumed at last the formal education I so pitifully began at Wake Forest. Loretto and I parted with wet faces and choking admissions that this wrenching moment was the worst of our lives. We had always wanted passionately to be together from the first hour of our meeting, but we were never confident of making a go of things. Now at twenty-four I had absolutely no professional prospect in front of me, nor even a wish for one, only a dreamy intention of writing things one day. I was—and knew I was—as palpable a specimen of inadequacy as a girl then twenty-eight could imagine. We both, of course, fell in love again and happily proceeded into lasting marriages.[1]

Why did I enroll myself for a degree in journalism? I found myself not long ago thinking about it in public—why I once wanted to be a reporter, a newspaperman, above all other callings. I was asked the question as a guest on the *Charlie Rose* TV program, and I replied that the press was less rank then than now, but just as biased and misleading. I concluded that forty years ago I was silly.

What I newly observe is the vile style of the press—vile the world over, but nowhere so deeply ingrained as in the most highly developed "civilized" countries where the press is jubilantly "free." Free, that is, of government interference and dictation, though effective government pressure is common enough; but not at all free of the interference and dictation of its corporate owners, who tell their publishers and editors what

---

[1]She married Bill James, editor of *The Great Falls Tribune*.

they wish, and do not wish, to see in print. The writing of news and editorials is expected to be conservative, that is, to humor the owners. And it must be fictionalized to excite the readers. The mass of readers do not demand accuracy, honesty, ethics and good taste in the pages of their favorite newspapers; and the owners' hearts are gladdened by their liberality, feeling themselves free of obligation to give them much of what is good for them. They may give them instead much that is false, prurient, sickening and cheaply acquired; for when such stuff is not cropping up in the real events of the day, it is fabricated like paper grotesqueries in offices, and boldly published as genuine, not only in the supermarket rags but in the presumably respectable rags, the big city dailies, the news-and-picture mags and even the news programs of network television, wherein the hot inventions of the tabloids are nowadays quoted and respectfully credited. Big circulation and big revenue are more than ever the goals of the press. The tiny inhibitions of taste and propriety remaining from my day are shrugged off with a leer.

Charlie Rose asked me if I really thought of the tabloids as press. I replied "Why shouldn't I? Everybody else thinks of them as press. If I were to advocate interfering with them in any way, you'd defend them with the battle cry 'Freedom of the Press.'"

The University of Montana—then called Montana State University, for no reason worth remembering—is in Missoula on the Clark Fork River in a valley in the Rockies called the Bitterroot. I studied at the university from the summer of 1948 until the summer of 1950, when I took the trip to Ireland with my brother Hugh for the purpose of getting him into medical school.

The first thing to say about the university is that I met Nancy there in 1949, and in 1951 married her in Dublin, Ireland, whence she had come to join me in that happy arrangement. She was tall, six feet, slender, shapely and beautiful. She was nineteen, an artist, and she was majoring in art and drama. Her parents and older brother had been graduated from the university—her father and brother with degrees in forestry, her mother in journalism. Missoula was nestled in a beautiful foothill environment, a richly forested campus in a charming old western town. The Northern Pacific and the Milwaukee Road provided rail service, passenger and freight, into Missoula, and Nancy went from there by train to New York, where she met my mother and brother Bob, and two uncles and two aunts of mine; and thence by steamship to Cobh,[2] Ireland. She left behind her a small city with a residual old-fashionedness about it that was soon afterward shucked off in favor of "the latest of everything."

She and I returned there in 1955.

But I want now to tell a sea story.

About those voices I referred to, those spirits within me—two have long dwelt insistently and possessively. That may not be remarkable: my mother was an O'Connor before she married; I am of the Kerry and on my father's side the Galway branches of that family; in short, all Irish.

Now by Irish spirits I mean personalities that make themselves known by commanding whispers. I mentioned them earlier. One of them is a Ghost. Whose? I do not know. The other is a Divil. He is very much a low-class creature given to grumblings and tauntings and teasings, and he is not deeply influential. Taking a portrait as an analogy, I would say that the Ghost has colored my life, the Divil has spattered it. While the Ghost is visiting, the Divil may visit too. He does not bother me. I often remind him of the madness of his counsel.

Let me give you some idea of what I mean. When in late 1943 I first saw Ireland I could have put a golf ball on the shore if one

---

[2]Pronounced "cove" and meaning that in Irish; called Queenstown under the British, it is the principal harbor of County Cork.

had been available on my ship and I had been a strong man with a wood. Yet I could not by any proper means set foot on that shore. The Divil nevertheless urged me to it.

The ship had arrived in the early morning at the mouth of Lough Foyle and had stopped. I came up from the engine room to have a look round and saw that part of our convoy had left us and gone to England or Scotland or Russia. We were holding position, gently under weigh, apparently awaiting our own orders. To the east a good distance off lay Derry in Northern Ireland. Just west before my eyes, as near as I have said, lay Donegal in Eire. I must here swear that the fabled green of Ireland is no fable: it is indeed green like the emerald, a startling green in the dewy morning before the sun gilds it. The sight was hypnotic, and as I stared at it feeling wholly unaccustomed sensations, welcome and unwelcome—surprise, delight, inexplicable sadness, lifted up, thrown down, and I cannot say what else—the Ghost whispered to me "That is Ireland looking at you, boy. Our home. We may allow ourselves a few tears." Being alone on deck, we did.

But the Divil happened to be also in brief residence, and no sooner had I cleared my emotion with a noserag than he piped up "Swim over!"

"What's that?" I snapped.

He giggled at my irritation and said again "Swim over, Jack." He always called me Jack for fun. My first name was John and he liked to play on my boyish resentment at always being called my second, Carroll, the family's preference.

"That's neutral Ireland there" he said.

"I know it" I replied.

"Begob they might detain you—that'd be great! But whether they did or they didn't you could stay as long as you liked. Faith you'd be warmly welcomed—they'd make much over you there—and you as Irish as a bush in Buncrana, with relations from there to Kinsale."

"I've no relations in Donegal."

"Well but you've friends there, a *chara*[3] and friends are as good, and better."

"What friends?"

"Sure isn't your grandfather great with Paddy the Cope?" (One of the leaders of the cooperative movement in Ireland, Patrick Gallagher.)

"My grandfather doesn't know the man" I argued. (For all I knew he did.)

"Arrah the two are known to each other—that's the big thing. Swim over now. We'll saunter about, say hello to the country folk and have a lovely meal or two, and then we'll find a way down to Dublin. Oh man dear there's the town for fun! Never sleeps! Burstin' with people from all over Europe and the ends of the earth—a Constantinople of the West!"

"A ridiculous idea" I murmured, conscious of a lack of conviction. "And" I firmly added, "a dangerous idea."

"Dangerous?" he scoffed. "And what do you call ridin' this tub in and out of the war zones? Look here at the stern of her, the way she's driftin' nearer the land as we're talkin'. Now—there's no one about save only the Swede mate on the bridge with the one bad eye—slip off here. I'll be with you. And we'll put a hand on shore before we're missed."

"Are you seriously telling me to jump ship?"

"Aye!" he exulted. "Jump the bloody ship! To hell with the war! Do you want to get killed? A U-boat hasn't sent you to the bottom only by the mercy of God. But listen you, Jack, that can't last."

"The mercy of God can't last?" I reprimanded him.

"Now, now, now" he countered quickly, "no sacrilege intended, but why put a strain on His Honor's generosity?"

"It's out of the question" I said. Yet at the same time, hard now to believe, I was giving the outrageous proposal intense consid-

---

[3]Irish for "dear friend."

eration. Should I run first to the cabin and grab the little rubber-lined emergency bag with papers and money and change-of-clothes in it? Who or what might delay me below? In an instant I had become, to all intents and purposes, a fugitive. Don't go below! My hands were gripping the rail. Abandon the bag? Yes. This moment was the moment of best chance. Wait—off with the shoes—tie them to the belt—

And then I stopped. The Ghost was laughing gently. "You must be daft—" he whispered.

I stepped back from the rail and looked down at the deck in embarrassment. I agreed: "Yes. Nuts. Completely nuts."

"The time to go to Ireland" said the Ghost, "is when I tell you to go, not before. Trust in me. And the back of your hand to the Divil."

Desertion! Any list of odious offenses would surely have desertion near the top, and I had been powerfully tempted to it. Guilt dogged me a while after, but not too long a while, I must confess; and nowadays I reflect only that I might have drowned in the swim. Thus does growing old denature shame. Within the half hour the ship was at full speed carrying her cargo of weapons and munitions and me south through the Irish Sea to the Bristol Channel. Not till we were alongside a dock in Swansea did I hear again from the Divil. I was looking to the east where long lances of light were probing the sky and guns were thumping the dark, and he spoke again, quietly and caustically.

"We'll hardly find a bacchanal in these regions."

"Go away" I told him.

"Wales!" he sighed. "T'was never in the best of times a happy corner of creation."

In the summer of 1950, the Ghost told me it was time to go to Ireland. "Take your brother over" he advised. "If he wants to be a doctor, that's the place for him." My younger brother Hugh did want to go to medical school and lacked the two requisites for admission in America: high marks in premedical courses and a member of the family in the medical profession. In Dublin Hugh would at least find the latter, Dr. Matthew H. O'Connor, Professor of Pathology and Dean of the Royal College of Surgeons, Ireland. We did not advise this gentleman of our coming. We just boarded a ship and hoped we would be cordially received.

Now there happened to be at that moment a war in Korea. I did not have to fight in the war or suffer personal loss in it, yet it left me with some unsettling thoughts about American life—our politics, institutions, popular myths and weaknesses—that ultimately found their way into my work as an actor. This is not unusual; the development of dramatic character is affected a little or a lot by an actor's societal perceptions, and probably the plainest example was to be seen in John Wayne: he perceived America as the preeminent hero-nation, virtually a land of heroes in which he himself felt heroic (and actually was, as I knew him) and infused that perception into all his roles as naturally as if it were one of the primary emotions.

Before Korea my feeling about my country had differed little from Wayne's. Though I had been a critical American, a constant complainer, very different I am sure from what the Duke had been in his twenties, I too, in my own way, thought we were a hero-nation. No one was more certain than I that America simply could not, by its constitutional nature, go far wrong. If someone had asked "Do you believe that no matter who is at the helm of America, God is the captain,"[4] I might have flinched at the religiosity of the question but I should not have debated it. After Korea I was more than willing to debate it. The Divil was at my ear saying:

"The Lord gave man the free will to sail his own ships of state. But His Lordship is not personally enjoyin' Himself on board any of the wretched tubs." The Ghost said "Ah, maybe he is. Sure it's

---

[4]Written by some clergyman on a page of a religious calendar.

a dear thought to think he's on ours, anyway." But the Divil's argument was a stronger one.

As we all know, if motives have to be explained in high moralistic language there is usually something wrong with them. A right motive—e.g., we fought Japan and the Axis because they attacked us and declared war on us—requires no moral decoration. Not to beat about the bush, the White House deceived us about Korea. The press deceived us too. I began to despise the newspapers, and I haven't been a newspaper reader since. The circumstances of that war so many years ago have faded out of public memory; anyone today under fifty would hardly remember it. Besides, a war in Vietnam yet to come would displace other wars in our minds; it would be the longest war in our belligerent history, and public anguish over it would become more intense than in any previous war. Yet in Korea we suffered about as many battle deaths as in Vietnam in less than a third of the time, and the causes, purposes and conditions of the Korean War were equally obfuscated, false and terrible.

When Hugh and I were sailing to Ireland the war was three weeks old, having begun the last week in June. We were members of a Montana National Guard unit and expected it to be called up.[5] We had thought at first of postponing the trip until the military matter was settled, but second thoughts (the Ghost, I should say) persuaded us to go. We simply had to look at the trip as a summer holiday that might be cut short. The commander of our Guard unit had no indication of immediate call-up; he himself thought we had no more than an even chance of being called at all.

It was a presidential war, a policy war, an option war. A president other than Truman, or Truman himself, might have chosen another option, might have formulated another policy. Four years later during the war between the French and the

---

[5]We joined the Guard for the pay—small but helpful in those college days.

Vietnamese, Eisenhower considered going in, but opted for staying out. Kennedy opted for measured participation. Johnson plunged in. Nixon plunged further in, then backed out, then started a new war against Cambodia. Nobody had expected Truman to take part in a Korean civil war, if one should begin. His military chiefs had no battle plan; on the contrary, they had a plan for getting out of the way—withdrawing to Japan.

I thought Truman was totally wrong—his political vision faulty, his practical leadership unintelligent, his moral justification false. For me the issue of morality in war—whether or not it is a "just war"—turns on the question of choice. When you wage war because you have no choice you are acting justly—probably you are. But when you have a reasonable choice and choose to wage war you can't call your war just—clearly you can't. The fiction promulgated by Truman—that the war was not really a war but a United Nations police action against "bandits," in which we were merely part of a lawful international posse—was derisory; and it was insulting to American troops who were soon looking round the battlefields and seeing mostly themselves.

Nobody in the country was given any facts to judge by, other than a report that North Korean tanks were clattering into the South. Our newspapers printed only our own official version of events, as handed down from MacArthur in Tokyo, and if you were a right-thinking person you accepted that version. Communist North Korea was said to have plotted and committed naked aggression against free and democratic South Korea. This was absurd. The communists of the North, despite their public blustering, knew that the South was a prize that was within their grasp without a fight. The South's "president," the dictator Syngman Rhee, had recently invited his people to confirm him in an election and his people had confirmed only that they wanted to be rid of him. Rhee, though still crazily hanging on to his palace, was definitely out. The United States seemed disinterested and vaguely disgusted. Acheson, the secretary of state, had declared that Korea was no longer within our "defense perimeter." The North Koreans could look forward to a coup in the South—Rhee frog-marched out of the palace, and a deal worked out for reunification of the country. If the Northerners rushed the process, if they invaded the South needlessly, they would run straight into a small American advisory force; they might bring on themselves a ruinous American counterinvasion from Japan. For them war was foolish.

But for Rhee the American counterinvasion was his one chance of survival; he had to induce the Northern Reds to act rashly, provoke them to attack him, and draw in the United States. I believed then, and still believe, that he accomplished this in the simplest possible way: he attacked the North Koreans. His charge that they had committed unprovoked aggression against him was ludicrous. He had attacked them before, and they had attacked him. Border incidents had been frequent and the Reds had deployed troops near their border to repel a big decisive attack on them, an attack Rhee had always promised and was still promising—an attack our own military men on the spot were nervous about.

On board the ship to Ireland the war was the main topic of conversation. There was no enthusiasm for it; nobody knew why we were in it, but nobody was prepared to say that it was a bad war, a cockeyed war. At the same time everybody wondered whether it might not be the start of World War Three. Some were certain, on the basis of no evidence at all, that this was Russia's opening gambit. Well—that was the assumption of the American president himself, according to his daughter's later account—she was with him at the time. A man who was with Stalin at the time, Khrushchev, who could never be accused of sweetening the memory of his predecessor, said that the Soviet dictator would have preferred that the North Koreans avoided war. Stalin withdrew a Soviet military advisory force of several thousand when the fighting started, and it was to this perplexing action that Khrushchev attributed the Korean communists' subsequent reverses.

Those Truman days were timorous days, a time of deep uneasiness, of security mania, loyalty oaths, witch hunts and stool pigeons. It was from Truman that the infamous McCarthy drew his inspiration. To strangers one talked about important things only after a lot of conversational feeling-out, and then very carefully.

"They say they have FBI men riding these ships."

This remark was made to me by an unhappy-looking man of fifty or so who was a teacher at a New York City college. We were on the deck of the liner *America*.

"They say?" I said. "What do you mean?"

"You know what I mean."

"Who are the FBI supposed to be looking for?"

He whispered "Guys who might be, you know—" he twitched the fingers of his left hand, "politically over here."

"You mean Reds?"

"Sha!" he hissed, glancing forward, aft, and over his shoulder at the waves. "No, not Reds. What Reds? All the Reds are dead. Or being indicted. Or working for the FBI. They're looking for people who are maybe a little too liberal—against this lousy war, for instance."

"And if they find them?"

"They jerk their passports. They report them to their employers, and to the American Legion, and the smear committees."

"Well, I'm not a liberal" I said, "though I'm against the lousy war." I noticed that I too was whispering.

"See that guy that just came out, moping around with the smile? With the baseball hat? He's the FBI agent for tourist class—our guy. That's the word. Sha! Here he comes."

The guy with the baseball cap joined us. He sprawled in a chair next to me and remarked on the beauty of the day, the calm of the sea, the speed of the ship, the danger of icebergs in summer, the beautiful bodies of the seven girls at table twenty-eight. I looked at my teacher friend to discover his reaction to this reassuring dose of the commonplace. He was staring wide-eyed at the man in the baseball cap and displaying a tiny smile wholly unnatural to his features.

The Cap kept on talking. "I hear" he said casually to me, "that you're getting off in Ireland."

I was startled. He hears? How, I wondered, did he hear that? Was he asking around about me? Whom did he ask? What was his game? I who always claimed not to give a damn was suddenly giving a damn. "What's in Ireland?" The Cap went on. "Poor relations?" He threw his head back in a joyful whinny, and my friend took the opportunity to press my right toe hard with his left toe.

The Divil was suddenly in my ear and he hummed "Tell this bloody spy to go check for cypher on the men's room wall." But the Ghost whispered "Lightly, lightly, he's too silly to be a spy."

"I'm going" I said, "to see a certain doctor, a cousin who, by the way, happens to be rather well off."

"Problems?" he inquired.

"Yes" I said, "left eye is constantly wandering, driving me crazy."

"Oh geez!" he exclaimed. "You'd trust a foreigner? Why didn't you let an American eye doctor look at your eye?"

"I did. The American wouldn't do what I want."

"With your eye? What do you want?"

"I wanted to replace it with something that doesn't move" I said.

At my right my friend the teacher exploded in laughter. The Cap looked coldly at him, then at me; but in a moment he too was laughing. So was I. It turned out that he was an ice cream distributor from Providence.

My teacher friend and I had panicked like fools, but such was the tension of the time. A lot has been written about the great fear of the fifties and I need not chronicle it here. I will say, though, that the American press was to blame for it. The Congressional inquisitions violated the Constitution, and the Supreme Court ultimately ruled them foul, but the press, instead of denouncing them, whipped them to further frenzy. Unchallenged, urged onward, the president violated the Constitution, arrogated to himself a power reserved to Congress, and made war de facto. He demonstrated that an American president unrestrained will equal any dictator in contempt and disregard of law. In fact no dictator in history had ever moved troops more swiftly, secretly and illegally than this American president Truman. (Though he would be matched by others in years to come.) American reporters and editors, though they were under no pressure from a ministry of propaganda, a Dr Goebbels, demonstrated that they could be counted on to keep themselves nicely in line with any fast-moving führer. Let the führer make the great decisions about life and death, right and wrong!—just as Hitler and Stalin had done with no reference to a *reichstag* or council of commissars. If Truman, in order to work his will, had padlocked the House and Senate and cordoned off the Capitol with Marines, his flouting of the Constitution might have been more alarming, but no less outrageous.

There were a few voices heard in protest: presidential candidate Robert Taft raised the constitutional question; but the press tuned the voices down and out. I was not surprised. In nearly every international crisis of the past hundred and fifty years the newspapers had howled for war, and howled most loudly when the nominated enemy appeared to be a pushover, as in 1940 when editors were chary about fighting the Germans but eager to take on the underrated Japanese. And in the sixties, when the Viet Cong looked easily beatable, the press gave massive backing to two other presidents who, in imitation of Truman, committed the United States to a bloody wicked decade in Vietnam. The *New York Post* (in its pre-Australian days) invited its readers to consider the benefits of a tranquil world, but most of the rest, the important dailies of America's big towns, advised us that we were already at war with the "communist world" and that any contrary doubts were probably Red-instilled and could only weaken our will to win.

One might have thought that the Second World War had worked a change; it was like no foreign war in our history: it was no dispersal of rag-tag Colombians in Panama, no rout of demoralized Spaniards in Cuba and the Philippines, no naval strong-arm stuff in Central America, no gallop into Chihuahua after Pancho Villa, no seventeen-month expedition against the Kaiser's exhausted armies in France;[6] it was the most appalling slaughter that had ever been loosed upon mankind. But the spiritual corruption of war, the old ugly policies of competition and encroachment, the old dreams of power, would now at last and for all time be extirpated. The men of the press, above all men, would see to that: a press reborn, a press that had seen what the old habits could bring us to—the devastation of countries, the staggering loss of armies, the annihilation of urban populations, the death camps, the banishment of reason, the Bomb—a press that could foretell the final utterly unthinkable war. But in the summer of 1950 our press, still the creature of the remorseless right wing, was actually trumpeting the unthinkable. American armies were battling the North Koreans, we were anticipating a clash with the Chinese (and got one), Truman was talking about dropping nuclear bombs again, and the American people were being told to dig holes for themselves in their gardens.

I imagined, and so did most people, that whether or not the unthinkable happened, the Korean War itself would be very short. MacArthur confidently said so and the White House was saying what MacArthur said. Little did we know. MacArthur was soon fired by Truman for insisting on extending the war into China, and three more Julys came and went before another president stopped the awful folly at a stalemate. Were the American people blameless? No. We went along with Truman. We like to think of our presidents as possessing a charisma

---

[6]Which had ceased fighting but had never surrendered.

bestowed by the Almighty upon their inauguration. And we rather like a war if it can be quickly won. Only when a tough enemy prolongs it do we find we hate it—begin to question whether our real interests were ever at stake in it—question the honesty of it. Always we question last the thing we should have questioned first. Pain, not conscience, evokes the moral squawk in America.

In any case the president in the summer of 1950 moved too swiftly for the public conscience to follow. The public eye could hardly follow him; he made his decisive moves while the public slept. The news of the war was deceptive and remained deceptive to the end. In all wars, as Senator Hiram Johnson observed a generation earlier, truth is the first casualty.

From Dublin I wrote to Captain Foster in Missoula and told him where I was and what I was doing. In spite of what he had said I expected a cablegram from him daily. But he never sent one. We were never federalized. When I saw him again five years later he told me that our unit, a tank-destroyer artillery company, had been inspected by the army and found wanting in equipment and therefore preparation; 105-mm howitzers were not notably good at destroying tanks. I must confess here that I had thought about refusing to report if summoned. Would I have had the courage to refuse? Few men go willingly to a foreign war; few believe in their secret hearts that the war was unavoidable or necessary; most go along obediently, preferring to be a casualty than to be prosecuted and disgraced. I probably would have boarded a ship back, cold with fear, hot with anger, and filled with contempt for myself. I was securely tied, without knowing it, to what the hippies of a later decade called "the uptight establishment."

Twenty-two years afterward, writing and rehearsing and performing a TV episode in which Archie Bunker confronted a defector from the Vietnam War, I was able to satirize, albeit grimly, the mixed emotions of that uptight majority. Archie was a prototype: his variants were, and are, on all levels of American life, the highest, the lowest and the in-between. They are all bound to the heroic vision of America, though not as Duke Wayne was bound to it in perfect belief; they are all bound by a fearful apprehension about national life: that to analyze its weaknesses and contradictions is to destroy it, to gaze steadily at the mythology of it is the only way to preserve it. Nothing new in this; it is known as patriotism. But there is a sadness in it—the sadness of unspoken disbelief, unacknowledged shame, painful pretense—and I have infused this sadness in some measure into all the American characters I have been asked to represent, just as the Duke infused in his characters the ebullient confidence of the hero. Animated in this way were all my unheroes from every walk of life—little roles and big roles, in movies, TV dramas and stage plays, and the TV series that comprised more than a third of all my work. Was the infusion of sadness observable? Probably not.

How observable could it have been anyway? Millions of people thought Archie was a happy hero.

6

• • • • • • •

My father's family in New York, though I knew them a little, were unknown to my brothers, Hugh and Bob. There were interesting reasons for this, and I will come to them. But Hugh and I became very close to my father's family in Ireland. When we arrived there in the summer of 1950, we telephoned Dr Matt O'Connor, who was my father's first cousin. He greeted us familiarly, as if he had always known us. Matt, as he asked us to call him, had an unusual history for an Irishman: he was born in New York and was brought as a very small immigrant to Ireland. There he stayed for the rest of his life. He was instantly charming; indeed he stands out in memory as the most completely charming man I ever knew. He was a medical scientist, a discoverer of causes and effects, yet a practical physician and teacher. He was an engagingly witty talker, conversant in politics and the arts, a theatre- and concert-goer, a notable host, a reliable friend—an Irish gentleman of the first rank.

His warm hospitality did not extend, however, to placing a relative in the College of Surgeons. He said that no one had ever been admitted by mere passage through the office of the registrar. The annual entrance examination in science, mathematics and English, a pretty formidable barrier, was to be held six or seven weeks hence. The candidates list was complete but Hugh's name would be added. Nepotism it was, but not crass nepotism. Hugh would have to pass the exam; he would have to start studying for it immediately. We went into a little hotel in Earlsfort Terrace, a short walk from St. Stephen's Green park, where Surgeons was located. Hugh enrolled in a "grind," which we here know as a crash course.

My plan was to return to New York, report on the trip to my mother, then return to Montana to finish my junior and senior years at the state university. I was just then twenty-six, rather old for a college junior, a straggler of the war years. I had allowed myself two weeks in Ireland for touring about, perhaps visiting some of my mother's family in Kerry, but for some reason I decided that Hugh needed me in Dublin. He did not. He was a mature twenty-two, well traveled and confident of himself. He had served a hitch in the U.S. regular army and, while a sergeant on occupation duty in Japan, had been offered an opportunity to prepare for West Point. He declined, wishing to go into medicine above all things. He left the army and completed two years of premedical studies, one of them at UM in Missoula, where he and I roomed together. Still I felt needlessly fatherly and remained with him in Dublin.

I passed my time walking about, looking into shops and pubs, the Trinity library, the art galleries, writing letters. I went to the theatre. The Abbey was closed for the summer, but there were variety shows (vaudeville to us) at the Queen's and the Olympia, and touring musicals from England, like Ivor Novello's *King's Rhapsody,* playing at The Gaiety. At the famous Gate Theatre Lord Longford's company were performing plays in repertoire; I saw Sheridan's *School for Scandal* done very cleverly and stylishly by a fine bunch of actors, some of whom later became friends of mine. And I began to form an impression of the Dublin character.

Walking beside the River Liffey, I stopped a pedestrian and asked "Is that an army barracks over there?" We were on Wolfe Tone Quay standing in a blowing mist. The Dublin man was wearing a tweed hat pulled down and a mackintosh pulled up; his face was visible from his brows to the end of his nose. He stared at me and never so much as glanced in the direction I had indicated, but in a weary voice a little muffled by the collar of the mac he said "That's Collins Barracks. And you can call it an army if you like; it's more like a mob."

My Divil whispered to me "They're all like that here, dour as a crepe on a door knocker. Come on, Jack, we'll run down to Italy for a fortnight, the land of songs and smiles! And then back to the States before the leaves fall." I coughed him away. I said thanks to the man in the mac.

"Are you lost?" he inquired.

"No, I'm all right" I assured him. "I'm on my way up to Thomas Street."

"To visit the brewery?"

"No, to see where they hanged Robert Emmet."

"They!" said the man in the mac. "You mean the English. Why don't you say the bloody English?" It was a bitter question, yet he asked it with a laugh.

"Yes of course" I swiftly emended. "The English."

"And not satisfied with hanging him—" he continued laughing, "they split him in two from the top of his head to the bottom of his bollocks, then cut him crosswise into four pieces!"

I nodded. "Yes. True."

"Good day to you" said the man in the mac. He stepped round me and went briskly toward O'Connell Street.

The Divil was still near. "Isn't that a dour specimen for you!"

In fact the Dubliner is not dour; he has a very merry soul. He merely regards the works and institutions of nations as ill conceived, with his own, far from being excepted, the first to be cited. Argue with him at your peril. Stand up in a pub and extol the protected myths and doctrines of society, any society, and incur a barrage of hilarity. A polite drawing room is no security against the risk: there the attack will be subtler—perhaps only a small yet crushing sigh of ennui—but no less memorable.

Dublin is not a carping town, though Yeats in pique once said it was, and so did Shaw. (Everyone hates his hometown now and then.) Dublin is exceedingly hostile to pretense, it is a place where the emperor dare not proclaim that he is dressed when he is naked; nor may he expect more than a modicum of approval when he is covered in his best, for every intelligent Dubliner knows that somewhere there is an emperor covered in better. An American could find this upsetting, coming from a land where praise of naked emperors can earn him anything from a drink at the Elks to an exalted political sinecure. But not I. My mother's side of the family, the side I knew, though all but the parents were born and raised in New York, had regularly produced the scorn of the man in the mac. I was inured to it. To tell the truth, I loved it.

The New York family were informed, opinionated and critical. They saw bunk everywhere; they were chary of all the powers-that-be, the politicos, the industrialists, the bankers, the union bosses, the press lords, the clergy, the radicals, the conservatives, every strident voice aspiring to authority. They would be called today, both by the right and the left, a gang of chronic dissidents, but as I have said, they were discreet, more inclined to wit than to action, content to do their debunking round our big dining room table on Sunday afternoons. And I remember the table for fun, not fury. Education was the one institution that escaped the fierce joke, for there were often four professional teachers present: my mother, two of her sisters, and one of her brothers (the real Jack). Present too were my father, a lawyer; my mother's father; and sometimes an uncle who dealt in rare books and prepared genealogies for well-off people who yearned for such things.

That talk, which went on for about ten years, the decade of the thirties, had a strong influence on me. I became prematurely a skeptic, mistrustful of everything I was hearing on the radio and reading in the papers. I wanted to emulate the table gang and marshal facts and logic and hurl them against sham, and I thought of becoming a famous journalist who would debunk and enlighten a grateful world. When the thirties were over I was away from the family far more than with them, and heard no more debunking. We were at war, and the prosecution of war required of everyone a wholly uncritical state of mind. After the war another war, the Cold War against our recent ally Russia, and still another, the hot war in Korea, required the same. Dublin, a neutral capital in World War Two, had known no such constraint; its teasing of orthodoxy had continued normally and energetically, and when I arrived there in that summer of 1950 I felt as if I had come back again to the dining table.

Dr. Matt O'Connor was able to arrange a little social time for Hugh and me. He drove us here and there sight-seeing, and to meet his sister Aileen. This was a most important visit. Everybody in the family in Dublin referred to Aileen's residence in Pembroke Road as The Flat, and nearly everybody turned up there on Sunday afternoons for five minutes or five hours. The Flat was the family's central news exchange, and also a place where one could get lunch, tea, high tea, supper, nightcaps, one after the other into the early hours of the morning. People never felt they were imposing on Aileen because she all but forbade them to leave. She hated going to bed where, she reminded us, "most people die." She said she needed no more than two hours of sleep. The Flat, with its stream of weekend visitors, was a microcosm of highly opinionated Dublin: doctors, lawyers, poets, writers of articles and plays, students, business people, and ordinary working people.

Aileen was happy to see Hugh and me. She professed to be out of touch with America, but she was eager not so much to hear the news, of which she was really well apprised, as to hear our particular version of it, and to observe how we looked and sounded telling it. She was unmarried, about fifty-six, small, with a pretty face and smile and very keen eyes. She liked to stand in front of her sitting room fire facing her seated guests, hands clasped behind her back (perhaps a military habit, for she had been in the British army, a twenty-one-year-old nurse in the trenches in France in the First World War), a cigarette held in her lips, its long ash bending toward the floor, where it usually landed.

Dr. Matt O'Connor's brothers and sisters, all but one, had like himself reversed the usual flow of Irish emigration: they emigrated from America to Ireland. Matt's father had traveled the usual way from Ireland to America, and so had my father's father, and those two brothers, Tim and John, were business partners in New York in the 1890s. They owned two prosperous saloons on the Lower East Side of Manhattan and they went broke. The father of Matt was, as they say, "his own best customer." This led to other excesses, and his wife left him and took six children born in New York to Ireland, to her home village of Ballinasloe in County Galway. Of these second cousins of mine Aileen was the eldest, Kathleen next, Matt next, and after them Joe, Dewey and Nora. Joe, a lieutenant in the Dublin Fusiliers in the first war, was killed in France, and Dewey died of coronary disease. Kathleen worked in the Irish civil service and Nora was a nurse. Both were widows. A seventh child, Lily, who was married to a policeman in County Monaghan, was the only one born in Ireland. Her father traveled back from New York to effect a family reunion, failed in that, but was permitted evidently to assist in the matter of Lily.

My father's father died in New York of influenza. He left my grandmother in tight circumstances but she and her children nevertheless managed well enough. My father, Edward, and his sister Margaret became lawyers. Another son Hugh (after whom my brother was named) became a newspaper reporter and worked for the old *New York World* and *The New York Times.* The eldest son John went into publishing and must have been good at it because he was president of Grosset & Dunlop when he retired. John and Hugh are long dead. I seldom saw any of my father's family, though we lived in the same city. They steered clear of us, for interesting reasons which I will come to.

It was in Dublin with Aileen O'Connor at The Flat that Hugh and I spent our Sunday afternoons that summer of 1950. And there the notion of my remaining in Ireland was broached. "Isn't it a pity" said Aileen, "that you won't be staying on with Hugh. Couldn't you finish your B.A. at Trinity or the National?"

"I doubt it" I replied. I was then engaged to Nancy, who was about to enter her senior year at UM and expected to see me back there in September. I assumed, wrongly as it turned out, that an Irish university would be unwilling to validate a multitude of American course credits, and also that my costs would be too high in Dublin. But I did not dismiss the idea. I began to think that if a transfer was manageable I might profitably and pleasantly spend the next couple of years in Dublin. After all, this was not a small university town but one of the oldest capital cities of the world, once a center of Western learning, and though completely foreign to an American, it made its unique culture entirely accessible through a common language.

I wrote to Nancy: "The time would pass quickly and you could come over next June as soon as you're graduated and we could be married here." Her reply was at once sad and glad. And she said that I ought to stay.

Matt O'Connor introduced me to the president of University College Dublin (one of the three branches of the national university system; the others are at Cork and Galway), and that gentleman, Michael Tierney, referred me to Professor Jeremiah Mahoney, registrar, and Professors Dudley Edwards and Roger McHugh of the arts faculty. I asked UM to send them a transcript of my record and they fixed a day for a "kind of examination." I came prepared to write essays on God-knew-what, but no, I was received by the three professors in one of the tutorial rooms of the college and was asked simply to talk to them about world history and literature and any and all collateral subjects for about three hours. The professors were most cordial; they provided a lot of tea and sweet biscuits and smoked all of my American cigarettes and finally, after expressing approval of the transcript and the talk, told me I would receive in a few days a letter of admission. I was to pursue a B.A. in European and Irish history with a subsidiary (minor) in English literature.

Hugh was pleased and so were Matt and Aileen and the rest of the family. I wrote the news to my mother in New York and she responded happily; Hugh and I would still be together. She said that she or her sister Pearl or her sister Jo would probably fly over to see us at the first opportunity, and she sent me some money. I was receiving no educational support from Uncle Sam. Merchant seamen of World War Two were not recognized by our military as members of the armed forces, though we were enthusiastically recognized as such by the German navy. We were not therefore entitled to the so-called G.I. Bill of Rights.[1] My only benefits were monies willed by my mother's father and other monies lent by my mother. Hugh of course, being a veteran of the regular army, was in a better position. My outlay for the college year in Dublin would come to about 750 pounds, or in those days something under two thousand dollars, which would cover fees, books and living expenses.

Hugh passed his entrance exam for the College of Surgeons and he and I took a flat in Lower Leeson Street, which we invited another student to share, an American, Arthur Fedel, who became a lasting friend. He was studying for a master's degree in Irish literature, and in time he became a teacher and a dean at the University of Pittsburgh.

We had already made friends of two other students, Americans of Jamaican descent raised in Harlem: Herbert Holmes, whom we met on the *America* on the voyage from New York to

---

[1] Congress in 1993 officially made merchant seamen veterans. But I cannot now go back to school.

Cobh, and his cousin Eric Williams, already living in Dublin. Herbie, like Hugh, was hopeful of getting into Surgeons. Eric, now dead, was a student at Surgeons in his second year. Holmes now practices medicine in New Jersey and through the years has remained our closest friend. We four and Art Fedel were much together in Dublin.

I liked Dublin and liked the university, but by the third week of Michaelmas term, about the end of October, I was in depression. My classmates at UCD were all eighteen- and nineteen-year-olds and I felt like everybody's uncle. I had lunch at the college with my contemporary, ex-Marine Art Fedel, and moaned about the matter. Art too, on his postgraduate level, was about five years older than his fellow students. He said, "Listen, let's be glad we're ahead of these kids in something." The Irish teenagers at UCD, and of course at Trinity and Surgeons and the colleges of Cork and Galway, seemed to be bursting with all kinds of knowledge. A visiting teacher, an Englishman, told me they were astonishingly well grounded in the art and science and history of the world. I can testify that in modern literature, though their traditional formal study stopped in the vicinity of Milton, they were as familiar as I with Hawthorne, Melville, Whitman and Poe and contemporary Americans like Faulkner, Fitzgerald, Bellow, Tennessee Williams and Arthur Miller. They knew far more than I about current British and French writers and were steeped, naturally, in their own great literature.

But apart from that, I could not shake off a feeling of foolishness—a man of twenty-six plodding through the days and months on funds from my mother with no plan, no answer for anybody who might ask "What are you going to do with yourself?" And everybody I met did ask that very thing. And the trusting girl I loved was coming over in the summer to marry me. How did I intend to manage that?

I told people I would probably teach; it was the farthest thing from my mind, but I knew it was the answer that in Dublin always seemed to repel further interest. (In fact I did begin teaching in New York a few years later and very nearly went on teaching.) I might have gone back to Montana but for the good company I had: Holmes, Williams and Fedel, and of course my beloved Hugh, one of the most cheerful and witty men I have ever known. The five of us went about the town together in twos and threes and sometimes all in a group. Soon we made six; we met an Italian of about my age, Renato Sidoli, who had come to Dublin to learn English. "They speak it best here" he told Art Fedel, who had met him at Newman House,[2] the UCD student union. Fedel, who spoke Italian, had to translate Renato's assertion for the rest of us. Renato became in time a very successful and popular Dublin businessman, the owner of the Unicorn restaurant, an importer of Italian wines and various produce—and a very dear friend of mine.

One of us always knew where student parties were going on, and there were a lot of them, Dublin being a three-college town. We went to the theatre; the Abbey was open for its regular autumn-winter season, and the Gate Theatre Company under its founders Hilton Edwards and Micheàl MacLìammòir had opened its season with a new production of *Richard II*. We caught Dublin's movie fever, rushing to all the cinemas, like everybody else in town, whenever there was a change of program. The cinemas were always jammed. And we found our favorite pubs: they were on the South Side (of the Liffey), within easy walking distances of where we lived, and they were the pubs frequented by writers, newspapermen, actors—the "talking" pubs, Neary's, Synott's, The Palace, Davy Byrne's, The Bailey, the Horse Shoe bar in the Shelbourne Hotel. Our little gang must have studied some of the time, and I vaguely recall the boys in Surgeons hunched over books, but my most vivid recollections are of not studying, and I have to think we did more of that than the other.

---

[2]John Henry Cardinal Newman who founded the National University.

The Divil told me that our flat in Leeson Street was too gloomy to study in (and indeed the Ghost agreed with him), and I did not have to be told by anyone that the National and Trinity College libraries were too cold. Besides, I hated disciplined reading and had always got by somehow without it. I never got by in good style, though. I suppose the diversions in Dublin balanced the depressions, and I stayed. The Ghost said, "Don't worry about your young lady who's coming over; she'll manage everything for you."

7

•••••••

One day Art Fedel told me that a couple of the students in the dramatic society wanted me to be in a play but were shy about asking me. I seemed to them a little stern and distant. I was delighted. I had wondered whether the students did plays. The college had no department of drama; like its sister colleges in Ireland and England it regarded activities like play production and publishing the student literary magazine as merely extracurricular, though it did fund them in a modest way through the department of English. Art introduced the students to me and I made them happy by agreeing to play the father in Thornton Wilder's *The Happy Journey to Trenton and Camden.*

They staged it in their Little Theatre at the top of Newman House, which had only thirty-five seats. The evening they planned also offered a scene from Marlowe's *Faustus,* and when an actor had to withdraw from this they persuaded me to take his place. I was the plumpest Mephistopheles ever seen on a stage. I was acclaimed the hit of the evening and could hardly wait to be in another production. I was not a raw beginner. I had played at

UM in *Life with Father, Winterset, Our Town* and *Antigone*. I had taken a couple of drama courses and even joined the Masquers, the student drama club. I met Nancy while acting in those UM plays; she was acting too, and also designing stage scenery and costumes. Art and drama were her major undergraduate studies.

The next production of the UCD dramatic society was Chekhov's *The Cherry Orchard,* and it was done in the large theater of the college, Aula Maxima; it was most important to the students for it was going to tour to Galway and be part of a national student drama festival. The colleges of Cork and Galway, and Trinity of Dublin would be represented, and so too would Queen's University of Belfast. And there would be a prize. I do not remember which college finally got that prize. We did not. But the adjudicator gave a spoken critique of each play and she highly praised our *Cherry Orchard*. She gave especial praise to the characterization of Lopakhin, i.e., to me, and I was profoundly pleased. She was a professional director and she said there was "something professional" about me, and I thought then and there that I should be happy to have the chance of acting professionally.

The chance came in the spring. The dramatic society put on a very interesting and celebrated modern verse play and I was "discovered" in it by a professional producer. The play was T. S. Eliot's *The Cocktail Party* and it was publicized and reviewed by the Dublin press as if it were as important as anything the professionals were doing. Our press notices were very good and everybody in town attended including Miss Shelagh Richards, actress, producer, director, and soon to be a friend of great importance. She sent a note offering me a part in a play she was going to present at The Gaiety, Dublin's most beautiful theater. I accepted at once.

My part in *That Lady* by novelist Kate O'Brien was small but good. Shelah Richards played the leading part with great presence and skill, and everybody was glad to see her again. She had been a favorite as a leading actress at the Abbey, and she had been absent for a while from the Dublin stage. Her great ability, however, could not by itself give the play more than two weeks of life. Set in the court of Philip II of Spain, it was nicely written as a piece of imagined history, but it offered no thought that followed one out of the theater. I became aware of a theatrical truth, something I never had to consider as an amateur playing in established old hits: people want to leave the theater with some insight into the human condition, something that, in the light of their own experience, they can find value in. I suppose it may be said that anything on the stage gives value in some measure, and the point, being subjective, asks for no argument. But since that time my own test of value has been the amount and kind of conversation the play evokes over supper, and not only supper the night of the play.

"You remind me a little of Arthur Sinclair" Shelagh told me at tea one afternoon. Sinclair was an Irish actor who had been very successful on the English stage. I had heard deeply respectful things about him and felt greatly flattered by the comparison. "I hope you'll stay with acting" she said, "and I'm wondering if you'll go with me and Lennox Robinson this summer to Edinburgh, the annual drama festival. The Abbey was invited and refused—it's their no-tour policy[1]—and Lennox and I think we can put together a representative Irish company. We think we should. The festival people are thrilled. We'll do Synge's *Playboy* and Yeats's *Cathleen ni Houlihan* and Lennox's *Whiteheaded Boy*. And we'll have Siobhan McKenna and her husband Denis O'Dea from the Abbey, and Denis Brennan and Liam Gannon from the Gate, and me of course and a few others on holiday from the Abbey, and you."

"Me" I said, "in a representative Irish company?"

"Well" she replied, "you've got the right sort of name. And I think the talent. And you do remind me of Sinclair."

---

[1] At that time.

Nancy was with me on that tour to Edinburgh; it was our honeymoon. Nancy was also part of the company as understudy to Siobhan McKenna and assistant to stage manager Josie McAvin.

Nancy had got her bachelor of arts degree in art and drama in June, and arrived on a ship at Cobh in July. I met her, we came up to Dublin by train, and she took a room in a little hotel in Hatch Street. On the following day we went to see the pastor of St. Kevin's church in Synge Street and applied to be married. We were indignantly refused by the priest, who ordered me to send Nancy back home for six months until a dispensation could be got from Rome. Nancy was not a Catholic.

Marriage without benefit of clergy was possible at a registry office if the couple were willing to affirm that they had no religion, but we declined to do so. We went instead to a Church of Ireland, which was spiritually close enough to Nancy, who was raised in the American Episcopal Church,[2] and it was close enough for me, who, at the time, was not attending the Catholic Church or any other church. We were accepted, the banns were posted, we got letters from home verifying our unmarried state, and in due course were married: that is, in the middle of rehearsals, the 28th of July 1951. Nancy and I asked for the Saturday off to do it, promising to be back at rehearsal promptly Monday morning, and the day was given to us gladly, though not without astonishment and hilarity. It was not the way people got married in Ireland! Hugh was back in New York for the summer, so Art Fedel and a girl he knew stood with us at the ceremony in St. Ann's in Dawson Street. My bride was twenty, I was twenty-seven. We four and the celebrant made up the occasion. There was no one else in the ancient little church.

---

[2]The Church of Ireland was related to the Church of England but was not nearly as ceremonious.

Renato Sidoli discovered that we were staying for a day and a night at the Royal Hibernian Hotel; he found the floor and the room, and discreetly serenaded us with voice and guitar. I seem to remember that he sang "Parlami d'amore, Mariu."

Shelagh Richards directed the Synge and Yeats plays and played Cathleen in the latter, and Mr. Robinson directed his own play, and our company was the hit of the festival. The reviews were raves and we were obliged to do extra matinees to satisfy the demand for tickets. We were asked to do *The Whiteheaded Boy* for the BBC and in late September the company reported to the Alexandra Palace in London for our first—for most of us—live television appearance. I was as happy as I had ever been. I could not see the outline of the future but the distant glow seemed healthy enough. All depression was, I was certain, forever gone, and the Ghost proved to be right again: as soon as we got back from London Nancy applied for and got a job at the Abbey as assistant scenic artist. And I got a phone call from Josie McAvin. She had recommended me for a part in a new play at the Gate. I wanted it. I had registered again for my last year at UCD but I was determined to keep on acting, to do both things, to study when I could. Something had to suffer neglect: it was the studies, and when I got my B.A. in '52 it was not honors but a pass.

"They tell me you're an American" said Hilton Edwards, cofounder of the Dublin Gate Theatre Company, and a superb actor-director. We were in his office in his house in Harcourt Terrace.

"That's right" I owned, "but I think I can play an Irish part for you. I've been doing Irish characters all summer in Edinburgh and London." I gave him the details.

"Would you mind reading this for me?" he said, handing me a copy of *God's Gentry*, a verse comedy written by a Dublin poet, Donagh MacDonagh. The author was also a judge, and his father, Thomas MacDonagh, was one of the fourteen Irishmen who were shot by the British for leading the Easter 1916 rebellion. Donagh's play, a charming comedy, had nothing to do with those sad and glorious events. "The part is the first policeman, and he's from Kerry. Do you know Kerry?"

"I do" I answered. A lie. Yet not altogether a lie. I had not yet visited Kerry but the speech of my Kerry grandfather was vivid in my memory, and my Ghost and my Divil, who had always been with me, were patently Kerrymen, both of them. Hilton took up a script and read with me, and it was amusing to hear the Irish-accented lines delivered in his rich bold English voice. He was a born Englishman, a Cambridge man, an Old Vic man, and he never attempted an accent other than his own. We read a page or two and Hilton put down his script. He went into another room and brought back his partner, Micheàl MacLìammòir. He asked me to repeat the reading. He was exuberant. He had not believed that a foreigner could exactly represent the Kerry brogue. He had auditioned a couple of Dublin actors who had not managed it. Micheàl MacLìammòir merely smiled at me and said "You'll do very nicely, my dear, and we'll see you at the theater." He shook my hand and went away.

Getting into the Gate company was thought by everyone a great stroke of professional luck, and with good reason. Edwards and MacLìammòir at that time had been for more than twenty years among the most highly regarded actor-managers of the English-speaking theatre, and were now very nearly the last of their kind. Of their kind they were remarkable. They were unique. Their peers were the dozen or so most luminous names of the English-Irish stage. Hilton at his best was the most knowledgeable and theatrically imaginative director I have ever known. Micheàl was a writer of plays and of books on theatre (his autobiographical *All for Hecuba* will grandly repay the interested reader). He was a talented designer of sets and costumes. He was a translator, a linguist fluent in Irish, Spanish and French. He and Hilton were both musical, Hilton more so— over the years he composed and conducted scores for a number of Gate plays and pantomimes—but Micheàl at the piano was a delightful entertainer at parties.

What these two partners had brought to the Irish theatre since they conceived their Gate company in 1927 was a world presence; which is not to say simply plays from other lands, for such had been seen on the Dublin stage for three hundred years, but productions that displayed the evolving theatrical art of their own time. The Boys, as Hilton and Micheàl were affectionately known, had never been content to stay idle between seasons. Excepting the war years, they had spent their holidays on the continent looking at theatre in Germany and France; they had always stopped in London to catch the latest British hits and the imports from Broadway, and what they observed with keenly comprehending eyes, and found innovative and important, they applied to their work at home. An appreciative Dublin looked forward to each new Gate season with delight.

The Boys were, as a French actor who knew them once said, *formidable*. Knowing of their standards, I expected them to be authoritative, demanding and hard to satisfy, and they were all of that. But they were patient and instructive, kindly even when abrupt, and exceedingly generous with all the theoretical and practical knowledge they had in store, including even small precious bits of advice about makeup and the care and wearing of costumes. Hilton gave me my first voice lesson. He said "You're bringing it out of the throat, over the tongue and straight through the mouth. Wrong! It must go up and out through the mask, the whole face—the whole head must resonate like a violin. Suppose a violin were merely a wooden box with one round hole in it. Weak, my dear boy, very weak. When you speak, think 'Face! Face! Face!' It'll come. It'll come."

On method acting he once said to some of us "Stanislavsky meant it for rehearsal, boys and girls, emotional rehearsal, for you alone. As for them out there," he waved a hand at the empty theater, "don't show them your rehearsal, only the character that comes of it. But please, show me the character first."

Sometimes at rehearsal Micheàl would stand staring silently at an actor. The actor would stare back at him wondering what could be the matter. Seconds would pass. Suddenly Micheàl would strike a physical attitude, a bit of mime. The actor would see before him the key quality of the character he himself was trying to play. Micheàl would smile and say softly "He's something like that, don't you think, dear?"—and without another word he would stroll away. The actor would have it: "Yes! Yes, Micheàl, thank you!" But I never heard Micheàl speak an actor's lines for him.

He once said something to me that turned out to be my most valuable acting lesson. My part in the play *Ring Round the Moon* was very funny but the audience wasn't laughing. I felt terrible. I felt out of place, miscast, a drag on the show, and I was grumbling about the situation. I said to Micheàl "You know, Hilton really ought to replace me in this one."

"That might put you at your ease" Micheàl replied, "but not us. Your replacement might make the same mistake."

"What mistake? Tell me!"

"The mistake" he said calmly, "of knowing, as the character, that you're funny. As the actor you know it of course. But in comedy, my dear, the funniest character is the most serious man on the stage."

It seemed the simplest thought once I had grasped it, yet it had not occurred to me. That night my character spoke every speech as seriously as if his existence depended on it, and laughs came back to the stage in waves. I have often passed along MacLìammòir's words to others just as he said them to me.

They were ever after in the front of my mind, and I used to say them to myself years later before every performance of Archie— worried, confused, flustered, inflamed, serious, serious Archie. I owe Archie to Micheàl. Archie made the people laugh.

I put in a summer of solid study before the degree exams in September 1952. We were examined at that time orally and in writing by "externs," professors from other universities, Irish and British, and the whole two-week process was Judgment: all one's prodigal ways and sins of omission were called sternly to account. With this in view, I had to withdraw from Hilton's production of *Hamlet* at Elsinore in Denmark, and I was deeply sorry. Micheàl was to play the prince and Hilton the king. I was to play the grave digger and Fortinbras. I rejoined the company in the fall.

The playbills of Gate productions in 1951, 1952 and 1953 listed an actor named George Roberts. Who was he? He was I, and I took that stage name, the name of an old friend in Montana, because I was a college student. I never hoped to conceal what I was doing from my professors, who were bound to learn of it, but I wanted to suggest to them that I was, in the words of one of them, "a good fellow who did not want to flaunt his unconcern for the views of the college." The words were Dudley Edwards's, whom I mentioned earlier, an Irishman and no relation of Hilton's, but my model as an historian as Hilton was a man of the theatre. He was the preeminent authority on the Tudors in Ireland.

I now had a contract with the Gate. My roles in the plays were larger, my time for anything but acting virtually gone.

Not without some regret I went to tea with Professor Edwards and told him I would have to give up, or at least postpone, the idea we had talked about—going for the master of arts in history. He was nothing but kind. He had seen me perform and allowed that I might have a stage career.

"I don't like to be the sole judge of these things" he said, "to push people toward one thing or another. What does your young wife say?"

"She thinks I ought to act."

"And your cousin, Matt O'Connor, good man that he is, what does he say?"

"Matt said what you just said."

"Well, you seem to be in place on the stage, into it, as it were—the man for the role. That's in your favor. And you couldn't be in the company of better men than Edwards and MacLiammòir."

"Geniuses" I agreed.

He smiled. "You Americans are notoriously fond of that description, but in this instance I won't quarrel with you."

I played in eight productions at the Gate, the better known being *Darkness at Noon* and *Ring Round the Moon*. The latter we took to the Opera House in Cork and at last I saw a little more of the rest of Ireland. The Gate was my drama school. I have often thought that all I know about acting and directing I learned from those dear men now gone, Edwards and MacLiammòir; that I have only been using ever since the tools they gave me. I had a chance to say that publicly a few years ago on one of Merv Griffin's talk shows. The occasion was Merv's bringing me together with another alumnus of the Gate, Orson Welles, who at age eighteen had gone to Dublin and played his first role with "The Boys." Orson's opinion of them was much the same as mine.

Other well-known Gate alumni are Geraldine Fitzgerald and the late James Mason.

The Irish theatre in our century will be identified chiefly with the Abbey and the Gate. There were of course other ventures like those of Shelagh Richards and Cyril Cusack. And Lord Longford kept a reputable company running for many years; it shared the Gate Theatre with Edwards and MacLiammòir. Less well known ventures were headed by actors like Maurice O'Brien and Ronald Ibbs. There were two or three provincial touring companies, the best of them that of the Shakespearean actor-manager Anew McMaster. There was a little-theatre movement in the late fifties, notably The Pike Theater, which introduced the playwright Brendan Behan. The Abbey has always been preeminent because its prestigious founders, W. B. Yeats and Lady Gregory, made of it a wellspring of writing genius. Styles and standards in acting and production lend reputation to a theater, but great playwrights give it lasting status. The Abbey was also from its beginning a subsidized theatre; a fact of considerable importance in its creative life.

I stayed in touch with my professors at UCD. My larger interest in Irish life generated by my studies has never lessened.

Nancy and I changed flats three times and each time she secured one with a room for Hugh. She was painting scenery at the Abbey and she had enrolled for postgraduate work in education at Trinity, which required practice teaching and the preparation of a thesis, and she did all the necessary housekeeping for the three of us. She accomplished everything with little help from me. She got through her crowded days with extraordinary energy and joy. She had no familial tie to Ireland (she is Anglo-German and American Indian) but she was utterly enchanted with every feature and quality of the place: the look of Dublin lanes and squares and Georgian houses, the cobbled walks of Trinity, the flowers and ducks in Stephen's Green and the swans on the Grand Canal and the Liffey; the shop people, the twinkling craftiness of Moore Street, the Anglo-Irish mannerisms of Grafton Street; the teas in Roberts's and Bewley's, the chats, the soft rain, the biting wind. Daily she gave an excited account of the busy world of the theatre and all our new friends. She had begun to sound as though Ireland was, and always had been, the original fabric of her life.

I have been asked frequently to elucidate the tragedy of Northern Ireland. The impression is strong in America, an essentially Protestant land, that Northern Ireland Protestants have been gamely resisting coercion and violence in order to maintain the Protestant government and the dominantly Protestant society that they want. I am asked whether they, as a majority, are not entitled to do that. I say they are. People should have a right to be whatever they wish to be. But when we have agreed on that happy principle, we must face two perplexing questions: whether people may impose their societal choice wherever in the world they choose to impose it, and whether we may rightly approve their imposition and support it.

Suppose for the sake of discourse we allow the funny idea that people who wish to be British may hold forever a British enclave wherever they like outside of Britain? Should we approve the enclave if it is unconstitutional,[3] undemocratic, unfree and unable to hold itself together but for the arbitrary brute force of the police? In 1969 we saw an exasperated British government set aside the deplorable local government of Northern Ireland and govern in its stead. It now remains for an enlightened and determined British government to take itself out of Ireland altogether.

Such a government there once was, eighty-five years ago, a government that on the eve of the First World War assented at last to independence for the whole of Ireland, a "home rule" under a native parliament in Dublin, something on the order of Canada. But organized Unionists of Ulster vowed to fight that liberal British government[4] and, incredible though it seems, bought weapons from Germany to do so. More incredible still was a mutinous warning by British army commanders in southern Ireland that they would not obey any order to go north to enforce the will of the British parliament. Unionism-Masonism, the *ne plus ultra* of conservative Toryism, had its fanatical believers in many persons very highly placed in British life, as high as King George V himself; it was a creed dearer to the military and the king than the very law of the realm. The well-intentioned British government took fright and backed down: it said that it was obliged to defer the home rule question to another time, the war against Germany being then its paramount

---

[3]With reference to the British constitution.
[4]Under H. H. Asquith.

concern. The Ulster Unionists wanted the question deferred to the never-never. The British government silently acquiesced, and then proceeded to hang Roger Casement for trying to buy German arms for the Republicans in the south.

Ireland never got what she wanted, the whole island-country to herself, free and independent. How and why she got less, and settled for less, are questions that cannot even be approached in these pages. A small part of that complex agonizing history occupies several shelves in my own library. Will Ireland ever be whole and independent? I think so, but not until England finds a leader of the stature, courage and vision of a De Gaulle. The stature of Madame Thatcher was not above that of a prison warden, and Mr Major would have looked perfectly correct behind the reservations desk of a Midlands hotel. DeGaulle towered above them, though he was really only a colossal autocrat who, by fiat, wrenched his country out of an old Algerian mess not unlike in its bloodshed and colonial depravity the chronic mess of Northern Ireland.

Would an Ulster no longer monitored by the British army burst into civil war? Would the Unionist majority with their Ulster Constabulary and auxiliary amateur storm troopers massacre their Catholic neighbors? No. The Unionist ascendancy, cut loose from its artificial British life-support system, would see itself sinking as an upper class, a socioeconomic consequence that brutality could not reverse. In the Irish Republic to the south Protestants are a minority, but there is not now in the world a minority more happily placed. Protestant Irishmen are not merely equal in every respect to all other Irishmen, but because of their historic preeminence in Irish revolutionary history, in government, in the professions, in the arts, they seem to be valued even more highly than the Catholic majority, and by the evaluation of that very majority! A "pampered and cosseted minority" are the words used to describe them by the English historian A. J. P. Taylor.

*   *   *

The subject of Ireland requires some words on terrorism.

For our own sake, if we are intelligent people who are committed to the proposition that there is no peace where there is no justice, we should try to think of "terrorists" not as invariably crazy killers, but rather try to see them as they see themselves: as partisans who are fighting a righteous war against overwhelming odds using small means and improvised strategies. They say they are fighting because of the unwillingness of their rulers to talk to them and negotiate conditions of even relative, let alone absolute, justice.

Why, we ask, should a state talk to "terrorists"? Because—still presuming that they are not necessarily crazy—their political aims are invariably the aims of an oppressed minority within the state. They are not transitory bandits. Their cause is validated by long years and respectable tradition. "Terrorists" were once peaceable men. The established government, bent on dehumanizing the rebel, denies this with hot indignation. Sad to say, the ordinary man in the street denies it too; he prefers always to believe in his government—he is afraid to disbelieve—and he deems it entirely intelligent to inquire: "If men are peaceable, why do authorities send police and soldiery against them?"

The straight answer? To turn them from peaceable men into violent men whom everybody can confidently join in deploring and hunting down.

The peaceable man with a reasonable cause is formidable; he knows it, and his oppressor knows it. The oppressor knows that the rebel can succeed by lawful means if he has a decent argument, if he forms a party, publishes his goals and shames a significant segment of authority into admitting he is right. The authorities will not risk allowing him to do this, but will physically attack him, drive him to the gun, put him on the run. If he is forced into common crime to survive, so much the better: military law is proclaimed against him, he is arrested without warrant, jailed without hearing, or simply shot in the streets or a sitting room or the pew of a church. If he shoots back he proves what the state has always said about him. Only when he loses all possibility of public sympathy, when indeed his own intimidated brethren begin to turn away from him, will the state feel safe from him. He is now finally a threat only to the simpleminded policeman who is ordered to go out and do battle with him. But of course the rebel need never be wiped out. On the contrary, the oppressor government, by its excesses, will always create a useful number of "terrorists," because this kind of government must feed and live on perpetual internal war.

If we look at Northern Ireland we find a typical case. The Ulster Orange Unionist Protestant government from 1921 to 1969 was determined that its system, though parliamentary, should never benefit the Catholic minority. The Catholic, though entitled to the protection of British law, had to be somehow deprived of it, shorn of his civil rights and his voting rights and, in brief, his status as a free and equal subject of the Crown. True representative government could not be permitted. Crown law somehow had to be superseded by a corrupt Ulster law, and indeed it was.

But corrupt law alone was not enough. Corruption might be cured in time, in the passing of generations, for it was said that Catholics, in obedience to a direct order from the Pope, were spending more time in bed (they might as well: they couldn't get work) and multiplying five times faster than Protestants. As well as this, fair-minded Protestants might themselves decide to change Ulster law, so disgraceful was it. The strategic expedient was to turn Protestant fair-mindedness to fear, as well as turn the Catholic into a violent enemy of an orderly Protestant Unionist society.

To this end the government created a special civilian police auxiliary; its men kept arms in their homes and, like the regular Royal Ulster Constabulary, were given powers of search and arrest without warrant. Known nationalists were defined *a priori* as violent revolutionaries, and any sort of political activity was said to be violent. Catholic homes were regularly entered by sudden force, ransacked and brutalized. Harassment of all kinds began and continued regularly year in and year out, and probably the most psychologically effective of them were the inflammatory marches of Orange societies on Orange holidays straight through Catholic neighborhoods (where muscular opposition proved that the men were not in bed after all). And of course the victims of this violence and torment finally struck back. The revolutionary body known since 1916 as the Irish Republican Army was revived and its latter-day nonviolent policy was renounced. Violence replied to violence. The nationalist Catholic minority of Ulster, which in fact was becoming larger, began to support the IRA at least passively, but in one way or another.

The Belfast Orange government in 1969, when the Crown in dismay nullified it, was called blind and senseless for provoking the guerrilla war of the sixties. Not so; its lawless vision was perfectly clear and its method made perfect sense: only a never-ending war, supposedly against "terrorists" but actually against the whole of a despised minority, could preserve such a regime.

This is so whether the regime be in Ulster or in any other place. So much for "terrorists." So much for another view of the matter.

Ireland was, and is, a charming and endearing land, and it is also a culture passionately misrepresented by a few who hold it ignorantly in contempt and a few who hold it idiotically in reverence. Often one gang promotes the foolishness of the other. I offer in evidence the old movie *The Quiet Man*, which turns up now and then (God help us!) on late-night television. It is about a visiting Yank's difficulty in wooing a stubborn country lassie, and it asks us to believe that the contemporary Irish are a simpleminded, pugnacious, alcoholic bumpkinry clinging to the rustic manners of the eighteenth century. John Wayne performed very well as the honest, straightforward American seeking a peaceful life in Ireland. The role was well conceived. But watching the picture one longs to see one other character with a glimmer of intelligence. None appears. But the "stage Irishman" of old abhorrence bounds forth from behind every wall, bush, bar and doorway; he is the sozzled Everyman; he is both of the reverend clergymen in the picture. And yet the Irish-American director John Ford loved the Irish and intended his movie to be, in a funny way, reverential. Faith and begorrah! 'Twas all cross-purposes and the grandest union ever of contending distortions.

Ireland's Irish are a modern progressive people as smartly up-to-date as the rest of modern Europe, as well informed by press, television and radio as people anywhere. There are first-class daily newspapers in the counties Limerick, Cork and Kerry, and three in Dublin. All employ their own correspondents as well as international news services, and all are written and edited as well as newspapers I have seen anywhere. The Irish are widely traveled, and of all the earth's island peoples I think the least insular in outlook. American and British movies about Ireland are absurd. Movies generally have made Irish characters inveterate boozers, but the Irish, though they are uninhibited consumers of strong drink, are usually well down on the international dipso lists one sees from time to time, topped by the French, the Swedes, the Russians, and the Americans.

Asked to sum up the Irish quickly, I would call them a nation of readers, writers and talkers. Their devotion to, and production of, literature and drama needs no survey here. I would say though, in passing, that American and British editors who have sometimes included Goldsmith, Sheridan, Swift, Farquhar, Wilde, Yeats, Joyce, Shaw, Synge, and even O'Casey in anthologies of British writing might have considered the identification more carefully.

Critics of Irish society point to restrictions of freedom in such activities as divorce, abortion, and birth control. But facts may be less important than the ways in which people respond to them. The Irish have freely chosen in parliament to restrict themselves in certain ways,[5] but they have full freedom to change their minds and choose otherwise. And it should be noted that old moral precepts are no longer sacred cows protected from political kicking and buffeting; they do not today enjoy the run of the street. The trend in Ireland is away from legislating morality; meanwhile people find ways to do as conscience privately persuades them.

As Nancy and I were not anxious to evade parenthood nor to avail ourselves of divorce, we paid no attention to those matters. The one freedom I might have missed in Ireland, had I been aware of its absence, was "artistic":[6] there were censors of the publishing and film-exhibition businesses. I was told that the film censor invariably cut undressed, fervent, voracious love-making. Movies being what they are, i.e., mostly inconsequential, I never sensed that any of them might have been more impressive if some carnal caper I had not seen had been left in. I do not offer this as a serious argument for movie censorship; it is simply all I am moved to say on the subject. The Irish stage was uncensored, unlike the English, which was controlled by the lord chamberlain, and the Irish newspapers, like the English, were as free as the wind and frequently as raw.

Books of all kinds were in circulation. The bookstalls on the Liffey quays were always crowded with buyers and browsers, and new-book stores large and small flourished all over the city, including a little leftist nook near Trinity College. Works by authors like Henry Miller, James Joyce and D. H. Lawrence, supposedly banned, were readily available. The only publications that, to my knowledge, could not be acquired were violent

---

[5] Divorce is now legal.
[6] Let's say "artistic" for argument's sake.

children's comics and pornography, all from America. The Irish censorship was such that literature got in, sleaze stayed out. We in America have always felt that censorship was unacceptable in the smallest degree. Yet we whimper in pain over the amount of porn-corruption confronting ourselves and our children, and try to keep the stiff upper lip about the collateral plagues of hooker and junk pushing. I suppose the Irish do run the risk of artistic constriction; but they seem to think the risk is slight. Here in America, to risk anything is to risk all. In Ireland, so high is the value put upon the arts and artistic freedom that artists the world over are invited to come and work there tax-free. Where is the legislator here who would dare propose such an inducement. All things considered, I could not then or now fault Ireland for the censor.

I should mention an incident concerning Ireland's most cele-brated playwright, Sean O'Casey, who was all but deified by the liberal intelligentsia of America, not only for his genius as a dramatist but also for his supposed dislike of the church of Rome. He did cause a good deal of misapprehension of religious influence in Ireland. He complained frequently that Ireland was a priest-ridden reactionary society and once, in a spate of high temper, forbade further Irish production of his work. He first withdrew one of his plays, *The Drums of Father Ned*, from the annual Dublin theatre festival. Some dignitary on the festival committee had appealed to the archbishop of Dublin to bless the festival with a mass. This had not occurred to the prelate himself; he was not sure that a mass was appropriate, and in any case he could not have been eager to bless, among other things, a play that he knew to be yet another swipe at Mother Church. He declined to lend his spiritual offices, but did not suggest that O'Casey's play should be dropped from the festival. Ireland, unlike England, had never had a lord chamberlain who licensed and censored the theatre, and the archbishop had no wish to play that role.

But believing that the archbishop was putting pressure on the festival committee to rule out the play, O'Casey himself ruled it out. He went further and vowed that none of his plays would thereafter be seen in Ireland. In time he relented. The three of his plays that were most effective and popular were soon being produced again in Dublin. After all, the Abbey Theatre was the only place in the world where *Juno and the Paycock, The Plough and the Stars* and *The Shadow of a Gunman* had ever been regularly done and well done, and had earned a little money for the playwright. (Before we immoderately applaud the Abbey for this, Sean's widow, Eileen, now dead too, told me that the Abbey had never given them much money for performances of his plays. "I got a solicitor after them" she said, "but the situation was hopeless. I was alone and needed money and got nothing.")

Before Nancy and I left Ireland we went on a tour with a new theatrical company formed in 1953 by the renowned Irish actor Cyril Cusack. We played The Gaiety in Dublin and then went to Kilkenny, Waterford, Tipperary, Limerick, Cork and Galway. Our plays were Synge's *The Playboy of the Western World*, with Siobhan McKenna playing Pegeen, Shaw's *Arms and the Man*, and as a curtain raiser to the latter, an American one-acter, Saroyan's *Hello Out There*. Nancy was stage manager during that tour.

In Waterford a film-producing company from London had offered me a movie part, which, of course, I did not feel free to take,[7] and it struck me that I had best go where the big-time activity was, London or New York or Hollywood. I did not imagine that Ireland offered a character like me much in the way of upward movement, and I was right. When at last we sailed away to America, and the tender was bringing us out to the liner, Nancy could not bear to look back at the shore, and when she

---

[7]More fool I. I should have left the tour and taken the movie.

did risk a last glance collapsed in tears as though her heart was breaking. And what did I do? I looked stiffly toward the ship with the Divil in my ear whispering "Shut her off, for the luva gawd! The eejits on this barge will think you're murdering her."

I was entirely mistaken in imagining that my professional readiness, acquired through my prestigious Gate Theatre experience, was going to be the key to success in the States.

Nobody in New York in 1954 cared the least about me or anything I had done in Ireland and England. Within a month I was sorry we had come home.

8

• • • • • • •

We were staying at my mother's house in Forest Hills, and we had to make some money and find a place of our own. Nancy took the lead. Within a week of setting foot ashore in New York she had gone down to the Board of Education in Brooklyn and inquired about a teaching job. They arranged for her to take the art teacher's exam; she passed it, they granted her a substitute teacher's license and assigned her to a junior high school on the Lower East Side of Manhattan. We decided that I was to devote myself to making the theatrical rounds, but then saw, after a few embarrassingly barren weeks, that we were going to need some income from me as well. I too went down to Brooklyn, and finding that an exam in history, my field, was not being offered, took an exam for substitute teacher of English.

I was assigned to a junior high school in 47th Street on the West Side of Manhattan, and given a "home room" class of forty-five thirteen- and fourteen-year-olds, girls and boys, who spoke only Spanish. It was in fact an all–Puerto Rican class, and I was warned that it was also a "bad" class. I was instructed to teach English to all my classes, according to the syllabus for each grade, and to my Puerto Rican official class teach history and general science as well. As the kids couldn't understand me no matter what I tried to teach, my assignment made no sense unless above all else I concentrated upon English conversation and reading. In brief, I gave them three classes in basic talking—in English only, I being the leader and model—about every kind of experience they encountered daily in the streets of the city and in the school and home. I began each class with "Well, where shall we go today?" and together we made imaginary visits to all kinds of shops, and played the parts of shoppers and clerks, inquiring, buying, selling. I managed to introduce a little rudimentary history and science into all this.

I never sent my kids to the administrative office for discipline, so the principal and her staff paid no attention to them or to me. But one day an assistant principal visited and observed my class and asked me querulously whether I thought my pedagogy was approvable. I replied, hoping to be amusing, that as it was Socratic I hoped it would be at least allowable. My superior was not amused.

"It is not allowable, I'm afraid" she firmly told me.

"It works" I said

"Can't you teach the syllabus? Can't you send me lesson plans?"

"No, I'm sorry, the syllabus doesn't work with this group."

My superior's voice became quietly unfriendly. "Why can't you conform to correct method, Mr O'Connor?"

"I can" I said, "but the kids can't. They won't learn anything, and in that case I won't stay."

She knew of course that she was being challenged and would have to retreat. Anybody who could control these special kids was valuable to that extent and not to be driven off. Plainly, the practical strategy of the school was to keep troublesome, non-English-speaking children in a sequestered place so that preordained education could proceed elsewhere. She said nothing, turned and walked away, and I was not questioned again. I managed my kids simply by engaging their interest every day in our acting game. I disciplined them but rarely, and without the help of "the office." I threatened to torture them horribly— miming the torture, of course, since mime was all they could understand—causing them to howl with laughter, to take turns in miming even greater tortures, and to cease any behavior that I found unbearable. Yet, to my great amusement, they were pinched by the suspicion that they should not wholly discount my outrageous warnings. I enjoyed being with them, and taught them a lot of useful English.

During this first short teaching round I got my first job on American television. My very closest Irish friend, the actor Liam Gannon, who had been a regular member of the Dublin Gate Theatre for several years before my arrival, came over to New York to try for better luck. He looked up a young American named George Roy Hill, who had worked and studied at the Gate in the late forties, and was now becoming known in New York as a television director. Hill gave Liam a part in a TV play, and Liam recommended me for another part. TV plays were produced "live" in those days, and we performed this one during my leave from school at Christmas.[1] I had said nothing about it, and when classes resumed the place was agog about seeing me do my stuff.

Nancy was teaching across town on Second Avenue and she had some but not many language problems to solve; her kids were an ethnic variety and could speak passably well and understand her plainly. They enjoyed the methods and materials of drawing, painting, paper sculpture and construction, and the demonstrations Nancy put on for them. They enjoyed working and learning in a fundamentally nonverbal field. But Nancy had

[1] The Kraft Theater for CBS.

to handle a couple of serious behavior problems, like the bringing of weapons to school.

An actors' agent in London named Al Parker, an American, had represented me abroad, and he had written me a letter of introduction to a New York agent. That gentlemen was at first cordial but soon thereafter—indeed after two phone calls from me, neither of which he answered personally—ordered his assistant to ward me off. She said "We can't imagine placing you in anything, so don't call anymore." This lady, someone told me, was Conrad Veidt's sister, and I think now that she must have been—she sounded like Conrad playing one of his famous Nazi roles.[2] I began looking for a New York agent and referring once a week to a casting bulletin board at the Actors' Equity office in the old Hotel Edison.

When my teaching day was over at three o'clock in the afternoon I often met Liam Gannon for a cup of coffee, and then, like scores of jobless actors, made the rounds of casting offices; the three TV networks maintained them, and so did the advertising agencies that produced television programs for their clients. We "signed in" on long legal pads on the desks of receptionists all over midtown Manhattan—in the offices of, among others, Young & Rubicam, J. Walter Thompson, Ted Bates, and the one whose name most intimidated me, making me think of a hard-charging defensive backfield—Batten, Barton, Durstine & Osborne. Presumably directors and producers hopped out of hidden offices from time to time, scanned the yellow lists, and found a forgotten name that might be plugged into a small role. But I was never summoned back to see a director or any person of consequence, nor did I ever espy such a person in a reception room poring over a pad. I saw only receptionists, who all said "Hi" without a smile and pointed to

---

[2]Veidt was a brilliant German actor who made a career for himself in Hollywood.

114

the pads. But to be fair to these jaded young women, they had no reason to be merry; their days were never brightened by anyone more glamorous than I. Actors of importance were cast by way of agents' phone calls.

We did not quickly find a suitable apartment, and Forest Hills was depressing me, which is another way of saying that I was depressing myself.

Some time around Christmas, feeling like a cheery drink, I called up Hugh McDougall—who still lived in the old neighborhood, married, a father of three, like me working in the public school system but unlike me a permanent professional who had moved up from teacher to principal to supervisor.

"Max—we were both going to be important" I reminded him, using the old nickname I had given him. We were at the bar in the tap room of the Forest Hills Inn.

"Ah yes" he said—"that's when we were sitting on the steps talking till three in the morning." The steps: they were appended to a little Presbyterian church on Seminole Avenue situated halfway between his street and mine, and sometimes after we had been out doing whatever we did at seventeen— movies, a party, "hanging out" somewhere—we headed home together and stopped at the steps. There our talk might last two or three hours and it was usually fantastic—of the future, of ideas and plans and conquest and fame, things we felt secure discussing only with each other, which meant that we were close friends.

"What ever happened to us novelists?" I wondered.

He laughed and said "We never graduated to literary circles."

"What was it we wanted to write about—can you remember?"

"Sure" he said; "things everybody else had already written about."

"No sign of originality?"

He shook his head. "If there had been a sign, I'd remember it."

"What was I like?" I asked him.

"Fine" he replied; "we were all fine. You know what I mean—okay. A little stupid, I guess, like any kids that age."

"Are they smarter nowadays?"

He shrugged. "They experience more, see more—there's more to see. Innate savvy seems to be about the same." He asked me what he had been like and I more or less repeated his answer to me. What we had both left out, I later reflected, were descriptions like devious, selfish and untruthful, especially applicable to teenage relations with families. Not that I was feeling guilty about our long ago; teenage rottenness has ever been pervasive, and in spite of it I used to overhear our elders speaking fondly of all of us as "nice kids." We were not exciting the attention of the gendarmerie and we were managing to get through high school in the time prescribed.

It was easy for us to be "nice" kids; we were not preyed upon by dope pushers, our pop music did not issue thunderous invitations to a semisensate flight from normality. Our music used to be played by skilled orchestras; intelligible singers rendered tunes about dancing in the dark while orchids bloomed in the moonlight and nightingales sang in Berkeley Square and stars fell on Alabama—silly sentiments, but carried along by intelligent melodic phraseology, and if the words were doggerel they were often wonderfully compelling. I know my comparison is cranky, but there it is.

Over our drinks I grieved. I couldn't get over the change in the old village—very different from fifteen years ago when its residential capacity was hardly tested. Forest Hills was geographically the same, still divided by Queens Boulevard into the Gardens and Cord Meyer sections. And the Gardens was unchanged, still in the style of a traditional English village (things English have always been reassuring to our uncertain middle class) with half-timbered houses, winding little streets, places, crescents, trim lawns, blooming bushes, radiant flower beds. Forest Hills had remained countrified till after the war, but now

urbanization was in full frenzy—awful overcrowding, burgeoning of undistinguished apartment buildings and frowsy shopping
marts.

"But nobody thinks about it" said Max. "All these new tens of
thousands of people can't believe the old place was once nicer.
They say 'Nicer than what? This is as nice as the city gets.'"
Point of view was all. The newcomers were not insensitive or
otherwise deficient; they simply saw the place as city, not
country, and as city they found it exceptional.

And again a point of view—graying birds like us heard new
pop music, amplified rock sounds, and said "Do the kids think
that's music?"

"Of course they do."

But wait, maybe they did not. Maybe they were not so dumb.
Maybe they well understood what real music was but were
culturally at a distance from it, not in need of it, fed up with
the form of it, yet *faute de mieux* using the old word. Maybe
"manifestation" or something simpler—some easy dialectal
synonym—was wanted. In the fifties and sixties "happenin'"
was the word I began to hear and it seemed to me to serve aptly,
carrying with it the connotation of accident or misfortune.
But the kids applied "happenin'" to pleasant things of their
own choice and "music" continued to be whatever they said it
was.

In the summer of 1954 Nancy went to Missoula to visit her
parents, and I found work in a first-rate summer-theatre tour
of New England, playing a gentleman's gentleman, a small
part, in the play *Witness for the Prosecution*. We both went back
to teaching in September, this time in high schools, I on the
lower west side, the Chelsea district, and Nancy in the Ridge-
wood section of Brooklyn. When school holidays came round
again we bought a new Oldsmobile and drove to Missoula for a
short visit that turned into a long stay. Nancy's parents, Ralph

and Hulda Fields, welcomed us home. It was the summer of 1955.

I said something to someone at a party about the great pleasure it was to be back in Montana, and out of that came an offer from Professor Bert Hansen of the Department of Speech at the university. I could have a master's degree at no expense if I taught speech to freshman and sophomores for a year as a graduate assistant. I thought about the offer and told Nancy I wanted to accept it. She was agreeable but not enthusiastic. Being away from New York for a long time fretted her a little; she was sure I was on the verge of a break on Broadway. She herself loved New York—found it incomparaby stimulating artistically, and if she chose to teach art as well as create it, she had by now passed the regular license exam and could be appointed permanently as soon as she wished. Personally, I could foresee no break on Broadway, and didn't care at that moment whether I got one or not.

I let myself think of Broadway only as the junk-strewn thoroughfare that it was in those days. I felt idiotically that I had been rejected by New York, and was glad to be away from there, willing to be away for a year—willing to stay away indefinitely. Besides, I liked the idea of teaching college kids. If I returned to teaching in New York, if I decided to make a career of teaching, I would have a higher degree, would earn more money, and would have taken a step forward. To run right back to New York could mean simply to waste more time there. Nancy saw through the self-serving sophistry: she knew the truth—that I did not take rejection well, meaning that I was not one for stubbornly pressing forward to an objective. My tendency, of old habit, was to substitute an easier objective.

Nancy was invited by the Missoula County school authority to devise and set up an arts program for the elementary schools, and she accepted the job for one year—thus continuing to be the major earner under our roof. Our roof, by the way, was provided by the university and described as a faculty housing "unit," being by no stretch of imagination either an apartment or a house. It was an electrically heated, prefabricated tripartite box in which we could sleep and cook and, disregarding everybody's comfort, entertain two guests. The record player and the telephone required thoughtful planning. But we were soon enjoying Missoula and campus life. We were in a place where, in a sense, we belonged. Here were not only Nancy's parents but a hundred loving old friends, who were constantly feeding us, entertaining us, and joyfully anticipating our staying in town forever. I began mulling that over.

Our low-rent little unit was demonstrating to us that happiness is possible anywhere for a loving couple working at things of interest and merit. The ten hours a week of teaching speech that were required of me were fun. My own courses in speech were fun. For my thesis I wrote a pageant play to be performed in school stadiums about Indian emigration from the Bitterroot. Nancy too was apparently having a wonderful time

I had written a play about the warfare in Northern Ireland, and I gave it to the drama department to perform; it was rather well received by the students and the faculty, and panned by the student newspaper: the girl reviewer wrote "Who cares?" The head of the drama department, Roy Hinze, asked me to perform with the kids in a Shakespeare play. He wanted to do *Othello* for some reason and I agreed to play the Moor. I was silly in the role. Somehow I also found time to direct the annual all-school musical presentation, *Carousel*, and everybody loved it. The heads of the performing arts faculties seemed to want me to stay after I earned my degree, and when June came I too wanted to stay.

But things were not what they seemed to be. The department heads did not want me to stay; nobody invited me. I was sorely bothered, but Nancy took it all with equanimity, not to say serenity. On the return drive to New York she revealed exactly how she felt: she was completely delighted to be on our way back, and said to me over and over "Wait and see—good things are going to happen now." Derisively I said "Now! Right now?" She retreated a little. "Soon" she said.

But for the time being, we had to return to teaching. Nancy was assigned again to teach art at Franklin K. Lane High School, and I was assigned to the High School of Performing Arts in Manhattan. My assignment had nothing to do with my professional theatrical experience. I was not expected to teach drama or conduct classes in acting. My license was in English, and I taught a little literature, and some grammar and composition according to the syllabuses for grades nine through twelve. Here the teaching task was easy. Here the students were ambitious and very bright. The IQs of my kids were all well above normal, and some were quite high. For one of my classes the syllabus was too slim to occupy them, and I had to fill time with extemporaneous, though formal, classes in "arts appreciation," that is, compare-contrast discussions of modern fiction they were reading and movie/television dramas they were seeing. It was all trash, but useful in analyzing style, structure, and character. These impromptu sessions once or twice a week evoked intense interest, and made me wonder whether English- and history-teaching shouldn't be regularly pursued in this manner, that is, through both formal and informal classes. This would be new in public schools, and would for that reason alone be judged unthinkable, but the argument would also be adduced that overcrowding demanded strictly disciplined formal study—which is to say the same old thing.

There are no problems in public schools that money could not solve. Everywhere in the country we need more schools, more classrooms (for smaller classes), more variety in method, more reliance on empirical nontextbook approaches; and of course corresponding changes in teacher training. We need five to ten times more well-educated teachers, and we have to elevate their community status by paying them very high salaries, commensu-

With Loretto in a 3rd Avenue bar
(1947)

Dublin: with Nancy in a garden in
Burlington Road

Dublin: on O'Connell Bridge

Betty Bell Skibsted

John Suchy

My darling boy, age two

Venice: Hugh in Piazza San Marco

Venice: the Grand Canal

Elsinore: a future Hamlet looks things over

Carroll O'Connor

Robert Brown

Pacific Palisades: Hugh in garden

With Nancy

Nancy Ellison

Covington, Georgia:
between takes

Alan Palmer

Cast photo of *Heat* with
Hugh and me, Howard
Rollins, Alan Autry,
Geoffrey Thorne and
David Hart

NBC Photo

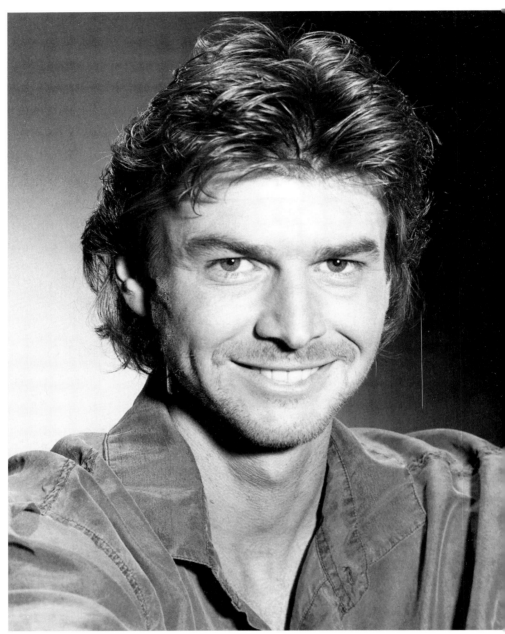

Hugh, age 27

rate with their national value. We will know we are paying them enough when their ignorant fellow Americans, who have traditionally undervalued them, begin to envy them and complain bitterly about them.

I hated leaving Performing Arts, but at the end of the fall term both Nancy and I had an offer from a producer who wanted to start a winter stock company in St. Louis, Missouri. This was a most uncertain venture, but then everything theatrical is uncertain, and if it clicked we would be reestablishing ourselves as actors and directors and designers in our first and best-loved profession. I should add that Nancy too hated leaving her school, but we were both afraid, to put it plainly, to let this chance go by. I shan't dwell long on the result. We folded. We worked in a good new theater-in-the-round, our company was not without talent, our work was more than acceptable, and showed signs of becoming quite good, but the worst winter snowstorms the town had seen in decades kept the customers away for weeks. The theater shut down and the company went back to New York.

Nancy read in the paper that Burgess Meredith was about to produce a stage version of James Joyce's prodigious novel *Ulysses*, the most influential piece of literature of the century. I was facing the old problem, no agent to submit me for an audition, but I grabbed a phone and called Meredith at the Rooftop Theater in lower Manhattan, Second Avenue and Houston Street. I did not get him on the phone, but got his assistant, the actor-director John Astin, and said "You can't do this play without me, and you have to give me an audition without delay." After a little spate of his defensive questions and my aggressive answers, Astin fixed a time for me to come and audition for Meredith—that very afternoon at four. When I got there at twenty minutes to four, Meredith, Astin, and a couple of other people were leaving the theater. I walked up to Meredith, whom I had never met, and said "If I had been right on time, you would have been long gone." Meredith said "What?" and I replied "You forgot all about me, didn't you?"

Meredith turned to Astin. "What's he saying?"

John Astin explained: he had indeed forgotten—hadn't written it down. He apologized to me and asked whether I could possibly return tomorrow, but Meredith intervened and said "No, I wanna hear him now." To me he said "Do you know this novel—*Ulysses*?" He held up a copy in front of my face.

I said "Yes, and if you're going to include the character Buck Mulligan in the play, I'm the best actor anywhere to play it."

"Let's go back up" said Meredith instantly. By "up" he meant up in an elevator, because the Rooftop Theater, a small five-hundred-seater, was actually on the roof of the building, and the building was the grand old National Theater. Meredith had no playscript for me to read, but he handed me the novel and said "Open to the first page and lemme hear you read some of it." I got up on the stage, turned to the first page and the famous first lines: *Stately plump Buck Mulligan came from the stair-head bearing a bowl of lather on which a mirror and a razor lay crossed. A yellow dressing gown, ungirdled, was sustained gently behind him by the mild morning air. He held the bowl aloft and intoned "Introibo ad altare Dei."* I read it in a strong voice and a proper universities accent, and read on for two pages until he stopped me.

"Okay" he called from the back of the theater, "you play Buck for me. What's your name?" This sounds like a scene from an improbable movie, but it is an exact report. Nancy came into the production as the designer of costumes, technical assistant to Burgess Meredith, and understudy for three women's roles, Bella-Bello, Mrs Tallboys and Molly Bloom. The memorable character Leopold Bloom, the Dublin Jew, was played by an extraordinary actor, Zero Mostel. The playscript *Ulysses in Nighttown*, was devised by Burgess assisted by Irish poet and teacher Padraic Colum, and by Irish playwright Denis Johnston, and it comprised a half-dozen delineating scenes in the novel. It was a major New York hit, though it was in the Off-Broadway category.

It closed in about five months only because the owners of the handsome old theater building tore it down. The reason given was that a new section of subway required a right of way. A lie. The site became a junk yard and then a parking lot. We did not have in those days in New York a Landmarks Preservation Commission. A more wicked and suspicious piece of civic destruction I cannot remember. Our producers were presumably sleeping a lot by day, because they failed to search for and acquire another theater.

But the play did not fade away. In 1959 Burgess got a call from Lord Furness, a theatrical dilettante in London, offering to bring *Ulysses in Nighttown* to the Arts Theatre in the West End, and afterwards to Paris, the Hague and Amsterdam. Burgess sent Nancy and me to London to cast and otherwise prepare the production; she and I, Zero Mostel, and the actress Pauline Flanagan were all of the original cast to go abroad. Again we were highly praised by reviewers, and played to full houses everywhere. Our reception in Paris, where we played the Sarah Bernhardt Theatre, was overwhelmingly rapturous; this was, after all, Joyce's home town, more so even than Dublin. In 1974 Burgess again revived the play, and producer Alex Cohen of New York brought it to the Winter Garden Theater, again starring Zero Mostel and one of the original cast, the great actor-dancer the late Swen Swenson. (Nancy and I and other original cast members did not appear, being otherwise occupied.) There *Ulysses* was for the first time unintelligently reviewed, and it failed to do business.

Nancy and I enjoyed a close friendship with Burgess Meredith from 1957, when *Ulysses* made its debut, until his death in September 1997. As an actor, he was unsurpassed, and yet he was undervalued; he was recognized most appreciatively, yet not much talked about. His work was completely satisfying. "No matter what he did" someone said of him, "you were always riveted to the character he had created." For a certain movie thriller he directed and starred in along with his two best friends,

Charles Laughton and Franchot Tone, he deserved the highest of honors both for directing and acting; it was one of Simenon's Maigret stories, *The Man on the Eiffel Tower*, and it was the most interesting of its genre that I have ever seen. We frequently traveled abroad together, and worked together as acting colleagues in feature and television movies. Our son grew up in his company, and when Hugh ended his life Burgess was shattered by grief; for a time he would not speak of Hugh's death, as though denying it. To me he was a friend of high importance, deeply fond of me as I was of him, of all friends the most admiring, encouraging observer of my work; and he gave me a priceless gift, a way of inducing a charge of self-confidence before any entrance. "Always remember this, *mon fils*—they're waiting for you."

My appearance in the first New York production of *Ulysses* brought me some attention. I had no agent, but I had been noticed by certain casting directors who serviced the ad agencies and the networks, and they—Caro Jones, Fay Lee, Marion Dougherty—called on me constantly for a wide range of character work: one appearance led to another. When we got back from the overseas tour of *Ulysses,* I resumed my TV activity and also found time to do another Off-Broadway production, a revival of Odets's *The Big Knife*.[3] My reward for doing this utterly humorless play was having a capable agent see me in it and offer to represent me. Lionel Larner signed me to his agency, Baum-Newborn, which later became General Artists Corporation, and still later International Creative Management. The last-named firm still represents me through its vice-president Jack Gilardi, and Lionel Larner has become my personal manager.

Let me here tell a tale of agents. Some time in 1960 a GAC agent named Don Wolff put me into a play to be aired by

---

[3] I played Marcus Hoff, an unscrupulous Hollywood studio boss.

Channel 13 in New York, the reputed outlet for better things. During my first rehearsal Don phoned me and said "Get away from there early and meet Sidney Lumet at NBC." I did what I was told, met the director, read for him from a script, and found myself accepting a part in another play. This was not fair to the first production, but Don Wolff said "Don't think about it. They'll blame me, not you. This is a career move."

The new production was an NBC Special, a dramatization of *The Sacco-Vanzetti Story,* and there were three very good roles in it: the two principals of the real-life drama—in which the state of Massachusetts in 1927 insisted on conducting two disgraceful executions—and the relentless prosecutor of the victims, Katzman. The title roles were played by Martin Balsam and Steven Hill, and Katzman was played by me. On the night of this well-heralded event, the head of GAC, Martin Baum, took movie producer Roy Huggins to dinner at Chasen's restaurant in Beverly Hills, and when *Sacco-Vanzetti* came on the air, Marty brought Roy into Dave Chasen's office to watch it—and, by the way, to see me. The result was that Roy signed me for his next movie at Warner Brothers, and shortly thereafter Nancy and I drove out to Hollywood. Don Wolff was right: he had pushed me into a "career move," and of course the rest of the GAC agents followed it up with ingenuity. During the next ten years—or until I started playing Archie on television—I made twenty movies and probably fifty television film and video dramas. Agents promoted this unusual run of activity. Movie script writers have always loved to portray actors' agents as soulless, unscrupulous creatures without whom we would all be better off. But movie writers, though marvelously reliable in inventing space creatures—shriveled humanoids and hugely swollen insects—are unreliable in depicting intelligent life on earth. Agents are generally shrewd, knowing, clever people; good company, good friends. They have made my career; they make all careers; they are the most important people in the business.

The very first movie I acted in was made on the East Coast before Nancy and I went west. I hate to count it because it was a bit part. I was never proud of playing bit parts, of "paying my dues" as they say. I always hated bit parts and hated paying dues. Like my first real movie, this preliminary was made by Warner Brothers; it was directed by Delmer Daves in Hartford and was an attempt at high melodrama about high-strung, high-living Connecticut tobacco tycoons, played by several bland Warner TV-contract people. I played a local volunteer fire chief with four or five lines. But my next picture for Warners, my real first, the one Roy Huggins engaged me to do, gave me a good supporting role, a newspaper publisher, and the cast included Herbert Marshall, Efrem Zimbalist, Don Ameche and Angie Dickinson. This movie, *A Fever in the Blood,* was directed by Vincent Sherman; it was a story about crime in state politics, but the writing lacked specific force, none of the characters could dominate the action, and audiences did not know whom to watch. I made little or no impression in the thing, but my agents, as I have noted, hustled me into one television job after another; and also into another movie, Kirk Douglas's *Lonely Are the Brave.*

Clearly Hollywood was the place. The work was plentiful, the money and billing were continually upped by my agents, and also—a perquisite most valuable to any indulged person—the treatment I experienced contrasted joyfully with that of New York, where, if I keeled over dead while signing one of those yellow pads, I would be thought of with relief merely as one less tiresome person. Roy Huggins, on the other hand (other coast is more appropriate), welcomed me into his big office on the Warner Brothers lot as if I were one of the stars of his movie, and I was afterward similarly welcomed all over the town. My representation undoubtedly had something to do with it: I was never sent by myself to see movie producers—always brought to them, to be introduced, by one of the young men at GAC.

The TV industry used a lot of film product at the time, not much videotape—the videotape boom came ten years later—and Hollywood TV was thriving. The film studios, Metro, Fox, Universal, Warners, Paramount, Columbia-Screen Gems, were all grinding out series stuff. These majors, as the old-time studios were called, were producing plenty of theatrical films too. I remember acting with Bob Redford in a couple of TV things—one, a *Dr. Kildare* episode. Independent TV producers, like Lucille Ball's company Desilu, were spreading into second lots. Agent Jack Gilardi had a thought about a series in development at Desilu, and brought me to see Desi Arnaz. A leading role was open in a new comedy series—the character was the only cop in Chicago who refused to take "juice," i.e., payoffs. His long-suffering wife, fed up with poverty, and forgivably larcenous, was to be played by the celebrated comedienne Nancy Walker. Desi gave me the cop's part and Jack made a deal with him, but Desi and Lucy decided at that moment that their marriage had stopped being joyful, and in the business maelstrom of their divorce many deals including mine went down the roaring spout.

The early sixties were busy years for actors. The Hollywood pool could not handle all the work, and New York actors were traveling constantly between the coasts. Still, round-the-clock television demanded product in quantities that could not be supplied by available talent. Two unsound theories about talent were then kited upon the wind: the first was that it was deep inside of everyone and naturally plentiful; the second was that it emerged according as opportunity required it. Help was consequently sought in every quarter, from everyone, however inexperienced, who looked interested; but the absence of first-class professional producers, writers, and directors ensured a continuity overall of low-quality television entertainment. Were audiences upset? Angry professionals liked to believe that they were, that audiences longed for high-quality product and were sadly resigned to low. But the truth was, audiences were delighted by either. This the networks learned from the ratings systems. What luck! Amateurism sufficed, and that being so, it could even be selected and scheduled by amateur network executives. Professionalism became marginal on the small screen.

Actors' pay was never higher. The cost of living in Hollywood was low. But the cost of living was rising steeply by the end of the decade, and actors were complaining that pay rates were dropping. Food and rent began to cost twice as much, but guest-starring roles on one hour film-TV episodes were suddenly paying $2,500 instead of the $3,500, and sometimes the $5,000, of a few years before. The explanation was that producers had decided among themselves to put a "top" on actors' fees. The collusion was a flouting of labor agreements, and probably of the law itself, but our actors' unions did not complain. Nor are they complaining about "tops" today.

The studios and the networks continued in the sixties to be ruled by the political blacklists of the fifties, though of course they were not, and never had been, under any legal obligation to do so. Readers under sixty-five will scarcely remember the Congressional Red hunts, the purge committees, the lists of suspected traitors that private industry maintained at the urging of the FBI. When Warners made a TV series about the FBI, actors' agents had to tell their clients that they would be "screened" by the FBI before being cast in it. Jack Gilardi phoned me one morning and said that the FBI series wanted me for something and asked that I meet an FBI man. I said "Jack, can you tell them I'm not interested?"

"They won't understand that" Jack replied; "you're an actor, you gotta be interested in everything. I'll just ask for a figure they'll never pay, something like twice their top."

That took care of that. It is worth mentioning that the press, on the whole, took no issue with the blacklists, or they frankly approved the blacklists. We were all expected to believe that communist doctrine was perfidiously (though of course invisibly) swamping us by way of the movies, and a lot of our patriotic super-Christian brethren lived up to expectations. But of course one did not have to be Christian to behave like an idiot. Over in Burbank Jack Warner was giving the most authentic idiot performance ever conceived within the walls of his studio. To advertise his passionate belief in government by inquisition—believing that some of us were laggard in accepting it—he raised a monster stars-and-stripes outside his gate overhanging Barham Boulevard. Jack's Old Glory loomed large enough to be a hazard for small aircraft; it seemed to be not a symbol of refuge, but a threat to safety.

The movies, indeed theatre as an inclusive whole, is not a useful tool of revolution. The rabble-rousing screenwriter or playwright, if he is a good writer, cannot help but make his piece entertaining, whereupon his audience depart the theater satisfied and leave the Bastille standing. If he is a bad writer the audience will hate him and his cause equally.

The theatre is unable to change people's attitudes. It has tried and failed: the world repertoire from the Greeks to Shaw, and well past Shaw, has shown us our iniquities and warned us to mend our contemptible ways. We have attended with joyful callousness; the theatre has put us beyond blame; the emotional catharsis it afforded us has relieved us, not cured us, and we are no better or worse after the play than before it.

9

·······

When Nancy and I and our son Hugh were in Rome in 1969 a friend persuaded me to meet "a kind of an interesting guy," another American who had been living in Italy since the end of the Second World War, a man, I was told, with a good idea for a movie. Which is why I had to be persuaded to meet the man: all Americans living abroad had "good ideas for movies," but the good ideas were all from movies already made.

"I am not a producer, Mr Liguori" I said when the man came to see me one morning.

"Ralph" he requested.

"Ralph" I repeated, and brought him to a table in the garden of the hotel. Actually I led him, slowly. He wore spectacles with very heavy lenses, and he held my arm tightly as we moved along. He was all but blind, and had been driven to the hotel in a well-kept black Chevrolet sedan, ten or twelve years old. He was rotund and small, not above five-five, and he appeared to be sixty-two or -three. I invited his driver to join us, but Ralph waved the man away with a brusque "Wait for me in the parking." His Italian dialect, cutting off the ends of words (*Mi shpett' in parchegg'*), sounded Neapolitan. The driver's accent, as he thanked me politely and withdrew, sounded Roman.

Ralph ordered campari. So did I. He handed me a Havana cigar, though he himself did not smoke, and he said apologetically "I know you're busy."

"No" I assured him. "Right now I'm on a short break from acting in a movie."

"I was told you know people" he said.

"Well, a couple of producers—but that doesn't mean—"

I stopped because I was unwilling to hear my own tedious voice explaining yet again the hopelessness of promoting a mere idea into a movie. I raised my glass, wished him health and said "Ralph, tell me your story."

He hesitated. He said "You look like somebody."

"Well, I've been in a bunch of movies."

"No, no" he smiled, "I don't see no movies." He waved a hand in front of his eyes. "The peepers is gone." His speech had all the character of poor New York neighborhoods.

"Ralph" I said, "is your story idea something out of your own life?"

"Reed told you, ha?" He was referring to Reed Morgan, the friend who had brought us together, an actor, one of the cast of the movie I was working on.

"He didn't tell me much" I replied, "though he did say you had to leave the States in '45."

Ralph nodded. He was smiling. He smiled a lot, faintly, even when later he talked about very serious things. "I got deported" he said, "with Charley Lucky. I'm talkin' about Luciano. They stuck us on a ship—over to here. I was put in Rome and Charley was put down south and the Italian cops said we was to never meet. We met. How they gonna keep us apart? Two guys like him and me, close so many years."

I waited, wondering whether I was going to be told a long story or, as I hoped, a short one. I was not surprised by the Luciano revelation. At least I was not surprised to learn that

Ralph was an alumnus of the Luciano school of life. Much about him proclaimed him so.

"Charley and me used to meet" Ralph went on, "halfways between here and Naples. He'd take a car from there, me a car from here, maybe two, three times a year. Then the cops found out. Some dirty guinea from over here put them wise. I hadda go on a curfew. Charley too. I hadda stay in my apartment after eight every night—they had stoolies watchin' for about a year. But I was doin' pretty good—had a night club goin' here in Rome, swell apartment to live in.

"I lived so good, Charley got mad—didn't like it, didn't expect it. Why, I don't know—'cause I always done good on my own even in the old days. See, I was in with Charley in the numbers, but I always had somethin' else goin'. Like the ice. I had the ice out in Queens and part of Brooklyn. Remember the ice?"

I remembered the ice. In the thirties many people still had ice boxes in their pantries, and every other day they bought five- and ten-pound cubes from "the ice man," who made home deliveries with his horse-drawn wagon. I used to marvel at the load of ice, how it retained most of its volume under sawdust and burlap even in the hottest summer weather. And we kids used to raid the back of the wagon while the ice man was carrying his cubes to kitchen doors. Our stolen chunks and shavings were ambrosial, and of course it was joy unequaled to be chased off by the ice man with his Sicilian curses and brandished ice tongs. But all we ever took was waste, to be swept into the street if not devoured by us, and one day when I glimpsed the ice man laughing quietly as he climbed back to his driving seat I realized that his fury was all show, all fun.

He needed a little fun too. His was a melancholy occupation. He had his morning rounds and his afternoon rounds, long hard days. His horse required after-hours care and so did his wagon, and his profit was low. He picked up his merchandise at wholesale "ice houses," which were operated by men like Ralph. The business was fearfully exclusive. The vendor paid a lot to get into it and a lot to stay in it—half of what he earned, plus extortionate interest on his loan from the ice house to buy his horse and rig. How many hundreds of people were involved in this seemingly innocuous and certainly beneficial enterprise I cannot estimate, but "the ice" was a big money mill, and when Ralph said he "had" it he was telling me that he was once a rich man, a racketeer who had staked out territories, laid down laws and usages, and maintained the system by brute force.

"Is Luciano in your movie idea?" I asked.

"Na, na, we leave Charley out. It's about me. I gotta get some money. See now I got nothin'. Next to nothin'. Well, somethin', but nothin' for when I'm gone. And I got married to a woman over here, and we got a little boy, not in the best of health."

He didn't look to me as if he was in the best of health himself.

He told me a hard luck story about his years in Rome, but he kept it brief and never slobbered off into self-pity. He had been doing very well until a certain man, a functionary at the American embassy (he said an FBI man) decided to finger him as the Rome link in the European drug network. This man persuaded the Italian police to arrest Ralph whenever a drug bust occurred anywhere in Italy.

"This FBI bum just wanted to give himself somethin' to do" Ralph explained, "somethin' he could write reports about—a dumb *stronz*."[1] His girlfren', who I got for him, told me he ruined her kitchen one night tryin' to kill cockroaches wit' a hammer."

Ralph said that he patiently endured the *stronz*s harassment. He got along well with the *Polizia Dello Stato*; he knew they meant him no harm, they knew he was behaving himself, but they wanted to show the Americans that they were nothing if not cooperative. Then the American agent began frequenting Ralph's nightclub, turning his visits into interrogation sessions.

---

[1]*Stronzo.* A shit.

"I had to sit with the guy, buy him drinks. I couldn't watch my business. And to tell you true, I was losin' trade—customers didn't want to be in there with this creep hangin' around. One night I blew up. I told him if he kept botherin' me they'd have to send him back to the States in a spaghetti box."

It was a bluff. Ralph admitted it was a bluff. The agent must have known it was a bluff because Ralph was in no position— would not dare—to harm anybody. But Ralph's outburst incurred reprisals. Daily raids by police and narcotics and tax investigators, repeated shutdowns, forced Ralph to give up the club. He had to vacate his large apartment and rent a small one and live thereafter on his savings.

I waited to hear the good idea. I wanted to help him somehow. I wanted at least to treat him seriously. "Why?" Nancy wondered when I told her about him, and I said I didn't know why. But I did know why. I just wasn't prepared to explain why at that moment.

Ralph began to talk his way toward the promised story, but he took a slow winding route through "the old times" in New York—the Prohibition years, old pals of his that I had never heard of, old "bosses" I had read about. Luciano was but one of many, though the most famous of all. Ralph told me how Willie Moretti, the old boss of the Bronx, had once saved his life.

"Three guys from Detroit come in lookin' for somebody by the name of Lagarone or somethin', somebody I never heard of. They didn't know this guy from your Uncle Luigi, but they was sent in to find him and finish him. Who knew why? Who cared? It was Detroit stuff. They pulled me into a car outside the Astor Hotel on Broadway—them and a driver from New York, who was the bum that fingered me, who I tried to catch up with later on but never could. I have to laugh: there was a cop on a horse, sittin' there ten yards away while the three of these mugs muscled me into the car!" Ralph chuckled. "The horse was watchin'—but the cop was lookin' at the other side of Times Square.

"They brung me to the back of a store down on Greene Street. I keep tellin' 'em I ain't who they want, they're makin' a bad mistake, and I write down my name and three phone numbers for them to call and check. One of them goes out to the front of the store and calls a number. He comes back very quiet.

"Meantime the driver has ducked out and beat it in the car. We sit there waitin' half an hour. This weasel who made the call, he starts talkin' to me nice—if they made a mistake they hope there's no hard feelins. I sit there sayin' nothin'. They even gimme back a gun I was carryin' which they took off me in the car. Finally there's some knockin' on the front door, and they let in four guys who come and say a big hello to me, so I know the first number this Detroit mug called was not Charley Lucky or Al Marinelli, but Willie Moretti, 'cause these four guys are Willie's guys. So that's how Willie saved my life." Ralph sipped his drink.

For Ralph, apparently, the story was over. I had to ask him "What happened to the Detroit guys?"

"Oh them—" he said, a bit surprised that I would inquire about people who, when he had seen the last of them, had been of no interest to him whatever. "We took 'em to Penn Station" he said, "put 'em on a train." His small smile spread a little. "We got 'em a bedroom all to themselves."

I thought a moment and then said "Did they walk onto that train?"

"They all got on the train fine. But I think they needed some help gettin' off."

At last I led him to the main story, his "movie" story: it was about himself and Thomas E. Dewey, a former governor of New York, twice a presidential candidate, who had been a "special rackets prosecutor" in New York when Luciano had been in lawless primacy there.

"Dewey framed me and Charley Lucky" Ralph said simply. "He got this madam and three, four of the *puttan'* who worked for her to say they brung money to me and Charley in a saloon downtown—few hundred dollars." His smile opened derisively. "Here was Charley doin' four mill a year with the numbers— like twenny fi' mill today—with a floor of offices up in the Chanin Buildin'—and me with him—and they grab us for a thing like that! The papers call Charley the Vice King, me Ralph the Pimp. They could get away with that in the papers, but anybody said that to me out of his face, he ain't got no face no more. It was the only way Dewey could get us. He could never make no case on the numbers or nothin' else, 'cause we had the city plugged, gagged and wired, and some of Dewey's own crowd was in with us. So Dewey frames the whore bullshit— scares the poor broads to death. He gives them money and they beat it to Europe when the trial is over. One jumped out a hotel in London."

He laughed, leaned across the table and said "I know what you're thinkin': the broad was pushed, ha?"

"No—thinking about other things" I said.

"She was crazy—everybody knew—no brain, gone on drugs, say anything, garbage. And for that me and Charley had to go away. But if she was pushed out a window it wasn't none of us done it. What I heard was—some newspaper guy talked her into spillin' everything about the frame-up, double-crossin' the Great Prosecutor, so one of Dewey's own guys went over and took care of her."

The driver appeared. He came hesitantly to the table and told Ralph he had just made a phone call—people were arriving unexpectedly at the apartment: *"Stan venendo la famiglia della Signora."*

"Cos'e?" said Ralph. The driver began to repeat his message but Ralph, uncomprehending, shook his head and said *"Gminge angor"*—Start again. I interrupted and told Ralph the message in English. His wife's family were arriving.

"See?" he said. "I can't even speak the language after all these years here, only a little crazy dialect from my mother. I hate it here. It ain't my country though I was born in it—I don't even know what place. In diapers they brung me to New York and my mother made it up I was born there. If only I knew the true I coulda got naturalized long ago—maybe they wouldn't deport me back. How you like my luck, ha?"

He got up and the driver came to lead him. "When I see you again?" he asked. "'Cause I gotta tell more."

I took his phone number and said I would ring him the next day. He started away, clinging to the driver but trying hard to walk erect—small and vulnerable and sad in spite of anything sinister that could be said of him, or that he had said of himself. He stopped suddenly and turned.

"Did I tell you look like somebody?"

"You did, Ralph, yes."

He shrugged. "But then with these peepers I look in a mirror and wonder if I ever seen *me* before."

We shared something, Ralph and I. He knew it, but didn't know what it was. I knew what it was.

I did not ring him the next day. I too got an unexpected call. I had to catch a flight to Belgrade, then speed by car to an old and ruined village where our film unit was simulating battle-torn France of a bygone day. The movie was a Clint Eastwood vehicle called *Kelly's Heroes.* I did not get back to Rome for a week.

Nancy meanwhile left a message at the number Ralph had given me. But when I finally called him myself he told me sullenly that he had been given no message. When I assured him that I wanted to hear more of his story, he grumbled a disbelieving "Yeah, yeah," and I had to say "Ralph, if I wanted to give you the brush, would I be calling?"

He told me he felt "watched" at my hotel, the Parco dei Principi, so I went to meet him at a table outside a bar near the Stazione Termini, the main railway station of Rome. We ordered coffees. He was not interested in my reasonable excuse or the events that delayed my return, like production blunders and unlucky rainstorms. I decided to try an amusing story.

I told him about a rooster that began crowing inexplicably at five forty-five one evening, making it impossible to film and record a certain scene. The assistant director sent two Serbian teamsters to hunt and destroy the eccentric bird. The teamsters obviously disliked the assignment but went off obediently with their long shotguns, and after a half hour of costly inactivity we heard four thunderous rounds, as if the hunters were bringing down a rhino.

The grim-faced teamsters came back and gave us significant nods. We resumed work. The recording equipment and camera "rolled," the director yelled "Action!" and we actors began to act. And the cock, evidently back from the dead, began crowing again, more loudly than before. We looked for the teamsters. They had vanished. In despair we "wrapped" for the day.

Ralph enjoyed this story. He smiled. "Them phony teamsters!" he said. "Didn't even have the balls to kill a chicken! Did you fire them?"

"Ralph" I replied gravely, "you don't fire teamsters, even in Yugoslavia." He laughed a little more at that. His glumness was gone and soon he was again talking about himself. We moved to a nearby trattoria for lunch.

Thomas Dewey, he told me, visited Europe after his electoral defeat by Harry Truman and came of course to Rome. His tour of the town brought him to the Pantheon, and Ralph was among the small crowd in the piazza observing him curiously, many of them not knowing who he was. A few extra police were on duty but their precautions were casual; it was not anticipated that anyone would offer insult or injury to somebody who was now nobody. When Ralph approached Dewey, no one prevented him.

What was on Ralph's mind?

He wanted to ask a favor of an old acquaintance. He touched Dewey's arm and Dewey turned with a smile. But the smile gave way to a look of shock and terror. Ralph in his soft voice said "Hi Tom, you're lookin' good." Dewey could not speak.

"Listen Tom" Ralph continued, "could you say a word for me back home? Could you say a word? I wanna go home, Tom, that's all."

Dewey, a small man himself, was staring at a slightly smaller one, a pudgier one in shirtsleeves, peering only half-seeing through thick eyeglasses, straining to smile, to ingratiate himself—hardly the fearsome bullet of a man the prosecutor had sent to Sing Sing. There was no hint of menace now in Ralph Liguori, yet Dewey took a backward step or two. A policeman came to his side.

Ralph said "Tell the cop it's okay, Tom, I just wanted to say hello."

"It's all right" Dewey said to the policeman. "All right."

"Just a word to the right people back home would help, Tom. I can't give you nothin'. I got nothin' now. I got a wife—she'll say a prayer for you. Will you say a word, Tom?"

Dewey nodded rapidly. "Sure Ralph, why not?"

"First chance you get, ha?"

"First chance" Dewey agreed. He headed for his limo. "Bye!" he called to the crowd. "Ciao!" called the crowd. And the "rackets buster" of old New York was gone.

Ralph chuckled. "And that was ten years ago. Scared to death he was." We sat in silence for a moment, and then Ralph said "Well, what do you think?"

"It's an interesting scene" I said, "but it's only a little piece of your movie."

"Well naturally we gotta fill it out, but that ain't no little piece, that's the big scene."

"Your movie" I told him, "if we could find a way to make it— probably begins with your mother bringing you to New York on a ship—ends with you leaving on a ship—and it's about everything in between, all the things you told me, everything about you and Luciano, and Costello and Moretti and Schultz and everybody else." He began to shake his head. "And" I insisted, "it would have to be very real, truthful, because we've seen a lot of pictures about the mob, mafia pictures—people want something different, new."

He said "I can tell a lotta things to you but I can't put 'em in my movie. We gotta leave Charley out—any of them guys I mentioned—out, out."

"Ralph" I argued, "I heard of a movie they're making now, about Joe Valachi—real stuff—the *cosa nostra*—"

"Yeah, yeah, somebody told me." He contrived a deprecating smirk. "*Cosa nostra!* I never hear them words in the old days. I never hear of Valachi neither."

"He must have been around."

"Maybe—a lotta guys was around."

"Somebody wrote a book for him. He told everything."

Ralph shook his head. "Valachi don't know nothin' because—"

He leaned across the table and knocked over his glass of wine; it spread about on the cloth and he dabbed nervously at it with his napkin. A waiter came to assist—removed tableware, glasses, the bottle, sponged here and there with napkins and arranged two fresh ones on the table as a cover. Ralph was embarrassed. His hand trembled as he took off his spectacles. Then he dropped them; they fell to the table and I said, "I'll do it, Ralph," and he let me pick them up and wipe them. Without a word he let me return them to his face. He looked down at the table. A spot of wine had bled through a napkin and he stared at it—put out a finger and touched it.

"I'll tell you why Valachi didn't know nothin'."

I said "Okay, tell me."

He hesitated. He was searching for words that would be convincing. Then, apparently settling for what to him was the simple truth, he made a little shrug. "Because" he said softly, "if he'd of knew anything he wouldn't of said nothin'."

We finished our meal without much more talk. I offered to find him a writer, warning him however that any writer would require far more than the scene at the Pantheon. But he told me not to bother; he didn't want anybody but me to write his movie, and anyway the movie could only portray himself and Tom Dewey—and "just actors, nobody real."

Back in the States I made the second revised pilot episode of an untitled series about a working-class American right-wing racist and bigot, a show I didn't give much chance of survival. When like the first one it was rejected by the ABC network I decided to return to Rome. I got a writing deal from one of the Du Ponts who wanted to go into the movie business—$10,000, not bad in those days for a first draft screenplay—and started working on a film to be made in Italy. (It was never made. Nobody liked the script. My friend the late Burt Lancaster said of it: "I don't know what's goin' on.")

I got in touch with Ralph and we met again at the café near the station. He moved more uncertainly than before, and had procured himself a strong cane. His Roman driver was not in sight, and when I inquired about the man Ralph said tersely that he had got rid of him—he was a spy. "Stayin' at the Parco again?" he inquired.

"No" I said, "I'm in an apartment in Via del Babuino—going to be here for a while—writing a movie." And then I added "But not about anybody we know, Ralph."

He laughed. He told me he had put his movie idea out of his mind, and was now thinking mainly, and seriously, of going home. There was a chance he could. His sister had been over on a visit; she knew a lawyer in Brooklyn who had a connection in Washington, and maybe . . .

It was a big problem obtaining three immigration visas: "Tough enough for my wife and kid, but real tough for me, for reasons you know. But if I can show them a passbook to a New York bank—good-lookin' numbers in it—that'll help. That's what I'm tryin' a finagle now, a passbook with the numbers."

"What kind of numbers?"

"Why?" he said quickly. "You got good numbers in yours?"

I hoped I didn't take too long to reply. "Twenty-five."

He laughed. "You went a little white there for a second. I need much bigger, and I wouldn't take it off you anyway."

He asked me to come with him to his apartment. He assured me his wife would not mind in the least, and would give us a far better lunch than "that dump over there where I spilt the wine."

The apartment was a pleasant one in a well-maintained prewar building a short taxi ride away. Going up in the lift, Ralph reassured me that his wife would be pleased to see me. When we walked in we found her dressed to go out and not at all prepared to give us lunch.

She was embarrassed—so was Ralph—but she had planned to take the boy somewhere; they were in fact leaving as we arrived. She was short and plump, yet a pretty woman, pleasant and frank, a good bit younger than Ralph. She called the boy, who was about nine or ten, and when he walked into the sitting room I noticed that he was a little lame. I told her that Ralph and I could easily go down to a bar and eat sandwiches— indeed I preferred them for lunch—and she, making me promise to come again for dinner, took the boy's hand and hastened away.

"Okay" said Ralph, "we'll go for sandwiches, but first we'll have the little something to give the appetite." And he went laboriously to an armoir containing liquor and glasses and poured two Campari with shots of gin. We sat awhile in silence, and then he said "So what's on your mind?"

The question surprised me. I said "Nothing, Ralph—any- thing—whatever we're talking about."

He nodded. "Just askin'."

"Why?"

"Oh" he said, "just the way you come up to me today. You gimme a little hug. First time."

He was shrewdly right, I had something on my mind. I had been wondering since I first met him whether he could give me some rather special information—about Sing Sing prison in New York. "Not for a movie" I said, "or anything like that. Just for myself. Just between the two of us."

He shrugged. Without enthusiasm he said "There ain't a hell of a lot to tell. The worst of it was bein' locked away. It could drive you bughouse. It helped if you had friends, and some dough. You hear the radio, see a picture show now and then, walk around a little, play games, read a lotta stuff." He smiled. "Up there, I got my health back—quit smokin', ate plain food, lost a lotta fat. People use' come and see me and say I never looked so good."

"Did they see you in those little pens?" I asked.

"The what?"

"The little spaces with the little wooden railings around—and the little benches—in the big room where people visited."

He did not reply. Some seconds passed in silence.

"When I used to see prison movies" I went on, "—I was about thirteen—I'd say to myself 'People don't visit the way they're showing it, talking through screens with a guard listening— hardly giving them time to say hello. They sit right next to each other in the little pens, and they can be together an hour or more—and they can hug each other hello and good-bye.' "

Ralph watched me—waited for me—to hear what was on my mind—knowing already what it was.

"You said once or twice" I began, "that I looked like some-body—"

"Yeah, you do, Ed O'Connor."

"When you were up there, did you know him?"

He nodded. "I knew him. Knew him well. How is he?"

"Gone now. Gone nearly three years."

"Yeah. Fine man. Hell of a lawyer. Charley Lucky used often talk to him about his case. So did we all. He helped a lotta cons with cases. Taught school up there too. How come it took you so long to mention him?"

I didn't know what to reply. Should I have mentioned him earlier? I rarely mentioned my father to anyone. Asked about him, I always replied "He was a lawyer—gone now," and said no more. Then why was I talking about him now?

"Were you ashamed of somethin'?" Ralph asked.

And that, of course, was the reason I hadn't talked about him. "I was ashamed of myself, Ralph."

"What'd you do?"

"It's what I didn't do. I never worked out a way to talk about him honestly, except now and then to my mother."

"He had some other family" Ralph recalled. "Charley Lucky knew one of 'em—a reporter."

"Yes. A brother. Wrote for the *Times*. And he had another brother, who was a publisher. No contact with them or theirs for years and years—since he got put away. They didn't want to be called—no interest in us."

Ralph chuckled in a mordant little way. "And who was they? Royalty? Listen, your old man was the best. He was a gent, and he was smart. He knew everything worth knowin', and he got big respect. He was like a Boss. Even the screws was a little scared of him. Know what we used to do?" Now he chuckled with amusement. "We use' make spaghetti in the yard! Would you believe it? We had a stove in the yard! The screws use' bring it out for us and light the fire. We even had wine. Your old man would come eat with us now and then. And we'd all talk over the news from New York, and laugh it up and have a swell time. And lotsa the cons was jealous; but nobody dast do or say nuthin', 'cause this was Charley Lucky's corner, and you wanna finish your time and go back to baby wit' your *gotz* still there, you don't bother Charley."

He fished for a few sprightly Big House yarns, obviously to lift my mood. This was a kindness. He recalled inmates Richard

Whitney, former head of the New York Stock Exchange; and Fritz Kuhn, former head of the German-American Bund, the Nazi party in the United States. He asked me how often I had visited my father in Sing Sing. I told him about my three trips. I recalled how, on the train moving up the Hudson shore to Ossining, my mother and I used to decide what and what not to tell him—how we planned our responses to his expected questions—preparing to assure him that nothing had changed at home, in school, in the neighborhood. All a lie. Everything had changed. But Mama made believe everything was the same. And my father made believe that he believed everything we told him.

Ralph nodded. "Like a Boss. Nobody would never know what he was thinkin'—nobody."

The irony of Ralph's comment lay, as irony always lies, in a deeper truth: the "nobody" included my father himself; he didn't know what he was thinking either.

Looking back, and I had looked back often, I was sure I had discerned in him the symptoms of a very bad old problem—a disease—a disease that had also afflicted his only sister. He was schizophrenic. Of course he was also, as Ralph had said, "a brain."

He had an uncommon breadth of knowledge and understanding, and it went far beyond his own field—into history and literature (where the run of lawyers seldom glance), and also into mathematics, physics and mechanics. He got me through high school geometry and trigonometry, helped me to perceive first principles, to follow constructive reasoning. Once merely in passing he explained to me the relativity of motion measurement—making a quick drawing with his gold pencil of the famous space-time illustration—the observers inside and outside of the moving train. He wrote well, he spoke well, he left people with a sense of being enlightened. He introduced me to "little Amelita" and to music generally.

Yet this charismatic mind could shift undetected to a mode of casuistry wherein fraud and larceny were blameless devices of good motives. He was kind and generous, and to his family and intimates most loving, and without being in the least self-congratulatory he clearly saw these merits in himself. To use an expression I hear at every turn these days, he "felt good about himself": that is, free of guilt and regret. He wondered what he had done wrong, how it happened that his defrauding other frauds of huge amounts of money caused so much horror in society, and he concluded that he was perpetually the victim of skewed analysis.

For the same pathology of delusion, though a much more aggravated form of it, his only sister was confined for half of her life to a mental institution, and there died. Schizophrenia, when its result is not grand larceny, is treated in hospitals, not prisons.

Ralph Liguori and I did not go out for lunch. We had another of his powerful cocktails, then drank beer and ate pannini and salami and cold pasta and salsicci and stared out the kitchen window at the rear roofs and terraces of Rome. We watched the women hanging out wash.

I didn't see Ralph again. I got deeply dug into my screenplay, and suddenly I got a hurry-up call to fly back to Hollywood and appear in thirteen trial episodes of that untitled series. We retained our Roman apartment, garaged our car, packed a few clothes for a short stay, and flew to Los Angeles. Nancy and Hugh and I didn't get back to Rome for three years.

And when I got back I didn't call Ralph. I had a feeling he was dead, but I didn't want to be told he was dead.

My Ghost said "That's daft! You're as likely to be told that he's alive."

The Divil said "Not at all! He was half-dead when we were with him last. I saw the Dark Angel in his eye—goin' he was, and glad to be goin'."

"But if he's here still—" the Ghost began.

"Arrah if he is, then" the Divil coarsely finished, "what odds? He'll have nothin' more to say, and maybe less than before."

"And have you nothing more to say to the poor man?" the Ghost asked me.

I thought about it and said "No, nothing, but I could try." But I didn't try. I've always been cowardly about sentiment. And that's where I and my advisers left it twenty-seven years ago.

10

·······

"I've never been good at predicting the popularity of any-thing. My predictions are unreliable, whether I predict success or failure."

I was saying this to a friend, who replied: "In plain words, which you're also not good at, you can't smell a hit." My friend (Gerry Briggs of Forest Hills) said it well. Norman Lear smelled the hit in the British comedy that became *All in the Family*. Not that he possesses a supersense; he has produced some flops, but he never doubted, as many did, that this venture was going to be a big success. To me, when I first read about the British comedy in an article in *The Saturday Review*, it was evidently an outra-geous piece of comic satire that only the fearless BBC would try to get away with, and did get away with, airing it as *Till Death Us Do Part* once a month for a year or so. It centered on a right-wing working-class fool who, in his home, freely vented his crudely racist, inhumane convictions. Everyone in England acknowl-edged the portrayal of a true British type, but many resented paying their TV license fees to bring this disgraceful specimen before the world. How did England benefit from that! But *Till Death* was nonetheless a great comedy hit.

Not two weeks after reading about the British show I got a call from my agent, Jack Gilardi, who said that someone wanted to talk to me about doing the same show here, an American version. I could hardly believe it: the ABC network was interested in doing this mad thing, and had agreed to work with a smart young fellow who had secured the American rights to it. ABC had told him to sign me to play the lead. I said "Jack, I'll talk to him. The thing is a sure disaster, but the explosion will get us a lot of attention." A pleasant young man with an eastern college look to him, Howard Edelman, came out to Malibu Beach, where Nancy and I and Hugh, six, were spending that summer of 1968, and I made a deal with him, script unseen. We began talking about where the principal character came from, and agreed on New York, though someone had suggested Texas to Howard; we talked about casting, and Howard began seeing pairs of kids for the parts of the daughter and son-in-law, and driving them out to Malibu to let me look at them. He mentioned some actresses' names to consider for the part of the wife, but didn't suggest that I meet anybody.

The part of the wife in the British original was very different from what it became in Jean Stapleton's unforgettable characterization. The British actress played perfectly what was written for her, a suffering soul, yet a crusty woman who was ready to do combat with her boorish cockney mate at the drop of an "h." I had the American actress well in mind if we were going to play the wife as she had been played at the BBC, but we could not get the gifted Marge Redmond, my choice, released from another series. Eventually the part of the wife got a completely new character, one that nobody else had in mind but Jean Stapleton. Jean's idea of Edith Bunker was not only original and perfectly suited to the American audience, but very comical and emotionally very moving. Jean invented the character that made the series work; the benign, compassionate presence she developed made my egregious churl bearable.

Howard Edelman told me one day that ABC wanted him to associate himself with Bud Yorkin and Norman Lear, a team experienced in producing TV comedy specials. He asked me how I felt about this, and I said I felt all right provided my deal with him went forward unchanged in any way, and that he remained prominent as the producer in control of the material. His tenure was important to me; he had agreed with me from the start that the leading character in this play, this TV series, was the archetypal American wage-earning goy.[1] Howard, being Jewish and educated, had observed this character only at a distance. He saw that I possessed a singular insight into the motives and behavior of the character, and he was happy to share control of the material with me. He assured me that none of our agreements would change.

A messenger shortly afterward brought me a script and I was given an appointment to meet Norman Lear. I read the script, and didn't like it from the first page to the last. The writer wrote jokes for four actors, but had no grasp of the characters of any of them. I decided to do a complete re-write, but having only a day or two to do it, and no secretarial help, I wrote everything over in longhand and then tape-recorded the whole script, reading all the parts. When I went to meet Lear I played this tape for him, and he gave it to his secretary to transcribe as a new script. The cast worked with this script as it came to them, with only a few technical changes, and it was videotaped as our first pilot before an astonished audience in New York. Lear did not inform the cast of what I had done, and I, assuming he had good reason to say nothing, said nothing myself. I didn't require a writing credit and fee for the extra contribution; it was enough for me to make sure the play was right. I knew the press would sanctimoniously

---

[1] Yiddish, also colloquial, for non-Jew (*goyim* = the others).

attack us when they saw and heard a television character open fire on the blacks and Jews and Hispanics, but I didn't want them to be able to say that the character, whom they were now meeting as Archie, was a distortion of his counterpart in the real world. Years later Lear told the story of my rewrite, as I have told it here, when he and I were guests on the Mike Douglas talk show.

The ABC network made our first pilot episode in October in New York. We rehearsed in the old Ansonia Hotel and taped the show in a theater on West 58th Street. During rehearsals Howard Edelman disappeared. Norman Lear directed us, assisted by an experienced video director with whom he shared credit. I left town without talking to Howard; he was unreachable—I don't remember why—at the phone number I had for him, and Nancy and I and Hugh were rushing for a plane to Europe. Returning from the vacation, we flew directly to Los Angeles, and on arriving home I learned that ABC wanted us to retape the pilot episode. Its raw honesty seemed exceedingly daring to the audience that saw it taped—some found it almost intolerable— but all were wonderfully entertained in spite of themselves and laughed longer and louder than any audience I had ever played to.

I was surprised by the demand for a remake. Lear explained that ABC wanted to recast the characters of Mike and Gloria, but the kids we used, Tim McIntyre and Kelly Jean Peters, had seemed very effective to me. We made the second pilot with the same script and two new kids, before an audience at the ABC studios in Los Angeles. ABC looked at the pilot again; the guiding minds said nothing about the second pair of kids, who were not as good as the first, but decided at last to say how they really responded to the product. They shrank from it. If we wanted to try another kind of Gleason show, another kind of Lucy show, fine, but they were petrified by the thought of anything as boldly unconventional as this.

Why they couldn't have spoken frankly after our first pilot is anybody's guess, because the change of kids had nothing to do with the content. My guess is that between the making of the first and second versions the ABC ayatollah in New York anointed a new mullah (vulgarly called the president of entertainment) to be in charge of prognostic sophistry. Only one network mullah gets this key oracular job; his acolytes rustle in and out with news of this and that, meditate agreeably at meetings and exude confidence. What else they do, no one can certainly say. Some of them, to be sure, have to take care of tiresome tangibles, say for instance the regular functioning of the multimillion-dollar industrial plant and all the departmental activities that the oracular mullah gazes absently upon from day to day. This anointed one, looking at our show, probably reflected that ABC had recently aired a new risqué variety show that had given offense to persons unspecified, and the network had felt obliged to kill it and exorcise the studio. No more heresy and its attendant fevers.

I wished the public could have seen our work, but doing it and hearing the big laughter of the audiences made the experience joyful and memorable to me. And then there was Jean. She and I had met before while performing in an episode of the old *The Defenders* series in New York, in which I played a murderer and she delightedly played a witness who fingered me in court. But it was on the pilot that we became friends, and on the series fond and lasting friends. Archie made everybody laugh; so did Edith (and so did Mike and Gloria), but Edith helped work a change in America, and she did this by signaling and encouraging a change in women. What we then called "the women's movement" (or sometimes snidely "women's liberation") was getting into stride, and Jean, besides being herself involved in it, and being a pace setter in the real world, saw to it that Edith, observed by twenty-five million people every week, was a courageous women's champion in her own imaginary Family. Before Edith came and endeared herself to America, women who lived with fellows like Archie were usually submissive and suffering in the face of roaring nonthink; after Edith, they confronted nonthink a little more sternly and stiffly, and gave hint of a serious readiness to rebel, just as Edith rebelled from time to time.

Did I run some kind of poll or survey to determine this? No. My mail informed me, and so did many conversations with women in many walks of life. Inexact measurements? Yes, extremely. I remain convinced. If ever anything on television changed the country, not radically, nor even obviously, it was the performance of Jean and the example of Edith. Did our series effectively attack bigotry and racism? We thought so at the time—our intention from first to last was to get on the flanks of the legions of Clucksbury and wound them to the death. But Clucksbury, while it howled laughing at us, ignored our serious stabbing instruction. Intellectuals too, both of the right and the left, howled laughing for reasons above the ken of Clucksbury, for instance, savants Bill Buckley of the *National Review* and Victor Navasky of *The Nation*. Everybody sooner or later perceived our motives, but those we had targeted for instruction declined to be instructed.

America meanwhile was undergoing a comprehensive change for which television deserves no credit. The federal government, namely the Supreme Court and the executive branch—omitting Congress, whose biggest constituency, like that of television, was Clucksbury—ordained the change: they stripped the Clucks of all their unconstitutional local powers and kicked over their unlawful race barriers. The great civil rights movement of the sixties achieved in the seventies all it had hoped for, equal access to all places and all things for all kinds of people. Today we are astounded reflecting on how long it took, how bloody was the struggle, and how majestic was the law's victory. Yet how widely and bitterly the Lord's exhortations about love and the brotherhood of man are evaded still. No court can rule out ill feeling. Nothing but the heart can change the heart.

I got busy again doing some television jobs, and a movie up in Utah with Bill Holden called *The Devils's Brigade*. Following this, my friend Gabe Katzka, who had produced and cast me in a Jim Garner Marlowe movie, asked me to come to Yugoslavia to make his new movie, *Kelly's Heroes*. Nancy and I and Hugh left for Europe again, this time aboard the Italian liner *Michelan-gelo* sailing from New York to Genoa. There we rented a car and drove east to Trieste, and from there, at the highest allowable speed, east by south through Slovenia, Croatia and Serbia to the city of Novi Sad on the Danube. We had hurried in response to a phone call telling us to hurry, and on arrival were told there was no hurry—which was no surprise, as the schedule, like that of every big expensive movie I had ever worked on, was spurious.

I had been in the country twenty-four years earlier in the Adriatic port of Split aboard a freighter delivering a United Nations shipment of food. Split was in the region that was Bosnia-Herzegovina, but the whole country after the Second World War, during my first visit, was a united Yugoslavia under Tito,[2] and it included of course the regions I mentioned above. Tito, an old communist who had once fought in Russia's Red Army, was a dictator who broke relations with Stalin in 1948 and made his country a model of socialist liberalism in Europe. Private ownership of small industries was common in 1969 when we arrived to do the movie. A Mercedes dealer in Belgrade from whom I bought a new sedan was a private entrepreneur. In this lively stick-shift six we made trips to Trieste and Venice and round and about the lovely Istrian countryside where we met and talked with hard-working, good-looking, friendly local people who spoke a lot of Italian and a little English and German. They seemed cheerful and hopeful of better and better times to come. Eleven years later Tito was in his grave; the nation

---

[2] Josip Broz, Marshal.

he created was breaking down once more into little principalities[3] whose pitiable rivalries had always made the Balkan Peninsula a battle pit.

Nancy and I made new lasting friends on the picture—Don Rickles, who was playing a principal role, and his wife Barbara. Another star of the picture, whom I knew from other happy mutual endeavors, was the late Telly Savalas. The original ending of *Kelly's Heroes*, though tragic, gave the thing some meaning, but it was changed in filming to something comically incongruous that left the work with no meaning whatever. Nobody cared. The picture was a success; it still plays regularly on television.

In the middle of shooting I was allowed to leave for what they said was "a month or so," subject to a sudden recall. Gabe Katzka gave me several thousand dollars in U.S. cash, and we drove away into Italy, revisited Trieste and Venice, and continued west to the region of Parma, to a little hill town named Bardi where Renato Sidoli, our beloved friend of Dublin days, was spending the summer with his family. All of us, one warm July night, stared at a television set and watched Armstrong and Aldrin walk on the moon. Renato, his wife Nina, Nancy and I and a couple of other adults found it hard to believe what we were seeing. But the four kids spread on the carpet, Renato's Sandra, Flavia and Lino, and our Hugh, the youngest at seven, watched the event with delight but no astonishment. Kids their age never doubted that they would see a trip to the moon and had been calmly expecting it for a long time. I hadn't realized how wonderfully the enlightenment of the young moves beyond us.

We went down to Rome and checked into a new hotel, the Parco dei Principi, because it had gardens and a swimming pool for Hugh and a garage for the car. Moviemaking wasn't booming

---

[3]There were five of them before 1914.

in Rome as it was seven years earlier when we were making *Cleopatra*, but it was brisk. At the Parco I met the busiest American actor in Europe at the time, one of my valued friends, the late Lionel Stander, who had gone abroad after being blacklisted in America, and prominently continued his acting career as if he had never been put off it. It was here at this time that Ralph Liguori came to tell me, as I have recounted, a story of the thirties and the old New York underworld, with its melancholy moment for me as well as him.

I had to fly back to Serbia for three days to film a scene, and Gabe Katzka told me that on returning to Rome I ought to start driving back to our final location, not Belgrade but the Istrian town of Umag on the Adriatic; there we would wrap the picture. Nancy's mother, Hulda Fields, had flown over from Montana to be with us and help us with Hugh, and she had never been abroad, so we made a little tour out of our return to the movie. I took a rectangular route, north to Como and Basel, the Swiss city on the Rhine; and east through Germany, the Black Forest, Augsburg, Nuremberg, Munich and Salzburg. Traffic on the roads made the going slow; those were the days of the Cold War and U.S. and West German ground forces were out on maneuvers. They never ceased maneuvering. Nancy and her mother were depressed by the sight, while Hugh and I loved it—the tanks and armored cars and weapons-carriers and rolling rocket launchers, always allowing us to pass them closely. We talked a lot, to the dismay of the women, about the differences between these new weapons and the old ones we were using as props in our World War Two movie. Male kids, myself included, have always been crazy about this stuff, God knows why, and there is no diverting them from it. We stopped two nights and a day in a couple of those German towns, and three days both in Munich and Salzburg. Golden-haired Hugh, wearing his Bavarian jacket and high socks, holding my hand as we strolled in the German marketplaces, was my passport to instant friendship.

The stay in Munich was memorable for a delightful Oktoberfest, a reunion with an old friend of student days, the American tenor Robert Hoyem who was brilliantly singing my old favorite *Hoffman* at the Statsspielhaus; and finally a melancholy pilgrimmage to Dachau.

Nancy and I and Hugh had been in Munich the year before, and I had avoided Dachau, but now Nancy decided that Dachau must not be avoided—this time we would see the place, and her mother too agreed that we ought to see it. Driving through the pleasant village it was hard to conceive that anyone living there in the war years—excepting of course small children who were probably discouraged from asking questions—didn't know what was going on in the neighboring concentration camp. The Third Reich, given its absolute control of news and the whole communications apparatus, could have disguised the exterminating activities of the camps; some Germans could have been kept in ignorance, but many must have learned the truth. What they should have, could have, done about it is still a subject of angry debate among people of my generation.

We who congratulate ourselves on our open society know very well how the authorities can fool us; how with the willing collaboration of a perfectly free press they can withhold and fictionize embarrassing and even criminal information. Most of us didn't know about our illegal internment of Japanese-American citizens during the war years. Most of us thought when we were fighting in Korea, Vietnam, Nicaragua, El Salvador, that we were fighting righteous wars and winning them. I have friends, however, who believe that all Germans knew of the genocide and were responsible, because the Holocaust was the ultimate fruition of abiding, inherent German tendencies. Anthropology and medicine have not, to my knowledge, addressed this genetic proposition, and personally I give it as much credence as the theory that Hungarians have a preternatural tendency to vampirism.

When Hitler won his last election in Germany only one third of German voters supported him. They were of course subscribing to his crackpot race supremacism and national-socialist state management. But even they—even that minority—were they really voting for an end to all future elections? For an end to all their own freedoms? For preparation for another war—Germany against the world once more? For national ruin? National suicide? The death of the fatherland? No. By a monstrous irony, these were national disasters from which the minority really thought *Der Führer* and Nazism would protect them. The two-thirds majority preferred to rely for protection on their existing republican government, but the majority found themselves suddenly leaderless; they were being locked up, tortured, silenced by fear or murder. The German congress, the Reichstag, was dissolved and dispersed, its very building burned to the ground, not by Hitler but by a fool who thought his act would hurt the dictator. The Nazis seized control of the press and the radio and even the pulpit.

Prior to this revolution the Germans supported the democratic Weimar republic, well regarded for its toleration of all kinds of political and religious thought. To be sure, there was always anti-Semitism in Germany (and everywhere else!), but when asked where it was most common, most violent, most characteristic of the ruling class, every European Jew I ever knew named not Germany but Poland. I never saw this in the press.

I have always simply said, when unwillingly involved in controversies over fixing blame for the Holocaust, that a German today would have to be older than I to be reasonably held in suspicion of Hitlerism and genocide. What about Germans my age and older? I say with old Hamlet's ghost "Leave them to Heaven!" And while this scant remnant wait for their judgment, God knows what anguish they will endure.

It must have been out of anguish that the state of Bavaria had memorialized the inhuman incumbency of the Third Reich in this camp of Dachau; it was a museum, and it comprised a newspaper exhibit in which the history of Nazism from 1932 to 1945, in enlarged press photos, covered a circular wall; also the preserved prison itself, dozens of concrete slabs marking the barracks surrounded by walls, barbed wire and gun towers; and finally the place where murdered Jews were burnt to ashes. The exhibits were appalling. Visitors began weeping privately in the newspaper rotunda, and wept openly when they confronted the barracks slabs. Nancy, Hulda and Hugh trudged on to the final exhibit, the place of cremation. I told Hugh I wasn't feeling well and wanted to sit down and rest. Nancy urged me to go along, but I hung back and waited. The truth was, I was afraid to confront what I had seen in news film and stunning magazine stills—afraid the black maws of the ovens would blame me and curse me. I had always felt like a passive accomplice in all this. I had heard "Hitler is doing many good things for Europe" over and over in the city of New York, spoken by people in all walks of life during the thirties, as late as the defeat of France; and I had been a nonreacting contemptible listener. Just a kid? Yes, but a smart kid who lived familiarly with Jews, who read everything and knew, at least from the newspapers, what was going on.

Now I reflected that if Britain and France and America had wanted to save Europe's Jews, all three could have threatened the Germans with intervention when the Nürnberg Laws introduced the policy of persecution and murder. But genocide was not then (nor is it now) reason enough for nations to confront each other with anything stronger than protest. Only when the Second World War was in full tilt did the Allies proclaim the one virtuous cause they had—their only truly moral cause—the saving of the Jews. But it was by then a cause without hope, for war had crazily trapped Jews on the Continent just as it had trapped Hitler. The doomed Führer no longer thought about merely deporting Jews, as in the days of Nürnberg,[4] but about leaving none behind him—his "final solution." As I have noted, he told his Obersalzberg roundtable

---

[4] He told Mussolini that Madagascar might be the right place to put the Jews.

that if the Allies landed in Europe the Jews would suffer destruction. Britain and France, though blameless of a horror they could not have foreseen, had doomed the Jews the moment they declared war.

Until I saw this museum I hadn't thought about the non-Jewish political pariahs of the Reich. They were all classified as Reds; the world was invited by the Nazis to approve their destruction and the world seemed happy to do so. Now I was learning in this press rotunda that of the thousands who died in that first concentration camp between 1933 and 1945, half were non-Jews who had bravely fought fascism and Nazism.

Salzburg's music season had not yet begun. The only music I remember was by the pianist in the bar of the Oesterreichischehof, who played Kahlman and Kreisler and Stolz for me during the cocktail hour. Hugh was always with me, dressed for dinner, permitted to sit with me at the end of the bar where the bartender solemnly served him a special fruit juice confection. The southward leg of our trip was over the Alps through the Brenner Pass to Trieste, and down again through the Istrian peninsula to Umag.

When *Kelly's Heroes* was finished, Nancy, Hulda, Hugh and I drove again to Rome, where we garaged the car at the Hilton and flew home to Los Angeles. I acted in a couple of movies—*Doctors' Wives,* starring my friend Richard Crenna, *Death of a Gunfighter,* with Richard Widmark and that remarkable star Lena Horne—and some television series episodes; and then Max Arnow of my agency made a deal for me to write a movie. He liked my script outline, and so did another client of his, the head of a new production company, John Du Pont.[5] The story was centered in Rome, and I wanted to go back to Rome to write it.

We took an apartment near the Piazza del Popolo. Hugh, eight, went into a school for English-speaking children; he took

---

[5]The man who shot the athletic trainer in Maryland.

a bus to it from the piazza every morning and I met him in the same place every afternoon—ice cream time. We would sit al fresco at Rosatti's and he would practice his Italian giving the order. He picked up the language easily. In the early morning, I would watch him from our terrace walk to the piazza, say *Buon giorno!* to the concessionario who had charge of the parking (and kept a special eye on our car, for which I rewarded him well), and chat with him till the bus came. The chat had to be mainly Italian because Salvatore spoke very few words of anything else.

For Hugh this was a third visit to Italy. His first was the 1968 trip following the taping of the Archie pilot. On his second trip we had flown to Dublin, then to Sweden, where we bought a car, then driven down through Denmark, Germany and Austria, and over the Alps at Innsbruck to Italy. Hugh, then six, knew all about his adoption, having asked Nancy some direct questions about being conceived and being born. We took him at that time on a visit to Salvator Mundi hospital in Rome to show him where he had been delivered to the world; he met Mother Johanna, the supervising nun who had attended his birth, and Father Coyne, the priest who had baptized him, and he was shown the nursery where, according to the mother superior, "You were sleeping right in there in one of those little beds, and you had a friend beside you, a little Sicilian prince who was born at the same time." Hugh seemed most interested in all this—seemed to be enjoying it—but of course we had no way of verifying his inner feelings. He was keen enough to know that we wanted him to react happily; he loved us and may have wanted to please us. Nancy, who, unlike her timorous husband, has never been afraid of drawing pleasant conclusions from the plainly visible, assured me that our darling boy was in a glad mood throughout the visit.

Next day, one of those special Roman days when the sky is a limpid curtain in front of heaven, the three of us were walking in the Borghese Gardens near the Casina Valadier, and we came across a group of twenty children five to ten years old. They were on a walk conducted by three Sisters of Charity. They went by, and six-year-old Hugh said "Why do their parents dress them all the same way?" I said I was sure it was the nuns who dressed them that way. He thought about this as he watched them walk out of sight. Then he said "Dad?" I said "Yes, son." He said "Do they live with the nuns?" I referred the question to Nancy, who answered "Yes, Hugh, they live with the nuns. They have no parents." I watched his handsome little face, wise and still, and took his hand, knowing beyond any doubt that he had imagined something that might have been: himself among the same-dressed kids.

Now, just over a year later, he seemed well adjusted to our new Roman life, which was full of movies and browsings in book stores, activities at school, outings with new friends, car mean-derings around the town and trips to see friends of ours at the beaches and in the countryside. He loved eating in restaurants, especially the *trattorie*[6] because he didn't feel confined to the tables, and the *camerieri* always had a perfect knack of making curious kids feel like a part of the restaurant family.

I felt fine. I was sure I was writing a very good movie script, but the first draft of *Little Anjie Always* was a disappointment to my partners. The story was about a Chicago industrialist who, on leaving for Italy—where incidentally he enjoys an old intimate friendship with an Italian woman—is asked by a business associate to look for his child, a runaway seventeen-year-old girl. He finds the girl, but his encouraging her to talk about her alienation evokes only a juvenile contempt for him, for her father, and her privileged life in the States. She and the drifters she has been living with conspire to rob her father's emissary. He's much too smart for them, outwits them, and physically beats off one of them, but the effort brings on a heart attack and

[6]Restaurants with sidewalk tables.

leaves him dead in one of the fountains of the city. The girl is unmoved, but we discover in the last scene that her cold detachment is a pose; she can't suppress her sadness. Lonely in the Roman crowd, she quietly cries. William Holden didn't like the script and Arnow and Dick Quine, the proposed director, soured on it. I had wanted to juxtapose a child of that bewildering sixties generation, loveless and angry, with a man who is now a rare specimen in the American milieu—the generous, well-bred, intelligent gentleman. A Dodsworth. Why? To remind us of certain traditional social characteristics that we were carelessly losing. But that is why the script made no impression: in that desensitized decade nobody thought we were losing anything. Nobody knew the man from Chicago.

I felt stupid for putting so much work and hope into the script, though I still liked it. After a couple of other people rejected it, I hated it. Dino De Laurentiis told me he would like to do it for Silvana[7] if I would make the woman the lead. I couldn't.

I began to get phone calls from Beverly Hills about the *Till Death* series that ABC had twice shied from. Jack Gilardi of GAC, the agency representing both Norman Lear's company and me, got me on the phone and said that CBS had picked up the discarded item. The roles of the kids would again be recast, we would do the same material we had done twice before, but this time it would be not a pilot but the first episode of thirteen on air. I had lost interest in it. I thought about it and decided not to do it. I still felt that it would not go far. Nancy disagreed; she reminded me that I had always wanted the show to be seen, even if a bad reaction chased it off the air. I replied that I would probably do it if we happened to be in Los Angeles, but we were now living in Rome. We had a duplex terraced apartment in one of the most desirable quarters of the city. We had a car, professional connections, good friends, and a life that seemed wonderfully removed

---

[7]Mangano, his wife, the splendid Italian star.

from the black cloud of Nixon's Cold War—though of course
there was really no escaping it anywhere in the world, and in fact
Nixon's enormous helicopter roared immediately over our terrace one evening as it conveyed our mysterious leader to the roof
of the Quirinale.[8] I had begun thinking of us three as being
permanent residents. Hugh liked Rome, and seemed delighted
to say "I was born here."

Nancy's advice was "Fly back and do a couple of installments
of this series. Do the thirteen the network has asked for, and then
we'll fly back here." I hesitated and she added "It'll give you a
chance to talk to Max and John DuPont and Dick Quine about
Anjie." That won me over, but we suddenly had a problem. I told
Jack Gilardi that since we had no place to come back to, Rome
being home for us, CBS or Lear would have to give us three first-
class round-trip tickets and some expense money. Lear refused,
and evidently CBS also refused, because the next message I got
was that Lear's offer, which included no travel or expense money,
was his only offer, and if I didn't accept it he would sign another
actor. I took note of the word "sign"; it meant that they wouldn't
be going on a search. They had somebody ready. They asked me
for an immediate answer and I gave them one. It was no.

Nancy was not altogether with me on this; she was as sensitive
to effrontery as I, but she had always believed that this show was
going to be important. She said "They're not nutty back there.
They're not going to drop you over a couple of thousand
dollars," and she said I ought to invite them to haggle a bit. I
declined. I said that what I wanted was right, that I was not
prepared to compromise the figure, that I could not overlook
their display of low respect, that I was sure they were the kind
who would indeed punitively drop me over a couple of thousand, but that it was a dead issue. For a couple of days I heard no
more about it, and then Jack Gilardi called again and said that a

---

[8]The Italian government buildings in the Via Venti Settembre.

GAC agent in Rome would deliver my tickets immediately—and that Lear wanted me to come home right away. "That's what I want too" Jack added. I told him we would need a week. I didn't know it at the time, but Lear had actually not weakened; it was GAC, which had a large packaging interest[9] in the series, that had provided the money. I telephoned a friend, the actor Robert Brown, who owned, with his wife Anna, a grand old hacienda in Santa Monica Canyon, and asked if we could move in for a while, perhaps for three months. Brown, one of two or three very important friends, got everything ready for us and then left for Miami to do a series of his own.

Our hard-won return-flight tickets to Rome remained unused in Nancy's file until long after the time we expected to use them. Three months! We didn't see Italy again for nearly three years, and when we went back we traveled again by ship. We had not retained our apartment in the Via del Babuino, but we had left our car with a friend in Milan. The car was delivered to us at Naples in the spring of 1974.

The history of my series, which we started videotaping as *All in the Family* during and after the holidays that preceded 1971, is too well known to brook a review here. It was the subject of more critical and analytical writing in newspapers and periodicals— sociological treatises, psychological disquisitions, university theses—than any television comedy or drama in the history of the medium—more, I would guess, than any other American theatrical offering in any medium. An interviewer once said to me "That show opened up a big window on America," and then immediately changed his statement to "No, not a window—it pulled down a whole side of the house!" This writer said that while Archie had a likeable vein, his character was exposing the whole American idiosyncrasy of faults—the enduring miscon-

---

[9] A fifteen percent commission on the money the network paid to Lear's Company.

ceptions, the cherished prejudices, the stubborn ignorance and heedless cruelty. I didn't know how to respond. It was a question for the cultural anthropologist. I was sure of one thing: we were presenting the only American satire that had been successful in any medium. Conventional show-biz savvy held that Americans hated to be the objects of satire. Comedy? Yes, give it to them by all means! But splash it with unreality, phony it up, make fun of the classes, high, low and middle, but leave the fundamental workings of society alone.[10]

Our "Archie" writers were the cleverest joke draftsmen in television, and what they delivered every week was the very special product they were hired to write. But I refused to play the naked joke, to do the setup-punchline routine, and asked them to recast jokes as characteristic thrusts and rejoinders, and rework sketch material to the emotional dimensions of a short play. They often balked and more than once threatened to quit, but I too more than once threatened to quit. Lear didn't write for the show, but he gave the writers orders, watched dress rehearsals and gave notes. He hated to tamper with a joke, and he and I had frequent arguments about jokes. He was glad to have other TV projects to turn his attention to—spinoffs from our series like *Maude* and *The Jeffersons* and several other sitcom plunges—glad to see less of me, as I was to see less of him.

Some people, but not many, thought we were presenting in Archie a false character. President Nixon thought we were making a fool out of a good man. George Meany[11] thought, and told me personally, that we were showing a distorted picture of the American working man. Whitney Young[12] said we were acquiescing in racism. We thought we were making people laugh at racism, Young thought we were treating it like a joke. Spokesmen for the black community generally doubted whether

---

[10]The playwright George Kaufman said "Satire closes Saturday."
[11]The late longtime head of the AFL-CIO.
[12]The late longtime head of the Urban League.

All in the Family was helping the black community, yet, being unsure, they declined to condemn it. The television shows they thought were helping the black community were the black sitcoms; and though these shows often embarrassed them by reverting to dismaying stereotypes, the spokesmen saw them as a long overdue employment of blacks in television, undeniable evidence that black shows could hold their own in the ratings and make money for the networks.

Lear was irritated by my calling the series a satire, but if it was not, Whitney Young was right: if it was not making fun of society, as its original model had lately done in England—and as all the great satirists had done in England long before—then Richard Nixon was right, and we were doing the persona of Archie Bunker an injustice. When I asked Lear how he would define the series, he answered crisply "Why does it have to be defined?" I could have pursued the matter with "Don't you think, in view of the scholarly interest in the show, that it should be defined by us who are making it?" But in the instant I said "us" I apprehended that my motive was really self-congratulatory. I myself was trying to usurp the role of Definer. Lear had good reason to be irritated; after all, he owned the show. I remained, however, the one insistent, and no doubt importunate, guardian of satire.

11

· · · · · · ·

With the end of the ninth season of *All in the Family* the cast members' contracts expired and all except me announced, with no regret, that they had different things they wished to do. Jean wanted to rejoin her husband, producer Bill Putch, in a couple of stage ventures. Sally Struthers was interested in getting a series of her own. Rob Reiner wanted to write movies. Rob and I were very fond of each other. His major interest at that time was writing, and acting was his next, and I had no idea that he was going to move suddenly into the directing game, turn out a half dozen successful pictures in a row and become a highly regarded moviemaker. I had no plans. As for Lear, I had been told by someone or other that his contract with CBS had expired, and he had decided to take *Family* off the network and release the just finished nine seasons to syndication. I was asked nevertheless by CBS president Robert Daly to keep the series going somehow in network prime time. He said he wanted to make a new deal with Lear. I told him I didn't see how Archie could carry on without his "family," but he wanted me to make it happen; he said the character was too strong and popular to be dropped. Lear didn't agree and he was obdurate. Daly could not persuade him. It appeared that money was not the issue.

William Paley, the ayatollah of CBS, happened to be in Hollywood and asked Daly to arrange a meeting with me. Paley had not asked to meet me in the nine years that my show had kept his network at the top of the ratings, nor had he communicated with me in any way. He had met and entertained the stars of all his big CBS shows, but though he had never had a bigger show than mine, he shied from contact with me. I don't blame him. Someone had told him—evidently in a convincing way—that I was in life, not merely in my series role, the man he saw on the television screen. He had no important reason for inviting a fellow like that into his home. Paley might have risked the distress of a visit by me and Nancy in order to confirm or dismiss what he had been told. But then why should he bother? Who was I, really?

But now he wanted to meet me at least in an office. I met him in Daly's office at CBS Hollywood and he asked me what it was Lear wanted. I said that Lear wanted to take his flagship show off the air. "That, we know" said Paley, "but what else?" I said I had no idea, but if Lear, in spite of the alarmed opposition of his gillies at Tandem Productions,[1] was rejecting another year or more of profit from the show, he probably had peculiar personal reasons. Paley said "Lear's in New York and I'll see him tomorrow. I'll bring him in, if you agree to do the show." I told him I would agree to try, but I warned him that without the regular cast I might not be able to devise and produce a continuing program.

He went to New York and failed to bring the quarry in, and Bob Daly called me and said "Carroll, you're the one that'll have to ask Norman."

---

[1]The name of his company, the first of several companies.

I went to his house and asked him. He told me he preferred "to see the old show die an honorable death," saying in other words that it would die without honor if it stumbled on under my direction.

I must digress to say that fourteen years later when CBS and I wanted to revisit Archie Bunker in a new series about a new life in Manhattan, Lear again stated his preference for the honorable death. I said "I thought we had long ago moved beyond that dear concern." But this time he stood firm. He suggested that I try a new series with Bette Midler, an outstanding comedienne who could make me look funny. "You need somebody like that." I said "What a good idea! Perhaps you could 'create' the show for us." He responded with the most amusing thing he ever said to me: "Well, one of my creative people tells me that if you really want to do something, it ought to be something new, and there are fifty brand new rejected scripts on every desk in town, waiting to be done. Pick one up."

How this little yarn plays in print I can't be sure, but it has rewarded me grandly in the telling. I keep it short: "A 'creative' person in Lear's office, when asked about finding material for me, advised picking through the rejected scripts in network offices."

Huge laughs every time!

But returning now to 1980, Lear at that time laid honor aside, overcame his sadness and let us proceed with the dear old show under the name *Archie Bunker's Place*. He insisted, however, that we retain the Edith character, even though Jean Stapleton would not be here to play it. Edith, he thought, would be retained in spirit. He thought the other characters could talk about Edith but never see her. She might be on a long visit to someone somewhere; she might be at home but not seen because we would play all new episodes at Archie's bar. Lear is the kind of executive who requires implicitly that one treat his most preposterous ideas with perfect seriousness, and once again I assumed the obligatory gape. Be it remembered, in mitigation of my sin, that falsehood is the irreplaceable fuel of forward motion in the television business.

I withdrew carefully from the meeting and gave Robert Daly the Edith problem to solve. I told him that Archie could live on only as a widower. Robert, wishing that I could have closed the "creative" part of the deal on Lear's terms, wearily undertook to get me my terms. He told me a week later that I could forge ahead without Edith, but I would also have to do without the old title and without the old song.

We opened the new season, the tenth, if like me you still thought of the show as *All in the Family*, with a one-hour episode called "The Death of Edith." I wrote it and codirected it and was delighted eventually to win the Peabody Award[2] for it. Archie was staying on at his well-known house on Hauser Street, and with him were his two nieces. He engaged a housekeeper to help him with the little one.

Something of human significance had to happen to Archie, or the show would become Archie Bunker's Joke Store, and the best way to make it happen was to expand his circle of friends and acquaintances. I hired the gifted actor, the late Martin Balsam, to come out from New York and play Murray, Archie's new Jewish partner. I hired Anne Meara to come out and play Archie's new chef at Archie's Place. The aim now of our scripts, of our series of small plays, was to show a man who was finding out not only that he could live without his prejudices, but that without his prejudices he could live better. Viewers now laughed in a different way, always copiously, less often explosively. But they kept laughing. I was enjoying the work more than ever.

As we were opening our twelfth season, the young man who was running Embassy Inc. for Lear, Alan Horn, asked me and my

---

[2]From the journalism school of the University of Georgia.

executive producer Joe Gannon to devise a series for Sally Struthers. Joe and two of our writers, Harriet Weiss and Pat Shea, got to work on a pilot script. The story: Archie drives his now divorced daughter Gloria to a new job and a new life in the country working for a veterinarian. Joe sold this vet role to the late Burgess Meredith. When our 1981–1982 season was over, our long-time director Paul Bogart directed the pilot for Lear's company and CBS. It was a success and CBS announced that it would appear on the network the following season. And so it did, but not with its originators running it. Lear had recently been in England and met the gaudy promoter Lew Grade[3] and a nephew of Grade's named Michael. The latter, a kind of *chachem*[4] who had worked in comedy at the BBC (he now runs his uncle's bingo halls, bowling alleys and snooker parlors), was imported by Lear to take over Embassy Television, succeeding the personable and valuable Alan Horn, who moved up to run Embassy's movie division. Grade's first assignment was to take over the Gloria series, i.e., take it away from Gannon, Weiss and Shea. Undoubtedly young Grade was a predacious fellow, but it was Lear, after all, who plugged him in and encouraged him to fire our talented people[5] with whom he did not wish to work. Lear's "creative people" brought in a producing team whose own sitcom had just been canceled, and who were expected to be docile, but the team baffled everybody by showing independence. Lear by now had had quite enough of that kind of carry-on; he trashed Gloria after a season, though I am sure the network executives, as dense as they were, wanted to keep it going. It was eighteenth or nineteenth in the rankings of ninety or more TV shows.

CBS told me that Archie Bunker was finished after the 1983

---

[3]Sir Lew (now Lord), the maker of forgettable movies.
[4]I prefer this tasty Yiddish word to our "smart aleck."
[5]Including me, the ever-looming menace.

season, the fourth. We pressed the network to keep us on the air for 1984, a fifth season, as this would give us a bloc of five[6] to sell to the syndication marketeers. I hoped for this because I was a partner, and also a friend of many performers, writers, directors and technicians who were looking forward to another year of continuous work. I was also thinking about Hugh; he had come to work for us as a general office assistant ("I'm a gofer, Pop!" he laughed) and I was scheming to work him into something better in the years to come. Robert Daly, who had moved from CBS to Warner Brothers, told me that he would have kept us in the schedule not only to do us a favor after thirteen years of remarkable service to the network, but to benefit further from a show that was still twenty-sixth in the rankings with a 28 percent household share. His successors, who canceled us as if they owed us nothing, now proved their show-biz perspicacity by guiding CBS rather briskly into last place.

Lear told me that at the urging of his partners he had personally appealed to Paley to keep us going. He said "I watched an episode with him, and Paley said 'Sorry, it isn't funny anymore.'"

"And you said?" I inquired.

Lear, with an odd moue of distaste and satisfaction, replied "I said I had to agree with him."

I enjoyed in every way my twelve years of playing Archie, and I wasn't personally sad about finishing a long job. I have indeed had great luck in being able to do as I wished in the television and movie business. Taking one day with another, my professional life in Hollywood, far from being blighted by disappointment, has been filled with joy and laughter. The hilarity is in the seriousness with which the entrepreneurial population regards

---

[6]The package likely to bring the highest price.

its "creativeness." The movie producer who yelled "Make the battle scene big!" soon sees on the screen an astounding twenty minutes of clashing armies and whispers to his girlfriend "I wrote that." The illiterate studio chief who threw a big blathery novel on a table and growled "Make this for Greta Gruyere!" soon invites friends to a screening of "My latest film." The television producer who fronted for a brummagem series premise, and then left its production in the hands of some larcenous gnomes, insists on the continuous billing "Developed By . . ." To hobnob with such oddities on a daily basis is to be laughing almost too strenuously to work. Frequent naps are required to restore one's vigor.

When you have given credit where credit is due—to TV's presentation of fine arts, of live events, of documentary science and journalism, there is little else to esteem. Angry commentators of all persuasions who talk these days about the "dumbing down" of America are staring hard at television.

Is any of it art? Not much. Popular entertainment is usually artistic, employing as it does the talents, materials, ideas and conventions of the recognized arts, but hardly any of it is actually art. The motive in presenting the work is definitive: is it merely entertainment? Decoration? Diversion? Do the pictures, the people on the stage, the movie images, the actors, dancers, composers, reveal to us something important about ourselves? These questions draw blanks, of course, from executives in the entertainment industry, which comprises movies, television and the stage, but the industry demands all the acclamations due art with the same fervor as a kid yelling for ketchup. The kid has more right to the ketchup.

The men who made the first movies had no apparent need of the dramatist. Directors, cameramen and silent actors seemed to be the essential personnel. Talented improvisation was the order of the day. The only writings required were an outline of scenes and action (scenario) and, when the picture was ready for the screen, certain "titles"—captions and short speeches—which from time to time clarified the silent action.

When sound came to film the playwright bid fair for eminence, but moviemakers observed that literary effusions seemed to hold up film action. Nevertheless, now and then, they gambled on art and put respectable dramatists and novelists on studio payrolls. They were disappointed; so were their lofty hirelings. The complaints of the moguls and the recriminations of the artists, chronicled often by the latter, were bitter and ludicrous and not worth recalling.

As time went by the writing that best met the requirements of the industry came more and more from a specialist class who, literate or otherwise (usually otherwise), were more than happy to write and collaborate in writing exciting material of no importance. These were the screenwriters, and they were well paid to take orders, avoid arguments, and suffer contempt. From the boss of the studio down through the ranks of producers, subproducers, directors, actors and schnorrers, anybody was allowed to batter to pieces and remake the work of a screenwriter. The finished shooting script is still today a product of chaotic interference. But then the whole film-making process is chaotic. Most completed films lack cohesion in the story. Many directors, even renowned ones, are never certain of their intentions. Editors cut and recut and reposition all sequences and sometimes contrive quite different stories from those originally planned.

The men who made the first movies were right. Film, being much extemporized, and arbitrarily altered in every phase of production, is not a serious writer's medium. The writer offers ideas but he cannot control their final exposition. His job, if he does it well, is to advise the camera. Seldom is his advice taken. Seldom is it sought.

A dramatic production on stage or screen may deal with the big subject—our Civil War, the Red revolution in Russia, Custer, Patton, George III; it may deal with the small subject—the piece of adventure, the love affair, the funny family of a TV sitcom; it may in ways be artistic and grandly entertaining, but does the work express insights into our brethren, our society, our condition of life in this time, or that time, or that other time? Does the work invite us to understand ourselves? Which is a plain way of asking whether or not the work is intellectual, whether it is art. *All in the Family* was intellectual; it was art.

The intention defines the thing, and even a true artist does not always produce art. The casual sketch or random strokes of a recognized painter, the notes of a writer, the notations of a musician, are not intrinsically works of art, though they may become art in due course, and are always of collateral interest. What then do we call the intensive, purposeful work that many people do in the forlorn hope that it will be considered art, or in the maddening friend-ending insistence that it is art? Best call it "artistic," which it may well be if it is done with some skill and has a pleasing quality, like the still lifes Aunt Lu produces for her show at the club. Say no more than that, "artistic," and head for the buffet. The alternative, of course, is to lie—say the work is important. I always lie if after trying "artistic" I see a glint of hatred in an eye. In the field of mass entertainment the producer is every bit as touchy as Aunt Lu, and expects you to say "Work of art, old pal!" when he has shown you his latest package of recycled notions that were unimportant when they were first hacked together in an earlier Hollywood epoch.

Most producers, writers and directors are not artists; they seem to be artists because they are milling and jostling in areas of enterprise that are distantly related to art. Their minds do not incline them to ponder the human condition, but the mind of the artist not only inclines but compels him to so ponder. The artist cannot help seeing and hearing everywhere, and constantly, indications of the state of man past, present and future. The artist's unique gift lets him tell us about ourselves.

Note the word "gift." We all take it to mean something delightful, and so it is, but to the artist it is obviously something burdensome as well. Does gift mean talent? No; talent makes, gift creates. Talent can be developed, gift is God-given. But artists have both.

All artists are intellectuals. Not all intellectuals are artists, though like artists they are inclined to ponder the human condition. The intellectual who is not an artist is in close touch with art, he is deeply informed by art. In this world there are comparatively few intellectuals and still fewer artists. The nonintellectual, as he himself will proudly confirm for you, is vastly in the majority.

Why trouble ourselves with these distinctions? The answer is that we need not. Lear saw no reason to call *Family* a satire, or anything other than situation comedy. Everyone knows that there is supposed to be a difference between Aunt Lu and Georgia O'Keeffe; studying the difference would enliven but few minds, and benumb many, still my own view of art demands that I give it this little survey in my memoir.

A Hollywood writer, as I suggested earlier, is not a writer from Hollywood, but a writer who earns his living writing for Hollywood. What he does, not where he does it, is crucial if we wish to distinguish him from the writer who gets his fortune writing books and plays. Should we make the distinction? Ask as well if we should distinguish between a contractor and an architect. But a Hollywood writer (HW) is not to be depreciated; he is a unique functionary and has to be considered and valued apart from all others. When the HW is well esteemed and in demand he makes more money than all other writers. The man who wrote and produced the worst movie in many years—or the worst ever, *Showgirls*—was paid a million for it, and was able to make a deal for three million for his next script.[7] Or so it was reported in the trade papers.

The finished film, after all is said and done, must inform us

---

[7] One Joe Eszterhas.

much less as readers than as viewers. The camera tells us all. The HW must know how to write the story for the camera. Too frequently this is all he can do, and viewers of his movie must listen to very bad dialog. When, as rarely happens, the HW writes very good dialog, he is a man in love with his words and his invariable shortcoming is in his visualization; he forces the camera off the wonderful scenes of the story and onto the talking faces. These imperfect conditions make rewrites necessary, not occasionally but always. The original HW is superseded by one or more HWs who rewrite his and subsequent drafts, and they are all finally superseded by directors and actors who want to have the last words. The HWs and their guild have drawn up rules that protect the writers' rights to be credited and paid no matter what happens to their material. The rules leave movie and TV producers free to do anything they wish with material they have paid for. Are we forgetting here the original author of the novel or play? No, he was forgotten long ago—but paid. What makes the HW unique, more than any other fact about him, is his capacity for happiness within this disdainful system. His own pure work cannot be, and is not meant to be, discerned; he will never be an important literary man. The important literary man will never be an important HW; he cannot bring himself to curtail his precious patter and write for images; he releases his work, allows it to be adulterated and disfigured to suit the movie medium, and tells you, if you question him, that he doesn't care.

Few HWs and directors have a formal humanist education, and these instructed few are constrained, no less than the uninstructed many, to keep learning, sophistication, artistic ideas, and all other such communicable diseases out of the workplace. The bosses have so ordered. The bosses always sigh in deep relief when the likes of Faulkner and Fitzgerald leave town. Are the bosses dunces? No, not all: I have known a few who quietly dislike what they produce. It is true, however, that being a dunce gives a dull young tyro a decided leg up in the industry; he naturally and quickly attains a level of production responsibility.

On the other hand, the inventive young tyro finds himself mysteriously blocked wherever he tries to push his ideas; in despair he allows himself to slide back into the purgatory of business affairs.

Turning briefly to the departments of business affairs: sound business practices therein are unknown. Enormous amounts of money are blithely wasted annually on big budget theatrical movies—wacky yarns unlike life, crazily effects-driven, spiritually deranged, and wholly without value unless you value bad dreams. But today gross movie returns rise to many times the costs, hundreds of millions. At the same time, many big grossers inexplicably[8] fail to reveal a profit—yesterday's feckless dunce is today's cruel and arrogant genius.

Movies that confine themselves to reality are vastly cheaper to make—the TV movies that lean to the sordid—true murders, celebrated shame, history as prurient fiction, disgraceful careers, the everlasting Mafia. But they too cost too much. TV series are proportionally the most wasteful of all. If a network wants five fresh shows to replace five moribunds, it finances the filming of thirty pilot shows at a cost of a hundred million, looks at all the finished shows, and chooses five. If two of the five succeed on the air, the ayatollah and his mullahs congratulate themselves. Obviously they could meet their needs more rationally: they could read thirty scripts and decide to make five at a cost of only ten million. There is no reason to think that two out of five would not be just as successful as two out of the thirty. Keeping in mind that this is really median-IQ stuff, requiring nothing more than any minyan randomly summoned in from the street to judge it, you readily see that this sane production process could be administered by five executives, eliminating nearly all of the hopeless hierarchy, probably fifty of them, as well as fifty staffs, fifty office suites, and at least one air-conditioned building.

---

[8]Because the audits are a joke.

Is the lean efficient plan a possibility or a pipe dream? It is a pipe dream. What it presupposes at the head of a network is a team of five shrewd imaginative people who have had plenty of professional experience both as writers and producers of high-quality drama and comedy. The network ayatollah in New York could never be brought to giving five fierce, decisive, talented men (and why not women?) the responsibilities now being bungled by fifty-five pleasant empty-headed men. Ayatollahs are always unnerved by decisive men; their word for a decisive man is "infidel."[9] But once over dinner in New York the president of a network conceded to me that my idea was patently right. His only question about it was: "What would become of all the producers in Hollywood who have been supplying us three networks with a hundred superfluous pilots every year?" A scary question. A hundred executives would be idled, and all the employment and commercial activity they generate would be lost. Some economists would say "That's right—cut them out, cut waste down to zero—make capitalism work." (Milton Friedman?) Soft touches like me say "Let all foolishness be; fools have to live, a lot of them are, unlike me, friendly and charming."

Having grown old and bent in the business, I am often presumed to be a sage whose opinions are worth having, and I am asked "What do you think is good on network prime time today?" I hate the question. My opinion is no better than that of any of the reviewers in the newspapers—which is to say, no better than any person one might stand next to in an elevator. When I am asked what I like, I can't say "Nothing!" Nobody can say "Nothing" without sounding rude. And I am unable to think up any polite answer that doesn't still sound suspiciously like "Nothing." I have to say "Prime time was never better!" and, as always, head for the buffet. But that slippery response is probably the truth. Prime time was never better because prime time was

---

[9]Not really. "Pain in the ass" is the phrase.

never very good. A rising demand forty years ago brought a rising supply of product, but, as we all know, quantity rises, quality does not rise—the well of talent remains shallow no matter how often we lower the bucket.

Sitcoms have always been cartoon caprices animated by live actors. TV drama has always been the tragic/scary situation retrieved and reorganized. We still have the brooding male, now badly dressed à la mode and stylishly ungroomed, shy of, because betrayed by, women; set against the new unsmiling female, shy of, because betrayed by, men; all of them, male and female, sensitive, pulsing young types—doctors, lawyers, sundry subexecutives, detectives (no plumbers or bricklayers), all repressed to a point of fevered glaring and sexual bursting. The bursting now occurs before our eyes. Violence occurs. Congressmen, parents, teachers, howl against sullying the kids, Hollywood shrugs, the kids laugh. What's to be done?

Science and technology have given screen entertainment an incredibly wide diffusion, as well as many laughably incongruous movies. Supply a hermit in the desert with an appropriate receiver, and a satellite will send him one of Aaron Spelling's TV tales of the opulent and ignorant, or a typical jokey setup-payoff sitcom, or one of the muscle stars' inscrutable big-screen tributes to revenge and the automatic weapons industry. The hermit may enjoy an hour or so of exciting product selling interrupted minimally by a shopworn movie. By day the hermit may watch terrible news read to him by jolly, quipping young women and men; studio talk shows, on which "guests" of low mentality offer disgraceful confessions to the judgment of unemployed persons; and the "soaps," which baffle explanation. Hermit and huddled masses are entertained by the same things, according to the ratings.

Let me here acknowledge the directors, men and women who presumably understand that in the processes of moviemaking they do have in hand the convention of an art. They may make in their careers a couple of movies that are works of art. They might make more but, as Sartre said, they cannot truly be artists until their art is as easily available to them as pencil and paper; and the tools of the film art, unlike pencil and paper, easel or piano, are never cheap and never in their control. The convention is wholly owned by an industry, and the director who wants to make art, i.e., meaningful, definitive, unforgettable moving pictures about ourselves in time and the universe, has to make it by stealth. Do many directors make it? No. Do many know what we are talking about? No.

An awful lot of poppycock is spoken and written about directing, and when the film festivals come round each year the explications become ever more cloying. I want to offer a few thoughts about directing.

Because of the persuasive powers of designers and the nearly unbelievable basal magic of movie photography, story plots that are barren of any sense or meaning can be made into movies by people who have never before made movies. So miraculous is the movie that it routinely makes itself, even though the director may doze. On its own, of its own power, the movie vivifies the lifeless morsel of nonsense and magnifies it into the big, moving, believable moment. Anybody can direct a movie; all he needs is the job and the title. Thousands of movies carry the names of directors nobody hears of ever again. A director on the set will at all times have at his elbow, welcome or not, a producer who will remind him of the story line he is supposed to be shooting, and a star or two who will tell him how they themselves want to be shot. His assistant director, always a man of procedural experience, will plan the order of shooting for him; his script supervisor will ensure that he achieves correct angular coverage; his head cameraman, now known as the director of photography, will give large beautiful life to the thing; and an editor will cut the thing for pace and dramatic interest. The composer of the musical score will imbue the thing with sentimental allure. Other postproduction processes will ultimately cosmeticize it.

Can a director fail? No, not even if he is a novice. His

collaborative cohorts won't let him fail; he will finish his picture; he will not fail. But his picture, like more than half the pictures shot, will fail. Let us remember that half the pictures directed by men of reputation fail. The acting? The characters of the movie story are naturally the main human interest, but the acting is not as important as one might think..For example, given a scene in which the working actors are not good and therefore have blank faces, or in which the faces of three good actors have been struck blank by stupefying dialog, an editor can yet find in his two-shots, over-shoulders, point-of-view cutaways, enough saving moments of animation to make the scene work. "It'll work!" is indeed the rallying cry most often heard on the set in the vicinity of the director's chair.

And now—some failures of my own.

12

· · · · · · ·

The title of my first Broadway flop was *Brothers*. I found the play in 1983 running in a small theater in Costa Mesa, south of Los Angeles. The characters were a father and four sons. Their sad story was that the youngest son required a kidney transplant, and one of his brothers, after agreeing to be the donor, changed his mind.

This play, following the cancellation of *Archie Bunker's Place*, was the vehicle I chose to carry me back to the New York stage, and I decided to direct it and play the father as well. I suspected of course that in impudently acting both as star and director I was giving reviewers a hook to hang jibes on. Still, I trusted my good luck. I firmly believed I was going to bring in a hit, but as I confessed earlier, I have no nose for a hit. This doesn't mean I don't know a promising play when I see one, but a hit depends not only on the merit of the play: the cast is crucial, the opening venue—the town and the theater—is important; so is the season of the year, and so also is the money it takes to keep the play open a while. But let me consider those and other things in due course. Here let me say only that by "no nose for a hit" I mean that I can never sense when the sum of all the requisites is healthy.

The characters of *Brothers* were well drawn. They lived in a certain ship-building town. Father and sons had always worked at the shipyard, except one who left to find a more prosperous life in the city of Boston. He is the donor who reneges on his offer. The father, a union delegate at the yard, is affable, witty and tyrannical. He was careless of the health and happiness of his late wife as well as of his sons, and the dialog was mainly accusations of selfishness, and angry recriminations. I asked the author whether there was not, far below the level of familiar bickering, an important elemental family defect. We discussed it. The missing element was family love, but he had not made that plain enough. He invited me to work with him, and what issued from the rewrites was the revelation that Pop, the old radical, had always been too busy trying to instill in the family a cohesive loyalty to socialist doctrine; he had neglected to nurture love, an emotion he was not, incidentally, entirely comfortable with. When he had to call upon it in a crisis, family love was not there.

We opened in Boston. That was a mistake, and I knew it was a mistake. How could I know such a thing? I knew because I was told by my ancient Irish counselors that I was headed for a fall in Boston. May I take a longer road round with this? It will be more colorful, I promise, than a fast train in the rain between New York and Boston. We must go back some years.

When I went to Boston for the first time I was not acting in a play, and had no notion of ever acting in a play. It was 1945, the war was not over, and I went to Boston under sailing orders. The Divil remarked glumly that I could have secured another assignment, adding "There's nothing but Irish in Boston."

The Ghost said "There's more, but it's the Irish you see, and a lovely sight they are!"

"My point" said the Divil to the Ghost, "is that the Irish he'll see are the same as the *bosthoon* that shkelped him in Hoboken, and he'll surely ask for a shkelpin' again."

"You'll find grand people in Boston" the Ghost assured me, "if you confine yourself to the elegant walks and ways of the town, and I'll see you do."

I went up there to sign on a freighter bound for France, and while walking to the dock, before encountering anything elegant, I was overwhelmed by a billowing cloud of aphids[1] and I swallowed one million of them. I lay sick in my bunk as we steamed out into the great bay of Massachusetts.

"Oh glorious epitaph!" groaned the Divil. "Sailed the Oceans but Drowned in Bugs!"

The Ghost maintained that there was high protein in the bugs, and I did in fact recover quickly; but the Divil argued that green bugs, nutrition aside, were always, historically, an augury of grief. The Divil was right. Boston became for me a town without pity.

A dozen years later, in 1957, avoiding the opinions of my shadowy old companions, knowing that neither of them would encourage me in the act of folly I was about to commit, I went back to Boston as an assistant stage manager–understudy in a bad play. Nancy hated the idea. Professionally it was a long step backward, and even the director, Burgess Meredith, who gave me the job, and with whom I had recently done the memorable first production of *Ulysses* in New York, advised me against it. I could have returned of course to substitute teaching, but that would have all but ruled out auditioning for parts and trying to interest agents in my faltering career, and worst of all it might have raised in me a psychological barrier to my returning to the stage.

The play was *God and Kate Murphy*, which first appeared in

---

[1] Tiny, green, flying biting bugs.

Ireland as *A Priest in the Family*. It was a modern play about a bossy widow who ordains that one of her sons should become a priest, and the other a publican. The publican longs to be a priest, and the priest longs to be a playboy; he can't keep his hands off his preseminary girlfriend. The errant young cleric was played by Larry Hagman, and the simmering maiden by Lois Nettleton. This was not a likely Irish family circumstance even in despotic days of yore, but whether or not you believed it, you didn't care. We were soon back in New York, where we closed after two weeks, though Atkinson of the *Times* gave the play a passing review. The only value of the thing for me was my meeting Larry and Maj Hagman; they have been very close friends of ours ever since.

I went back again to Boston in 1959 with a comedy called *The Goodwill Ambassador* about an Irish premier who gets hold of a nuclear bomb and threatens the British with it. The thing sounds grim but it was merely absurd. It was nevertheless very well played by Cyril Cusack, Arthur Treacher, Reginald Owen and some others including me. I also functioned, at the request of the producer, as the play doctor. He said to me one day at rehearsal "You're a kind of a professor, aren't you?"

I said "No, no kind of a professor, merely a lowly substitute pedagogue, an off-and-on instructor of the unwilling."

"But I think I detect" he said, "that you know about plays."

"Yes" I said, "I know about plays."

He said "Help me fix this one."

In my rewrites between New Haven, where we got a wounding review, and Boston, I practically wrote myself out of the play. My character was not merely vacuous, it caused a lull in the movement. As play doctor, I implanted a number of new jokes, and cut old fat, making the play livelier and leaner, bringing the laughs closer together. The surgery was all to the good; what was still to the bad was the incurable preposterousness of the thing.

On opening night in the Wilbur Theater, Nancy was sitting

beside the preeminent reviewer of the town and she reported at the end of the first act that he was laughing a lot. The customers were laughing too. When the final curtain came down and the cast went off in good spirits to an opening night party, the producer and I hiked, with hope in our hearts and a needling wind in our faces (Was it aphids again? No, merely tiny bits of hail) to the *Globe* offices to see the review. A city editor wearing a green eyeshade, who looked like Don Rickles, said "You really wanna see it?"

Stunned by the question, we nodded.

The editor called to a copyboy: "Pull a proof on Norton."

The producer dropped into a chair. To the editor I said "I can't believe he killed us. Did he?" Don Rickles nodded. "Showed you no mercy."

The review was carnage. We were dead, yet we lingered, indomitable corpses, for a another week in Boston and audiences greatly enjoyed our work. They liked the comic performances by Cusack, Treacher and Owen; we knew they would, and this is why we had all looked not for a rave but for a nice little "money" review. We couldn't move from the Wilbur to Broadway without one. Incidentally, if our engagement at the Wilbur had been an open one—if we had not been obliged to move out in a week's time—I think we could have run well and made money. So much for Boston in the distant past.

Now—back again to Boston in 1983, and there I was with what I now believed to be a well-prepared play. I was dismayed by having to play *Brothers* at the Colonial, a musical house far too big for us; this was our first production blunder. Before leaving New York I had consented to do a telephone interview with a leading Boston reviewer. This was blunder number two. The Divil had said "What d'you expect to get out of an interview with this boyo, a good review?" "Put it this way" I said, "I'd expect a bad review if I refused him."

"Talk to the fella" the Ghost encouraged me; "he's got an Irish name."

True. But like the *bosthoon* in Hoboken,[2] he punched me in the face when I wasn't expecting it. I put the bad review out of my mind and called a few morning rehearsals to fix technical problems and let the cast know that I was as confident as ever.

We went on to the Forrest Theater in Philadelphia, where the reviewers treated us a little more kindly, and then finally to the Music Box in New York, where we played a week of previews and rehearsed every afternoon. This theater was not at first available to us, but when its owner, Irving Berlin, learned that I wanted it, he opened it to us. The producers' practice in New York was to invite reviewers to review one of the previews, if they wished, instead of reviewing the opening night performance. Did it matter? I am afraid so. The *Times* man reviewed us on the evening of a day when I had scheduled a rehearsal of new material and new staging. A producer called me and begged me not to hold the rehearsal, but was afraid to tell me why. That was blunder number three. I held the rehearsal. We were not ready for the *Times* review, but the *Times* review was ready for us— ready for us to read at the party after our opening performance. The review killed any advance sale. I closed the show that night.

I lost some money[3] but I look back fondly on the experience because it let me bring my son into "the business." Hugh, then twenty, was with me throughout the production, rehearsals and run of *Brothers*. I gave him the job of assistant stage manager and told the production stage manager to show him how to do it. I never gave him anything to do that he did not do well, and he learned stage management well in those eight to ten weeks. The one thrill I recall from that show was hearing his deep voice outside my dressing room door: "Half hour, Pop," then going out to the stage and finding him in the prompt corner, his production script on the rostrum under the hooded light, earphones on his head, mike around his neck, preparing to order

[2]Which I will come to.
[3]My partners Orion Pictures lost $400,000, I lost $450,000.

the lights down and the curtain up. He was, as all the boys and girls on Broadway say, "a real old pro." He had earned his Equity card and he was on his way.

Following the *Brothers* disaster Orion Pictures and I produced a TV movie in New York called *Brass,* a police picture for which I wrote the script and played the leading character, the chief of NYPD detectives. The real chief at that time was Richard Nicastro, a man my own age, a shrewd, deeply experienced officer with a fine intelligence and a sense of humor. He did me the great favor of reading the script and correcting errors large and small, visiting the set now and then, and encouraging me to call him with questions. I noticed that his driver was a young detective, and for that role in the picture I cast two "cops" who divided the duty, one a beautiful Spanish girl named Begona Plaza, who played her character as a New York Puerto Riqueña, and the other Hugh, who became a favorite of my new friend and adviser, Dick Nicastro. Hugh said to me "I'll play the part, Pop, but do you really want me to be an actor?" I said "Son, your pop hasn't got a business to leave you. My 'business' is not a tangible asset, it's all experience and know-how, and I want to give you a chance at every phase of it." He accepted that, and asked me how to play his part, Detective Jimmy Flynn. I told him Flynn was utterly delighted to get this great job with the chief, and dedicated every moment to doing it perfectly. He said "That's exactly how I feel myself." He played his small part well, as I knew he would.

A young PR woman at CBS, distracted by her own need to be noticed and wanted (a girl begins feeling that way in a network job of any kind), told the press that *Brass* was a series pilot; it was not; it was made by the movie people at CBS, not the series people, and none of us who were working on it had a series-option contract. When CBS didn't turn it into a series, the press called *Brass* a "rejected pilot." I could have given them the accurate story. Network series executives make it a rule of self-defense never to use product that they themselves have not ordered, unless of course the Grand Ayatollah orders them to order it; and as I had often called their policies dumb, and identified them openly as dumbbells, the thought of ordering a series from me was never at any time in their minds. However, *Brass* as a series would have been a good one, much the same as *In the Heat of the Night,* which I began making for NBC in 1987. In both stories the chiefs were father images to their men, deeply absorbed in their profession, widowered but drawn to interesting women. The TV movie *Brass* was well watched and liked.

The reviewer on the *Times* hated it, by the way, and singled out young Hugh for a mean slash. The reviewer was a cousin of mine, John O'Connor.

But reviewers of television and movies don't do much harm. What they are reviewing isn't really important in the first place, and in the second place the public won't forego a movie or a TV show on their say so. But now let us turn to reviewers of plays. Let me recall a rainy afternoon in Manhattan when cabs were scarce, and three souls, no longer hardy, were leaning on the bar at The Players talking about "critics." One of us, an old acting colleague of mine, moaned "How do they pick 'em?" I could not help him, but the world-weary third gentleman, a writer who owned that he had once been a reviewer of books but never plays, offered this:

"They pick a guy who's written critical stuff before, not necessarily about theatre."

"Baseball perhaps?" quipped the venerable actor.

"Movies perhaps" replied the writer, "though I knew one who came by way of antiques and restaurants."

"What an entry level!"

"At all events" said the writer, "they want an intelligent tone.

But not a boring tone. What keeps a review from being boring is abuse. They want to know—can this man intelligently deliver abuse? They may also ask about family background, politics, religion."

"Do they ask" inquired the actor, "whether he ever wrote, produced, directed or acted in the professional theatre?"

The ex-reviewer shook his head. "They don't want an old theatre pro—he'd be too sentimental. The man they want has to be willing and able to draw blood for a laugh."

The old actor sighed forlornly. Raising his glass to the wall at his left, a picture gallery of bygone Players, he moaned "They're killing us, boys! First you, next me, soon the whole theatre!"

Allowing a decorous pause, I ventured to say that I didn't think reviewers and reviews were that important.

"Reviews not important? Listen—that matinee I saw yesterday was utterly goofy, totally lousy, and it was playing to a packed house. Because it got raves! Damn thing'll run two years—reviews are all!"

"Well" I said, "but you're now citing an example of a review keeping the theatre alive." It turned out, though, to be a faulty example. The play closed in a month.

The argument is old, inconclusive and dull, but I am sure that reviews are not as influential as people think. A success on Broadway depends on producing something the public wants to see; the key problem is getting the public to see it. If audiences are entertained, their talk will keep it alive; if they find it fair, poor or wretched, their talk will throttle it soon, sooner or instanter. But the show has to stay open a while.

The producer blunders when he blows his backers' cash on advertising.[4] Heavy advertising before opening is useless. Light advertising and a couple of good reviews will bring some

---

[4]And also on expenses for production office *schnorrers*.

customers to the box office; bad reviews will of course scare some of them away, but the producer's strategy must be to acquire enough money to push past the reviews, pay the "nut," the costs of running his show, for about a month. One of the running costs will be heavy advertising. A sensible businessman, a manufacturer or retailer, advertises lavishly when his product, whatever it is, comes on the market, not before. But I have seen some big money (for instance, mine) wasted trying to buy a hit in advance with advertising. I shall never forget a costly half-page ad for me and my play in a paper whose reviewer was clubbing me to death a few days later.

Incidentally, advertising managers of newspapers should be made to understand that only if shows run, only if the theatre business is healthy, can they expect to make any money on show ads. Am I slyly suggesting financial pressure? Yes, of course.

If I were producing something on Broadway and could not raise enough running money, playing money, I would go back to my California beach, contemplate the ocean, and recall yet again my peacefully uncomplicated years afloat, even with a war raging. If I were again invited by a producer to star on Broadway I would ask for the right to withdraw from the show if playing money were not securely available before opening night. Would that accord with hallowed practice and tradition? No. Would my fellow actors applaud me? No. Would a producer make that deal with me? No. Would that deal be entirely fair and proper? Yes, it would, and why not?

Some reviewer once said "Critics don't close shows, producers do." He should have added "Critics don't keep shows open either." (By the way, "critics" is his word, not mine. I prefer "reviewers," and I will come to the distinction momentarily.) But the run-of-the-mill producer cultivates and pets the reviewer, gives the fellow a free seat or two, favors him with an early performance opening night, and, if he prefers not to attend opening night, submissively invites him to attend an earlier performance, an unpolished preview, which he may attack in print as if he has seen the opening performance. Of the producer it only remains to be said that when he scores a hit, it is not because he hasn't tried everything he could to achieve a flop.

Our talk at The Players bar turned to other questions. What of the artist and what of the public? What does the reviewer mean to them? The old colleague thought that the "negativism" of reviewers was "killing off the playwrights"; the writer thought it was driving playwrights to the securer land of television, but I reminded him that if their defection had hurt the theatre, it had certainly not improved television. By "negativism" we all meant that we see many fewer raves than rejections, and of course this is true and always was. But did reviewers ever have a decisive influence on the artist or the public?

Taking the artist first, I can confidently say that to him only the reactions of other artists—of reputation preferably—are truly important. To the playwright the artistic evaluation of the reviewer and, say, the usher who seats the reviewer are of about equal value: in brief, no value. The playwright does like to hear from the usher on a level of simple emotional comments such as "wonderful," "awful," etc., because he knows that the usher is a normal person much like the people who paid their way into the theater. Yet even on this simple level he ignores the reviewer, because he does not regard him as normal. He does not believe that a normal person, a balanced person, would lean to review-ing—would aspire to a responsibility or crave a power that he is unfit to wield. He is right.

Reviewers of the arts, unlike practitioners, have nothing at all to do with creative work. They do not, and as a rule cannot, create. There have been exceptions. The artist-turned-reviewer is not unknown, though time has left him dimly remembered in the dual contour, and the other fellow, the reviewer-turned-artist, hardly rouses a recollection. (One man does come to mind: Shaw; he was both.) The reviewer is fit only to tell us of his own eccentric response, and artists, unless they are tyros or hysterics, never alter their work in consequence. Now and then in the theatre, revisions and alterations of a play may appear to have been prompted by reviewers, but invariably they have been long in other minds.

The playwright sees the reviewer as a rattled creature, daffy, campy, debauched and driven. He thinks of him as a person somehow deprived in early life, and therefore envious and vengeful; a person who at curtain rise is depressed, in need of a pill, on a pill—in other words, devoted only to himself and his dark impulses. Is this view excessive? No. For what it is worth, it is a printable redaction of opinions I have heard not only from playwrights but from different kinds of artists. The fact is, the reviewer does lack a relevant professional education, and it is terrifying to the artist to think that a man with no mastery of the dynamics of the art is going to pass public judgment upon the artist's work. The reviewer is his enemy, and if you would say to me "Oh come now!—always?" I would say always. I would ask you how the artist may otherwise regard a publicist who rarely supports him—and then never for the right reasons—but habitually tries to strike him down.

"Enemy" is the word. And the reviewer is a singularly detested enemy because he is, unlike the hapless artist, invulnerable. His wounding salvos are spewed from an unjustly protected position. If only, like the artist, he had something at stake! If only his appraisals put him at some risk! But no! He may write stupidly, viciously, tastelessly, yet he is safe. For him, no matter how shameful, no matter how fatuous his performance, his closing notice will not go up next day. His act may run for years. I once broached this matter to a reviewer over a comradely glass, and he stared at me coldly, one flaccid cheek trembling, and hissed: "That is a tired old issue. Get it through your head—I was hired

196

for general acumen, not specific experience." That ended that. I might have retorted that he was not delivering acumen either—his prolix output was always reducible to "I love this," "I hate that," rather like a child picking up and throwing down candy. But I forbore disputation. These fellows are very thin of skin; the nerves beneath induce spasms alarming even to impassive bartenders. The angry reviewer took my silence for surrender, which it certainly was, and issued a two-minute bill of indictment against the acting profession, setting forth such actors' crimes as extorting outrageous salaries from producers, clamoring for publicity, whining in public, torturing reviewers, and having a lot of sex.

But what then of our own bill of indictment against the reviewer? Should we lay it before the fellow's editor? No. Outrage only makes the editor chuckle. So long as readers are buying the paper, the editor is delighted to give proportional credit to the reviewer no less than to the astrologer, the obituarist, or the roving nosher.[5] At any rate, the particular reviewer I have been here recalling was moved eventually from the drama desk by his editor. The editor himself found the man's constant disdain chafing, his rare praise fulsome, his slashing prose redolent of violence. While the paper lasted, this reviewer was put to writing in the holiday section, and his last byline was seen over a piece debunking the charm of Seville.

Now to the public. How does the reader see the reviewer? I asked a number of intelligent citizens, and the synthesized answer was this: "He tells us what's on, what it's about, whether it's worth seeing—and I guess he's supposed to write an entertaining column."

"Are you" I inquired, "entertained?"

"Once in a while he says something funny."

---

[5]Eater, taster.

197

"Do you see or not see shows because of what he says?"

"If he says a show is bad and I don't hear any good opinions from people who saw it, I might not go. If people tell me good things, I'll go no matter what."

"And of course if the review itself is a good one?"

"No. I think I still have to hear from people."

So people don't trust the reviewer. They have the impression that he is wrong more often than right. They read him, and things trouble them: meanness, petulance, ill will or sometimes silly adulation, served up in a couple of columns of difficult hoity-toity language. Readers know that plays and musicals have been fashioned for them, not for the peculiar creature of the columns, and they prefer to judge things by their own lights.

The truth is, we really don't need reviewers, just first-night reporters who will tell us faithfully whether or not the audience liked the show. However, what we could certainly use is a few bona fide critics, and that brings me to the distinction I alluded to earlier. A critic is a different creature altogether. He does not produce art either, but he engenders it, and that function is a kind of art in itself; indeed criticism has no higher purpose. The true theatre critic is a man of learning who can speak to playwrights, directors and actors in the language of both aesthetic and practical guidance; and can also speak to them of the world and the times and the things that merit observation— the human experience that today wants artistic expression. The dedicated theatre professional will know that a true critic will be sympathetic and encouraging even when disapproving; never discouraging except to the slipshod, the opportunistic and the fraudulent. Nor will the ordinary newspaper reader and theatre-goer have reason to be chary of the true critic; for his prose will be lucid and light, its aim not to dazzle minds but to open them. But alas! where may we encounter this valuable practitioner? We search the papers and periodicals, even those abroad, and find ourselves everywhere confronting the conceited, the smug, the rude, the maker of cheesy wit.

But we must not be dashed. As Joxer Daly said to Jack Boyle, "Ah Captain, *nil desperandum!*"

Editors do make changes when first impressions fade: they replace eyeglasses, office furniture and reviewers. The public is not aware of the changes, though they do notice after a while that somebody else seems to be writing in the old place. Nobody cares, though actors take note, of course. We three at The Players bar were joined by two others, a lady and gentleman of the stage who, on learning that we had been talking about reviewers, brought up a name: they wondered compassionately why "poor old John——" (the name John is merely a convenience) had been replaced by his paper.

Poor old John! The lady had apparently forgiven the fellow for writing a paragraph of ferocious contempt not just for her performance but for her dear nose and neck too; and the gentleman had once seen himself described by John as a blundering misfit with a chronic Lower East Side accent. They both wondered at the time why he felt he had to slash so cruelly at their personal dignity and confidence. Yet now, strange to say, a year or so afterward, they seemed to be murmuring something or other generous about him. I can't recall exactly what, but I did hear the kindly phrase "poor old John," and then I heard it repeated. Actors never nurse grudges. There was a clap of thunder suddenly, and the conversation turned to the weather.

What about the press generally? Standard and tabloid, vulgar and obscene, the papers run rumors daily about people in show business, tales of wicked ways and witless affairs, inanity and misbehavior. Reporters develop these stories from tips and yarns they pick up, or buy, in hallways, parking lots, costume and makeup rooms, bars and toilets. They also reprint "releases" from press agents, though release stuff is always laudatory, tepid and bland. Army Archerd at *Variety* is the only columnist I know who checks his tips and rumors by making personal phone calls. He is a respectable reporter and commentator, and his specialty is straight news from authentic sources. In the main, show-biz buzz-artists, discovering that celebrities are dull, not vivacious and absorbing, do not hesitate to rush misinformation into print, usually adding a *soupçon* of scandal. Some celebs, being witless, are not disturbed; they are getting the publicity they crave, and if it causes the world to marvel at them, their hearts are glad.

Not all celebrities are dunces. Many get upset when misrepresented, misinterpreted and misquoted, but their anger gets them nowhere. The eminent journalists who wronged them assume a posture of plumb disbelief. The ungrateful staggering wounded are actually complaining about valuable publicity!

Some misinformation is funny and really harmless. The blabber merchants have always trumpeted show-biz salaries as feverishly as if the security of the commonwealth depended on the revelations. They have never given the public the right information. I, for example, was widely reported to be making twenty-five million when in my best year I was making five.

(There is a question, which I have considered elsewhere, whether the press ever gives us reliable information on anything.)

Now, everything worth having or doing in this world can be had or done for far less than the honest five I made, never mind the fictitious five-times-five. Why then did I launch a half dozen bitter contract battles to get the five? Because it was there. Much more was there. The television networks and the owners of my series were making many millions day after day from my work. I couldn't leave the whole treasure to be scooped up and carried off by those lucky fellows who, besides counting it, were doing little else to get it. The better question is, Why does all that incredible, unaccountable loot pile up in the first place? The study of the dollar values we assign to entertainment—why we are willing, and how much we are willing, to pay for entertainment, is beyond the scope of this frivolous opus: it is a subject for anthropology and psychology.

It seems, however, that entertainment is what most excites us pleasurably, and what we value above anything else. The most exciting and desirable entertainment seems to be having our imagination stimulated to the level of escape-fantasy, exceeding in pleasure any actual excitement: in other words, even lovemaking is less desirable than watching basketball, football, baseball, boxing, hockey, Sicilian massacres, sci-fi absurdities, Super Bowls and Academy Awards. The quietly churning inner ecstasy of these experiences goes on and on, far beyond the quick thrill of intimate human contact. Accordingly, performers and performances that pull us up into the realm of escape-fantasy can command, as we all know, fantastic price tags. Owners and controllers of the precious product charge the public, performers charge the owners. All charges are out of sight—there seems to be no upper limit.

But a word of caution to the fan before he lets himself become inflamed by outraged envy. Let him bear in mind that in a capitalist society persons who create capital (the athlete Michael Jordan, the movie-studio chief Michael Eisner) are given the staggering rewards; persons who use up capital (teachers, research scientists) are given no rewards: they are simply paid and ignored.

The year 1984 brought a fresh new opportunity to flop on Broadway. I signed to act, and only act, in a play called *Home Front*; it was about a father, mother and daughter terrorized by the son, a violent veteran of Vietnam who seemed to be blaming his family for the war. He had a fair case to make, but the slobbery play kept him from making it. We closed after twelve performances. Why did I do it? True to form, I guessed badly that it would be a hit and would redeem my blunders of the year before. O vainglory! A TV reviewer for ABC (Siegel) judged me unfit to work on the Broadway stage. A print reviewer thought me splendid. Many theatre folk told Nancy that I ought to come back immediately in another play. She replied that I would; she told me so. I said nothing.

I had made sure that Hugh was with me again on this venture; he worked for the producers as a production assistant. He had declined, or rather adamantly refused, to go to college, and if he had gone I think he would have studied marine biology; but by now he had learned more about my business, in a practical professional way, than any kid with a baccalaureate in drama, and at a time not far off, in a new television film-series, he would learn a great deal about movie acting and movie production.

In the meanwhile we went back to Los Angeles and devoted some attention to another money-eating failure, The Ginger Man restaurant in Beverly Hills. My friend and partner Patrick O'Neal, who had previously opened a popular restaurant of the same name in Manhattan, came out to Hollywood to play in my remake of the movie *The Last Hurrah* for Columbia and Hall-mark in 1977; and in the course of the shooting he mentioned to me his intention of opening in Beverly Hills. He asked me if I wanted to be a limited partner. I was delighted and told him I wanted to be his general partner, fifty-fifty, and we did the thing together. We opened about ten months later in July of 1978. That summer, by the way, was both grim and happy. In the June just passed Nancy discovered a tumor in Hugh's neck. I emphasize that Nancy discovered the thing because she had noticed the classic Hodgkin's lump in his neck, and when a doctor diagnosed it as a swollen gland she didn't believe him. She led an angry, unwilling sixteen-year-old to two other internists and found out that she was right. Hugh went into the John Wayne Cancer Center at UCLA to be treated for Hodgkin's disease. He endured three surgical invasions, the first into his foot to introduce a detection dye to the lymph system, the second into his neck to remove the tumor, the third, the most disturbing, into his midriff to remove the spleen, the lymphatic haunt of the disease. The happy news of the summer was that after effective surgery and radiology, he seemed to be headed for a normal life.

In 1984 our restaurant was in its sixth year on Bedford Drive off Wilshire Boulevard. The place had been a great success, making a profit till about 1983, but now it was just carrying itself. Losses loomed. I had by then bought out Patrick and renamed the restaurant Carroll O'Connor's Place. Had Patrick sold out sensing the coming decline? No. My dear friend, and colleague, never a doomsayer like his partner, merely wanted to go into a land deal in Florida and needed some cash.[6] The restaurant needed a night manager and Hugh, at my request, put himself under a day manager who trained him for a couple of weeks to take over. He was now twenty-three. His job was meeting, greeting and seating people, adding up all the covers at closing, reconciling the cash with the paper, stowing money in the safe, and locking up the doors. He was fast and accurate with figures, smoothly ingratiating to customers, very good looking, handsome in his dark business suits. The restaurant was elegant in an informal way,[7] but for Hugh there was nothing daunting about it; from childhood to the present he had observed all the graceful customs and modes of dining and serving on board the great ships and in the renowned restaurants abroad and at home. He knew what to do. He did it very, very well. But dark things were happening. The dope crowd were in and out, and neither Hugh nor any other employee offered to identify them to me; nor would my own people admit that even a little dealing and using went on from time to time. Even so, it was being bruited about that one of the places where one could "score" was my place.

---

[6]Patrick, a highly esteemed actor, died of cancer in 1992.
[7]It was designed by Patrick's chic and gifted wife Cynthia.

I always had, and still had, excellent chefs and service, but my good customers were vanishing. I held meetings with the staff. I reminded them that they enjoyed in my employ a health insurance coverage for themselves and their families that no restaurant in the city would equal; its cost to me canceled profit completely, but as they knew, I was running the restaurant for the fun of it. I simply enjoyed it—holding business lunches and interviews there, bringing friends there, being told by everyone, especially by smart women, how much they loved the place. It was "show biz" in many ways—like staging a popular piece of theater. I told my staff, many of whom were Mexican, that much of the pleasure it gave me was in providing a good secure place for them to work. I asked them to help me rid the place of the dope menace, and to bring down costs in about ten specific ways. The bar seemed busy, but the bar was losing money. Food was unaccountably missing, and I turned my appealing gaze not only on the bartenders but on the waiters and kitchen staff as well. It hardly needs saying that everyone agreed that we ought to solve the mysteries of losses, work hard to keep the place sparkling and attractive, and, as I adjured them, "Help me get rid of the things that are hurting us and get back the business we've lost. Think of ways we can help each other." But we didn't work hard, we didn't do any fresh thinking, we never reversed our losses, we never identified the dopers who were preying on us, we never recovered the popularity of our first five years. In general, my Mexican employees, including a highly talented chef, wanted to make a go of it; my americanos, most of them, didn't care,[8] and theirs was the slack attitude that prevailed.

Hugh really didn't know how to help me. Being a drug addict—a fact that I couldn't see—he ignored the many ways in

---

[8]Some cared.

which the losses of supplies, the increase of nonpaying sodden malingerers at the bar, the newly exceptionable look of "the crowd," were hurting our business. Hugh was always serene; he never saw bad people anywhere. What he thought was wrong with the restaurant was its old-fashionedness—what I ought to do was turn it into a jazz club and let him and a couple of his friends run it. He and the slow-witted, dope-smoking pals he had in mind were as fit to run a jazz club as to run a health club, but—not to put him down—I seriously discussed with him the restructuring and renovation that would have to precede this change. We agreed that five hundred thousand would be a low estimate and one million would not be too high, and we had a good-natured ongoing exchange of hot air over the matter until it was time to go south to begin a new series.

13

. . . .

One important lunch meeting at the restaurant was with Fred Silverman[1] when he and I talked over the new series *In the Heat of the Night.* He was representing himself and Ms. Lynn Loring, MGM vice-president in charge of TV projects, who must have been screening the old MGM movie and thought it would make a good series for me and a black leading man. She told Fred, and Fred told me and within two weeks—as Fred had promised—we were all committed to the deal. I wrote and directed a test scene in which I played Gillespie opposite five very good black actors who were testing for the role of Tibbs.[2] Howard Rollins was my favorite, but a couple of the production executives preferred one of the other four candidates, O. J. Simpson. Simpson looked superb and played the scene very well. The president of NBC Entertainment, the late Brandon Tartikoff, allowed me to make the final choice and I chose

---

[1]The well-known producer, former head of entertainment at CBS, ABC, and NBC.
[2]Characters that were played in the movie by Rod Steiger and Sidney Poitier.

Rollins. I saw in Rollins's acting a unique clairvoyant insight into humanity and character. He had a fine voice. He had an exceptionally good-humored amiable disposition. Acting was above all things his preoccupation; he had little interest in celebrity, and his sole ambition was to be recognized as an actor preeminent in our theatre.

If dear Howard had lived and had got control of his life, which drugs had so wounded and knotted, he would have been a towering figure in the theatre.

The *Heat* company went to Hammond, Louisiana, in the late fall of 1987, prepared to make six episodes of the series plus a double episode, two hours, a kind of pilot. Hammond is a town forty-five minutes by car north of New Orleans and the bayous, and its friendly people made us most welcome. But one had to search the town with diligence—and without much success—to find its southern aspects. Interstate and state highways had spawned a utilitarian culture that had pushed the ancient disposition of affairs out of existence. Shooting the series as we did— we wrote and shot unintelligently—we need not have gone south at all. The stories could have been filmed in Dubuque, Iowa, or at the MGM studio lot and the neighboring streets of Culver City, California. The South in the mind of our female producer was a kind of Transylvania with a sneering drawl. The South was the American locus of morbid souls and macabre events, of primitive brooding blacks, wealthy white lunatics, horribly spoiled racist bad boys, and devilishly grisly murders. Her scripts and the ones she ordered from her writers were preposterous. Nevertheless these scripts, when blown out into film through the intrinsic magic of the medium, and the razzle-dazzle artifice I spoke of earlier—of designers, costumers, composers and editors—these things got the show by. But getting by was not what I was content to do.

My contract with MGM/NBC gave me the right, as a story editor, of collaborating on all writing for the show. Despite this, my producer week after week rejected my work on the scripts, and tried to prevent my rewriting the dialog on the set. I warned of a breach of contract, and well before the short season was over told my friend Ms. Loring that I detested the work and was going to step away from it. Lynn told me that the producer took this with remarkable aplomb; she did not care what I did, confident that MGM and the network would be content to replace me and retain her. She was as unrealistic as her story plots. NBC told MGM to replace her. MGM then hired, with my ignorant, uncomplaining approval, a certain husband-and-wife writing duet to produce the next season, 1988–1989. This pair immediately did the show a service; they moved its location to the typical southern town of Covington, Georgia. But alas! their first service was their last. They chose to ignore the dramatic resources within the real environment and wrote what we may call "situation nondescript"—as if they were using a plot matrix spongy enough to suit all locales, all characters. The proof that this was their plan and method, as it was their predecessors', was their predisposition to produce the show by remote control from California: i.e., by telephone. Only spongy-matrix shows can be done in this way.

The spongy-matrix show is common in television; it is the explanation of why a curious sameness seems to inhabit everything in prime time. For this, the networks must take first blame. Network entertainment presidents judge what is right for their networks by what they see on the other networks. This fault is well known and well decried, but let us not lightly pass over it. Let us look at its roots. Entertainment presidents are not normally chosen from the entertainment professions; and they are not chosen for originality of mind either, but rather the reverse, the ability to replicate cheerfully and promote aggressively all that is wholly familiar. The prezes predictably place their series orders with writer/producers who exhibit the same dull *gestalt* as their own.

Imagine, however, a prez with an original bent and a lively

imagination. Presumably he would devote himself to finding at least one writer/producer who, like himself, is not yet in the grip of the recycling habit. How would he fare? Not well, because a truly creative man or woman willing to work for TV and movie executives (1) can't be found, and (2) even if found, can't be handled.

The reader may wonder whether the spongy-matrix, remote-control method of production should not be taken as a sign of enormous contempt for the viewing public. No. Contempt, like any other personal reaction, requires thought, and the viewing public is never the subject of any thought. But isn't it a valid argument to say that the viewers are being served what they want? Don't the ratings tell us this? No, the ratings tell us that of the programs viewers are offered, ten or twenty are well watched, and the rest range downward from now-and-then watched to rarely watched. The viewers are taking what they are given, not being served what they want.

My new producing team for *In the Heat of the Night* (new to me, not to the network) began their occupancy at MGM by presenting me with a finished two-hour script to open the 1988–1989 season. This did not augur well for harmony. I had not been invited to work on the script, according to our agreements, and I found the thing derivative and third rate even by going standards. I considered leaving the show, but Nancy argued me out of it. We reported to Georgia and I angrily barged into the new season, resolved, however, to bolt at the finish of it. Meanwhile I would save my neck as an actor by rewriting my own dialogue, let Hell and Culver City disgorge molten fumes. Culver City remained tepid though testy, and Hell showed no interest.

One Friday in late February, shooting beside a stream on a wickedly cold day, I felt tired, and blamed myself for getting too little sleep the night before. I went to my motor-home between takes, sat down with a cup of coffee, stared out of the window through a wavy film of ice on the glass, and decided to call it a day. Ed Ledding, my line producer, quickly rearranged the shooting schedule and sent me home to bed, asking if I wouldn't drop in to see the company doctor, who happened to be on my route. Neither Ed nor I thought there was anything wrong with me, but my quitting early meant the loss of a half day of shooting, and as our insurance carrier would be asked to pay for the loss, I had to see its appointed doctor as a matter of procedure. The procedure served me well. The company doctor, minimally competent, referred me to Dr Thomas Crews, a first-rank cardiologist of Covington, who examined me and sent me on to Emory University Hospital in Atlanta, where I became a patient of Dr Willis Hurst. Dr Hurst, formerly President Lyndon Johnson's doctor, ordered an angiogram and afterward he and his chief associate, Dr Spencer King, told Nancy and me that all three of my coronary arteries were closed, each one in two places, and would have to be opened not by angioplasty but conventional surgery. I asked him whether it couldn't be done immediately. I didn't want to languish in the hospital till Monday contemplating the knife. Dr Hurst called Dr Joe Craver, a peerless heart surgeon, who agreed to come in and scrub up the very next morning, Saturday. Joe, a big merry ol' boy, and former all-American from North Carolina, made six bypasses in seven hours, two in each of the three arteries.

On the eighth day of my recovery, Dr Hurst came in and said "Carroll, the gallbladder is frequently a problem after heart surgery, and we gon' have to go in and get yours." And next day I was wheeled downstairs and another surgeon, Dr John Henderson, went in and got it. The three-week ordeal was not as shocking to me as it was to Nancy and Hugh; she had prepared herself for loss by prayer and willpower, while he had looked for escape from panic in the transportive power of cocaine. When he came to see me, he was unable to make easy conversation; he was toxic—very hard to talk to. It was his first occasion to binge during a working season of the series. There would be other occasions.

I missed the final three episodes of the season, and when we went back to the West Coast, I was certain that the series was over for me. Nancy made me walk, firmly guiding and pushing me west along the Malibu beach and back east by the road every day. Going that route on foot for the first time—I never liked walking anywhere—I found myself meeting neighbors seen rarely or not at all in eleven years of occasional living on Broad Beach; and also some old acquaintances who sojourned there as seldom as we: the Jack Lemmons, Walter Matthau, Dick and Dolly Martin, Dustin Hoffman, Abbey Lane and Perry Leff, Steve and Edie Lawrence, Bob and Millie Wise. Such is the nature of showbiz—all of us most of the time on the move, missing one another, headed in all directions. They all said they had inferred from the papers in April that I was about to cross over Jordan (this told me that everybody was reading the supermarket tablurbs), and they were glad to see me still on the jolly side of that legendary stream. Being thickly ignorant of medical science, I began only then, weeks after the surgery, to understand what had happened. The arterial blockages in the heart had been forcing the old pump to find other routes, to push blood through by way of whatever tiny interstices there were in the muscular tissue. My heart had been laboring at this for a very long time and was ready to give up when Spencer King saw the awful condition in his angiogram. Cholesterol did not appear to be a cause; my count, according to the doctor, was that "of a homeless man," 38. The cause was tobacco, which I had smoked addictively in all its forms for fifty years. And in my hospital room the Friday night before the surgery, believing Nancy to be in a nearby office answering phone calls, I was actually inhaling a Charatan pipeful of delightful Dunhill. Nancy swooped in, grabbed the pipe, made a fast triumphant search for cigarettes, and threatened me with assault if ever again she saw me as much as light a match. She got rid of all smoking paraphernalia except a gift from Hugh, a beautiful lighter that projected a jet of flame into a pipe bowl, which I reprieved by explaining that it was good for lighting candles. I can't believe that any addiction is more tenacious than smoking, and but for the consecutive surgeries and the pain and distraction they caused, I would have remembered my need and satisfied it before I left the hospital. But when the thought of a smoke once or twice darted across my mind, I felt so abjectly stupid that I blocked all subsequent thought of it.

One effect of convalescence was a deep depression that I thought would never end. My heart doctor in Los Angeles, Ann Hickey, asked me to describe what I was feeling and I told her something I had not told Nancy: that certain surreal fantasies, both waking and sleeping, strongly implied that I didn't have a right to be here; that I was meant to be gone, and that there was something sad and wrong about my walking around on earth. The fantasies were short scenes in which I was moving about among people I knew who didn't speak to me but looked at me as if I were someone else, a stranger. The doctor assured me that this would pass, that it was a common consequence of heart surgery, and put me on an antidepression medication. Ann was right. My spirits were soon back to normal, and I couldn't remember when I had felt so well physically. The blood was flowing again and my oxygen supply was now plentiful.

Some time in May I got a call from Dave Gerber, president of MGM TV, to enquire whether I had thought about doing another season. I told Dave that I despaired of finding producers who could write and run the show to my requirements, and that if I returned I would have to take over full management. Dave said he didn't believe I could play the leading role in the series and do the big production job as well, and when I replied that I could, he said he could not make such a proposal to NBC. I modified it by inviting Fred Silverman to share with me the title of executive producer, and this proved acceptable to all. I became the hands-on executive producer working at the production site, Fred became the symbolic exec, remote from the site in the South, comfortingly close to the nervous network; his familiar presence in Los Angeles made NBC content that nothing about the show was going to be radically different. But it became radically different.

Plots were no longer about incredible persons from other places passing through Sparta—"imported drama" I used to call it when I was demanding that former producers stop relying on it. Our new episodes were about local people—the crimes and investigations, the chases and arrests and trials rising from local people in local situations. This alone guaranteed originality. Being in full control of the series, I was able to make the stories delineate the contemporary changing South, a South that in my opinion was far ahead of the North in coming to terms with the racial justice so recently won by the civil rights movement. Sparta became a town where there were socially prominent and civically important blacks, as well as whites; poor and working-class whites as well as blacks. Politeness and cordiality normally prevailed in the interracial encounters. Interracial romance was shown without comment.

In the last two seasons of the series the star, a dough-colored old leading man, fell in love with and married his costar, a doe-colored leading lady.[3]

Old familiar, well-loved police show dialogue was forbidden. *Heat* was barren of such succulent tidbits as "I want this cleared up fast," "I want to see this killer in twenty-four hours," "I want action," "The mayor wants action," "The governor wants action," "Move!" "Okay, let's move it—now!" "Let's get moving!" "Let's get atta here!" "What're you tryin' to say!" "Wanna keep your job?" "Only doin' my job, mister," "This could mean

---

[3]I, Gillespie, married Councilwoman Delong, played by Denise Nicholas, a renowned beauty.

my job!" "Be better for you if you tell us what we wanna know, and I mean all of it!" "There's a killer out there," "Find that killer!" "Freeze!" "Don't even think about it." The stories we now filmed were of ordinary people who spoke real idiomatic and true colloquial English in a southern community in Mississippi.

I did not always produce art—as I defined it earlier—but I had complete freedom to do so. I had full responsibility for every story and script decision; casting, costume, property, and location decision; music and editing decision. I also had line producers who, knowing what I wanted, made many decisions for me, and gave me valuable advice and assistance with everything. I think I did produce film art—not always, but much of the time. *Heat* was always thoughtful and reflective, like the *Archie* series, but where Archie was funny in his frantic efforts to hold back change, Gillespie was interesting in his maneuvering to accommodate it.

My working hours became longer, usually twelve a day, and more when I directed an episode, but they passed swiftly and happily. Being boss made the work easier. I venture to say that most bosses would say the same, given the talented assistance I had.[4]

Our series was twice given the NAACP Image Award for favorably depicting blacks on film. CBS discontinued the series in 1994. I have many people to thank for my success in the South. We all have many people to thank. But I must acknowledge a large debt to the doctors at Emory University in Atlanta for extending my life.

---

[4]Messrs. Ed Ledding, Herb Adelman, Joe Gannon.

14

• • • • • • •

T he last time I saw my son before he killed himself he was
going one way and I was going another—he into his house, I
driving away to mine—and I was relieved to be getting away
from him for a while. It is hard now to believe that that was my
thought.

I have to remind myself that I had spent the night with him, an
unforgettable night of watching him hunt through the house,
room after room, and then hunt again, driven by cocaine
hallucinations of enemies in the place, one of whom was trying
to steal his wife Angela. She had come with the baby to spend
the night with Nancy and me at our house in Brentwood, and
they were in a two-room guest suite. Hugh had twice knocked on
their door and had been told by Angela to wait till morning, to
go away and let her sleep, to let the baby sleep. He had twice
come back to me in the living room and reported with alarm that
Angela wasn't there. He reminded me of someone else, of
another cocaine frenzy, of other staring eyes, swollen and
inflamed—beloved and precious Howard Rollins, telling me that
voices, including mine, had attacked him from his fireplace,

insulted him about his sexuality and his talent. Howard later escaped the grip of cocaine. Hugh could not.

In the final deadly phase of cocaine intoxication, when suicide is likely, when suicide becomes an inviting alternative to mental agony, the victim cannot save himself by an effort of will; he has lost the power. People deride this: they argue "Surely he has a sober moment when he understands what he is doing and what is happening to him." True, and when I left Hugh at his door he himself was having such a moment. But sober is not drug-free; sober is toxic still, free momentarily from delusions, but far from being rational—being able to discuss the ominous meaning of his condition. In this lucid yet impaired state, pleas to the addict to return to treatment are worse than useless—they are adversely provocative. He is actually in a dying mode. The mode can only be reversed by prolonged detention in a rehabilitation hospital, and this cannot lawfully be imposed upon a person who is not threatening anyone else. The maximum lawful detention of an addict is three days. Allowed to go, the addict relieves the agony of being "down." He immediately orders cocaine from his pusher; riding this cycle, he finally overdoses and dies of heart failure or he insanely kills himself in a panic of paranoia.

Hugh on this cold morning, out of cocaine and oppressed by sorrow and self-hate, asked me to take him home. He wanted first to see Angela, and she came out of her room. She had spent many nights with Hugh like the night I had just spent. Hugh now tried to persuade her to come home with him, but she calmly, firmly refused, told him she loved him, and insisted that he put himself into the hospital. She knew, we knew, he wouldn't, and yet we urged him—it was all we could do. By now the only advice, the only words of sympathy and love we could offer were to him stale and useless. He asked me to drive him to his own house—he would leave his car parked in the street in front of mine, pick it up some other time.

I Think I'm Outta Here

I drove him home. I can't recall what we talked about; it wasn't important in itself, a little evasive chatter apropos of nothing, but significant of how our once comfortable feelings had changed. My diary of the day records:

Brentwood, Sunday, March 19, 1995

I stayed up all night trying to monitor Hugh, but failed to remain constantly awake. He damaged nothing in his frenetic moving from room to room—damaged only himself with the cocaine he had with him. How can I describe the deeply melancholy experience it was? He was docile, but quite insane the whole night. I had dozed on the sofa and wakened to find him standing near me, staring down at me. He looked worried. He asked me if I was all right, and I replied that I was. "You were making terrible sounds, Pop" he told me, "and I thought maybe you were having an attack of some kind." "No, no" I assured him, "I'm fine. The sounds are just extravagant snores due to overweight, bad breathing and whatever." "Does Mom ever mention it?" "Oh sure, plenty." "You better get a checkup, Pops." He was normal again. We went to the kitchen to make coffee and Nancy and Angela soon joined us. The baby was still fast asleep. Hugh asked Angela to come home with him but she calmly refused; she told him firmly, patiently, that he had to commit himself indefinitely to a cure facility, but immediately to St John's Hospital detox center. He argued bitterly, though quietly, that all he needed was a change in our attitudes—we weren't helping him, standing by him and making life comfortable again. He was now "coming down" the last few steps from the coke high, and getting into the mean-sober, rotten phase. His attempts to put Angela and us on the defensive, blaming us for his sad stupid life, were absurd and became vile.

I drove him home. He asked me if I wanted to come in and I

said no, I had to get back to take care of some things. He was a lonely figure crossing the street, finding a key, raising his hand in a small wave, but I was not moved to get out of the car and follow him in. Nance and I took care of Sean from about 2:30 P.M. till 5, and this for me was a great pleasure; he is such an interesting, amusing, bright baby. Angela was visiting friends in the Palisades—had lunch. She returned, picked up the baby and went back to the party for dinner. Nance and I went to 6 P.M. mass at St. Anne's Mexican church in Santa Monica, came home and dined by ourselves. Angela and Sean came back to our house at about 9 P.M. Hugh, having again gotten himself wholly coke-toxic, was phoning us idiotically at 11:45 P.M. We pulled the plugs on the phones.

I have wondered at times, remorsefully, what might have happened if I had gone into the house with him. Would we have sat down and as usual avoided looking directly at one another, and tried to find something to talk about, until he fidgeted and chafed and looked a little wild-eyed again, and said "Pops, I think I'll get into bed for some sleep." And I would have said "Go ahead, son, you need some." We would have suddenly tightly hugged and kissed each other. That kind of expression of love was always easy for us because it was primary and needed no words. I would have left, knowing that sleep was truly what he needed, but that what he really wanted to do was make a phone call. And I would have lurked in my car at the head of the street to observe the arrival of the pusher.

Why? I don't know why. What would I have done? Attack him? Take the .38 automatic out of the door pocket? Threaten him with it? Provoke him to some action that would compel me to shoot him? I wouldn't have required much provocation. I would have shot him. Dwelling on the last twelve hours with my boy, I could not make my mind work sanely: my unrelenting fantasy was of killing the pusher—a sign no doubt of derangement. I had had disturbing intimations of losing Hugh. I had been recalling incidents—Nancy and Angela seeing him collapse into unconsciousness and calling 911; tall powerful Preston Hagman[1] restraining Hugh while others begged him to go back into a hospital; his shouting coke-crazy imprecations at me in a sheriff's jail in Georgia—and confusing the real scenes with remembered dreams. The mix had always resolved itself into a single horror, someone telling me of the death of my son. So that long before his death—because I knew he was going to die—I wanted violent revenge on whoever was bringing death to him.

I could see only evil in the pusher. Hugh had said "He's not too bad a guy" when I once asked sourly "What kind of a human being is he, son?" Nobody, according to Hugh, was too bad a guy. What would the people who loved the pusher say? Such people existed. I saw them later in a courtroom. What could they see in him, this creature whom I thought of as a deliberate killer? They saw—they must have seen—a dear loving young man, a son, a brother, a sweetheart, for whom they would do anything in the world. Even if they knew what he was up to? Well, maybe they didn't know. Or, knowing, were persuaded that what he was doing was no great sin—something he shouldn't be doing, of course, but nothing a friend or relative couldn't prevail on him to stop doing. I, on the other hand, saw only a man who went willingly and happily into the drug trade in order to live well by selling deadly substances to the reckless and the unwary. A man who worked at developing a reliable circle of helpless, high-spending addicts who were too mindless to be deterred by the prospect of early death.

What would such a man say of himself? The pusher's simple complacent argument is always that millions of people want his wares, which are merely lay prescriptions for turning depression into delight, and that in flouting the law he is providing products

---

[1] My friend Larry's son, and a friend of Hugh's from childhood.

that are no worse than booze, and should be just as legal. He sees our efforts to punish him as crazy. But wouldn't legalization hurt him? No, this criminal could always compete successfully with legal retailers both in price and incidental services, like round-the-clock delivery. Besides, criminal wholesalers would far prefer dealing with criminal retailers. Legitimate commerce inevitably imposes enormous tax and regulatory problems, and in fact invites government to become an implicit partner. Can one imagine the drug cartels merging, and negotiating in a confident bloc with governments everywhere (like OPEC, for oil) to produce and deliver their salutary products on a respectable basis? Can one imagine governments contemplating this?—at a time when many of them are conniving benignly to extirpate the tobacco industry!

But as the father of a victim of marijuana, amphetamines, cocaine, heroin—all items offered on the pusher's menu—I ask first and foremost not the question of how legalization could be successfully established, but how it would diminish for us the threat of a spreading nationwide disease. By making the poison easier to acquire, how does law help the addicted self-poisoner?

Returning to this fellow Harry, I shall never forget him somberly staring at me when I was on the witness stand under attack by his lawyer, twisting his head about in dismay at my persecution of him, though it was he who was suing me—for ten million. His sad look may have been just an inapt pose for the eyes of the jury, but I could not be sure that it wasn't a genuine, however skewed, emotional response. His lawyer characterized him as the "little guy" whose rights were being trampled by a "big guy." The big guy (he pointed at me) wanted to shift blame for his son's suicide away from himself, the indifferent father who was responsible for it. The lawyer, as palpable a knave as ever I did see, told the jury that his case was really about championing the cause of the little guy. He implored the jury of little guys to be the righteous voice of one of their own. But the jury's unanimous resounding reply was that they rejected any identification with this particular little guy. I learned later when I met the jury that in fact they cared about as much for him as for a roach.

In December of 1994 Angela was deeply worried. She didn't tell us the worst of her fears. When we called her and asked "How are things?" she answered "Not much change. I just keep hoping." Note that an addict's loved ones use circumspect language. The question "How are things?" means "Is he clean today?" The answer "Not much change" means "I haven't seen him snort coke, or gulp vodka, but I think he did." Why do we talk in code? Code, we hope, will protect us from the awful truth of plain language. We are wrong, of course. We feel the pain of the truth in spite of any evasion, and we find that the evasion itself inflicts a pain. Angela was doing more than just hoping. She and Hugh were visiting a psychologist, a therapist whose specialty was addiction, she to get help in dealing with it, he to get himself off it, and they were consulting the therapist together and singly several times a week. She was working hard to maintain something like a normal marital environment. But Hugh was taking drugs: cocaine and vodka, and various prescribed "uppers" and "downers" he was getting from his doctor.

Angela told us that she wanted to bring the baby to Atlanta, to her mother's house, for Christmas. I assumed that Hugh would go with her, and I was content with that arrangement; he would be separated from his pushers, both in New York and Los Angeles, which hardly would be an obstacle to his "scoring," but would be at least a benign inconvenience for him. I was remembering our Christmas of 1993 in New York and praying that we could avoid another of the same sort. My thoughts are in my diary of the period.

New York, Friday, December 17, 1993

Bob consulted with Hugh at his apartment in the Dakota. Nancy had set up the meeting. They joined us afterward at our place at about 6:30 P.M., left at about 8:00 P.M. [Bob: my brother the psychiatrist, who lives and practices on West 71st Street. Our place is our apartment at 67th Street and Central Park West.] I don't know what Angela is going to do about the holidays— whether or not she'll stay here in New York—not that staying here with him is the best thing for her to do. Maybe all of us ought to accept his illness as something we have to live with, not fight. I don't know. I'm merely casting about for something new to say. Everything I say is old. *Is there* anything new?

New York, Saturday, December 18, 1993

He got into a big argument with Angela. These continual fights they have are exclusively about drug use. There is no other matter in contention between them. They have everything: love, youth, a career, a home, a precious baby.

Hugh walked out and flew to LA, leaving wife, babe, parents, family to spend Christmas without him. No 'bye to me, and his last word to his mother was that she is "a big mouth"—this because she asked Bob to talk to him. He is in a familiar mean mood; it can swing abruptly to happy, and then swing back again to mean in a day. Angela thinks he will fly back here for Christmas. I pray for him.

Nance and I went for a quick look-in at Mama at The Esplanade, then went to 5:30 P.M. mass at Blessed Sacrament. We said hello to the pastor, Father Robert B. O'Connor (no relation), who I understand has been over to see Mama. Then we took the Holmeses and Angela and Sean to Patsy's for dinner, 9:00 P.M. to 11. [The Esplanade: residence hotel on West End Avenue where

Nancy situated my mother and Jim, her brother. Holmeses: Dr Herbert and wife Carol.]

New York, Tuesday, December 21, 1993

Hugh came back to NY today. Three days in LA. Why? What did he do there? He coked without interference—what else? There is nothing else a cocaine addict wants to do.

He rang from the plane to say it was American Flight 80.

His plane, due at 4 something, got down at 6:45 P.M., and the car we sent missed him. He rang from the terminal sore at everybody, needing cash for a cab. Why? Where is his own cash? I didn't ask, just told him I'd leave money with our doorman—he could stop here and get it and continue in the cab up to 1 West 71st Street. That's what he did. But he soon came legging it back down here, having got a rough reception from Angela (his story). He started home again later, walked with me in the Park when I took Emma out at 10:15 A.M., and then decided to return with us and stay in our apartment until things settled down.

New York, Wednesday, December 22, 1993

Up and out with the dog before 9:00 A.M.

Hugh stayed in bed till after noon, then got up and went to the Dakota, was allowed in, and went back to bed.

Angela came down here with Sean at about 2:00 P.M. to show him to Lionel [Lionel Larner, my longtime friend and agent], who was here for lunch—delivering Christmas presents—he's off to Switzerland tomorrow.

Calls from Jim and Teresa summoned Nancy and me to The Esplanade [Teresa Monterosa: Mama's housekeeper]. We met Bob there at about 6:30 P.M. Teresa was there, and reported that

Mama hadn't been able to keep food down and had been in bed all day. As always, Mama looked fresh and clean. She opened her eyes when I sat beside her, and her eyes were clear and steady and pretty. She was not able to respond to me, but she seemed to be listening carefully to everything I said, and what I said in several ways was that we all loved her and were very grateful for the good life she had given us. I patted and kissed her, and she kept a knowing eye on me the whole time. She won't be joining us at the Christmas table. I'll be surprised if she lasts till Christmas. Jim said to me "Your mother's real bad" and I said "No I think she's good—she looks good. But she's 93, and it's the end—that's all."

New York, Friday, December 24, 1993

Too cold to go see the tree at Rockefeller Plaza. Besides, on all these sight-seeing occasions I become one of the "sights." Prefer to stay inside, lie on the bed and watch all the celebrating on television. Nancy always makes Christmas fun, but for me it hasn't been fun since kid days. My father made it fun, and that's why now it's sorrowfully nostalgic—a memory of times, love, laughter long gone, never to return.

What are my own son's thoughts about his Christmases past?

Amusing incident: a very fat woman driving a car cut in front of me as I was crossing CPW this morning—yelled out the window—wanted to know if I was who she thought I was. I yelled back "Madam, I'm trying to cross this street with this dog!" By the time I had entered the building and got to the elevator she had jumped out of her car—leaving a frightened male passenger in it—and followed me on the run into the building—with a camera! A doorman was in hot pursuit. "Just one picture!" she wailed. Emma tried to take the camera away from her. She yelped. Emma barked. I whined simplemindedly

"People like to be left alone!" and pushed the elevator door button.

John and JoAnn were with us all day [John and JoAnn Fields, Nancy's brother and his wife.]. So were Angela and the baby. Hugh was around, tight all day. Constantly smoking, agitated, moving around, trying to cover his unhappiness with artificial humor, his own real smart humor not available to him when he's high. He lunched here with us but said he would not be joining us for mass and dinner.

We all, including Sean, went to the 7:00 P.M. Christmas mass at St. Paul's, 59th Street. Ro Murphy joined us [Rosemary Murphy, the actress]. We were seven at dinner afterward at Patsy's. Many patrons there enjoyed seeing me and saying hello. I wished so much that my boy could have been with us. Fans of the show always mention him—expect him to be with me, especially when his wife, baby and mother are with me.

Angela brought home some pasta for him. He cares about nothing but being alone with cocaine—it transports him from his world of fantastic woes to a realm of beautiful (is it?) unreality.

Our limo saw everybody home.

I fed Emma and aired her at 11:00 P.M., and encountered a homeless man at the entrance to the Park, white, in his forties, shambling along muttering to himself, a little bent by the sorry pack of trove on his back, and I attempted to give him one of my twenties [I try to keep three or four handy at holiday times. I keep fives with me on ordinary nights]. "Nah, I got money" he said, and kept moving. Then he half-turned and growled "Thank you sir, but I don't want to spoil the spirit of Christmas."

New York, Saturday, December 25, Christmas Day 1993

Hugh came in at about 10:00 A.M. just as I was leaving for the Park. I didn't wait; he had come to see Nance.

The doctor visited Mama and put her on IV. He arranged for a nurse-aide to visit her on the hour and check things. Teresa was there for a while too; her husband drove her in from Woodside.

Call from Joe Sherman [old friend and composer of music for *Heat* and *Brass*] in Marina del Rey, and from Burgess Meredith in Malibu. We called Denise Nicholas. I couldn't reach Howard Rollins; the Georgia operator said his number had been changed to an unpublished number. I called Yavroyan and left holiday greetings on the recorder to him and to Howard [John Yavroyan, Howard's friend and manager.].

I called Claire [my assistant] at our house in Conyers, Georgia—said hello too to Joan and Patrick, who are staying there with her for the holidays.

Wonderful big gourmet Christmas dinner at Bob's prepared by Marie and the kids: Leigh, Elyse, David. At table, besides the cooks—Bob, Marie, Hugh, Angela and Sean; Nance and I—and under the table, Emma. We all assembled at 5:00 P.M. and got home between 10:30 and 11.

Hugh delighted me by being fine and sober at dinner, utterly normal and of course charming. Bob and Marie are very good hosts. Happiest Christmas family dinner in ages, even though Mama could not be with us, and Jim had to stay with her at The Esplanade.

New York, Sunday, December 26, 1993

John and JoAnn joined us for mass at St. Jean Baptiste, and for dinner at The Post House.

Hugh and Angela took care of Emma at the Dakota while we were gone, but between 7:20 P.M. when we dropped her off till 11:10 when we picked her up, she was neither fed nor aired, tho' I left food for her. At the apartment door Hugh said, turning her over to me, "We're both sick now—we couldn't go out with her." They have the flu, but he's been on something. What? Probably a couple of things. I think heroin, for one. He has a connection here in Manhattan, close by. Hugh and Angela, though they plainly love each other and are crazy about their baby, don't appear to be having any fun together. When poor Ugo [Hugh] is not blotto, he's ill recovering from blotto, or suffering trying to fight it off, leaving Ange in a permanent state of funk unable even to think of living a normal life. I hate to think it, but she may by now have had it with him. I think she's nearly ready to take the baby and bolt.

New York, Monday, December 27, 1993

Hugh here at 11:00 A.M. to see his mom about something. He seemed quite all right.

We were in all day and through the evening. Nancy and I grabbed some eats from the larder here. We took care of Sean C. while his mom and pop went out for dinner with David and Elyse. They came back and collected the little guy at about 10:30 P.M. and wheeled him home up Central Park West, asleep and well bundled up—weather was below freezing. It was 22 degrees at 11 when I gave Emma her last stroll.

New York, Tuesday, December 28, 1993

My blood pressure at 4:45 P.M. 147/76, pulse 78. Hugh and Angela dropped off Sean for "sitting" while they saw a movie. They picked him up at 8:30. N. and I dined alone at Des Artistes; we got a lot of things talked over, one of them being the matter of the inheritance for Hugh: he will have one, and a good one, but how and when should he get it? What will the conditions be?

George joined us for a chat [George Lang: owner of Des

Artistes]. The girl assistant manager (at the door) came over and told us that everyone in the place was murmuring about our being there. I should make believe—even to myself—that this kind of thing leaves me *blasé*, but the truth is, it pleases me and I let the pleasure show.

New York, Wednesday, December 29, 1993

Snow at noon, but it couldn't have been predicted from the sunny beauty of the early morning when Emma and I went to the park.

Angela and Nancy to see *Cats*. John and JoAnn to see the two-part play *Angels in America* and *Perestroika*. When the show broke I met everybody at the Russian Tea Room—for years a much overrated restaurant, which Nancy wanted the Fieldses to see. The borscht was as usual too thin. Angela and Sean stayed at our place for the night. And Manuela [our housekeeper] stayed too, the weather being bad.

Angela's reason for staying here was that it was yet another bad old cocaine day for Hugh. It's taken me a long time to accept the central fact of this addiction thing: a cocaine and heroin user wants to do nothing really but *use*. Angela tells me that passing the night with a cokehead at close quarters is "like being with a big mechanical toy that can't be switched off."

New York, Thursday, December 30, 1993

Angela went off with Nance, John and Jo to see the Miró show at MOMA [The Museum of Modern Art, of which we are members]. Sean remained with us—Manuela and me—and was simply the best-behaved baby in town—not an angry cry out of him all day, just gabbling and chortling in his playpen, napping in his crib. His mama came back alone and took him home about 3:30 P.M., but she fled back here with him at 7 P.M.—same old torment—by which time the others had returned and we were all fixing dinner.

New York, Friday, December 31 (New Year's Eve)

Small party here tonight, as usual. Not a happy day in the forenoon—Hugh in his dope pit at the Dakota, Angela deep in sadness here, wondering how long her marriage can stand this strain. And my mother over in The Esplanade dying.

But there must be something the matter with me, because I'm rather composed in confronting it all instead of being in a slough of melancholy. Am I callous coming into old age? I'm surprised that I have no tears. I wonder if Prozac should be credited. Or blamed? After two years of taking it I feel no ill effects—nothing physical—though I do feel in a way closed in, as though defended from strong emotions—sometimes unenthusiastic. But then I've always been odd about enthusiasm—stingy with it. Like Mama. And also like Mama—when we *have* been enthusiastic, particularly about people, we've often been amusingly wrong.

Bob yesterday told Mama's doctor that he didn't want him to keep her going artificially at age 93—injecting her with this and that—feeding her intravenously when plainly her system is no longer able to ingest food. She's barely semiconscious, not able to swallow—and what small evacuation she accomplishes evinces some bleeding somewhere.

Hugh and Angela did not come to the party—spent the night together trying to believe each other's vows. Jim didn't want to come—thought he'd better stay with Mama at The Esplanade.

The party began at 9. Florry and Noma got here at 8:30 [Florry Barnett and Noma Copley, NY friends whom we met in Italy].

231

Others: Anne and Jerry and Amy Stiller; Bob and Marie and their kids; Herbie Holmes without Carol (ill) but with his aunt; Ro Murphy; Domingo De La Cueva [Cuban friend, art collector and jeweler, resident of Venice, Italy]; half a dozen more. Paul Trueblood played piano from nine till two in the morning of Jan. 1. Manuela and her husband and son, Adam and George, served. Turkey, ham, meatballs, cheeses, cold beans, hot pota- toes *au gratin,* caviar, champagne, still wine, spirits of all kinds, tarts, cakes, candies, fruit.

N. and I were alone and got to bed by five-thirty in the morning.

New York, Saturday, January 1, 1994 (New Year's Day)

Mama died at about 6:00 A.M. Bob and Marie were hardly back home when they got the phone call—5:45.

Mama died as she lived—no trouble to anybody. She died, I think, peacefully—certainly not consciously. Nancy said "She gave us all a great life." True, she did. She was as old as the century; in April she would have been 94. I'm going to miss her more than I can imagine at the moment. I used to enjoy—so did she—going to her for long "family" talks with plenty of laughs—many more laughs than sighs—and going out in a gang in a big car for dinners in good restaurants—and my boasting to her about this and that. But all that ended a couple of years ago when she began to drift away from conversations, as we all drift from talk we are failing to understand. She always enjoyed speaking a little German with me, or some words of Yiddish, because funny comments and expressions are more available in these tongues, and she remembered them very well to the end— to the time, that is, when comprehension at last left her—per- haps two years ago.

N. and I met Bob and Marie at 4:30 at The Esplanade, and with

Jim talked over the funeral plan. Then we four went to Cooke's in 72nd Street and arranged a $9,000 funeral—nice-looking oak casket, three cars, one-day viewing Monday the 3rd, tomorrow; mass at Blessed Sacrament Tuesday morning at eleven-thirty and burial right afterward at Calvary. Cooke's is a neat well-kept but hardly elegant establishment. We picked it for convenience sake: like the church, it's here in our West Side neighborhood in walking distance from all our apartments. Nance, though not disturbed by the place, thinks Mama herself would not have chosen it.

We went to the All-State Cafe in 72nd Street for a meal at 7, then came back to our place to compose a message to the *Times.* I wrote it, Bob amended it, and I faxed it to the paper's city desk at about 9:30. Bob was tired. He had wanted a "private service," no embalming, no viewing, burial tomorrow. I understand him; his memories of many funerals hurt him. He's probably right—simple and quick is best. But I recall Mama's remarking on such funerals: she thought they were cold and too plainly *déclassé*, and at the same time she always cheered for economy, and economy particularly in this sad project.

New York, Sunday, January 2, 1994

Up and out at ten to the slushy park with Emma. When a small mutt snapped at her she snarled and attacked it, causing its woman owner to scream hysterically "Put that dog on a leash!" I pretended to kick Emma's ass and ran her off. No harm done, though the little dog may have a stroke later, in which sad event its owner will surely track me down and sue me.

I phoned Loretto. I phoned Bob Sias [old friend from Montana, who knew my mother well]. Long reminiscences about Mama with both of them.

Angela wheeled Sean down to our place and we walked a little in the Park—not much, because it was darkening and quite cold. She says Hugh is okay, but much distressed "going off"—in other words, quitting. Mama's death has something to do with his trying again to quit. Ange strolled back up to 72nd with Sean Carroll at about seven.

At 8:30 we joined Barbara and Brian O'Doherty for dinner at Des Artistes [Barbara is a professor of art at Barnard; Brian, a well-known painter]. Very good. George Lang came over and brought us a bottle of his own reserve Medoc. We came back to our place for a touch of dessert.

Got into bed before midnight, wishing I'd got in before ten.

New York, Monday, January 3, 1994

Mama's viewing began at 2 P.M. and ended at 9. Bob and Marie and Nancy and I were there the whole time. So were Jim and Teresa.

Many visitors came, but few were old friends of Mama's; the old friends are all gone. Visitors were friends of Bob's and Marie's and Nancy's and mine, and their spouses and kids.

And of course the young people: David and Elyse and Leigh, and one or two of their friends; and Hugh, Angela and Sean the baby.

The *Daily News* carried the story I gave AP in its obituary space in first position. From the *Times* I expected nothing, and nothing was what I got—no mention at all.

Mama's makeup was quite good. She looked very nice. The pretty woman she always was could be seen in her still face, and in a photo placed near her, of herself as a girl of about nineteen—in a dancing pose and costume for *A Midsummer Night's Dream*. Nancy had placed the photo within the raised cover of the coffin.

Jim, on arriving, said to an assistant manager "Cooke has places all over the city." "Yes we do" answered the man. Jim

nodded. "You're mob-connected, right?" The surprised employee simply said "No."

We took a dozen visitors to dinner at 9:30 at Scaletta's in 77th
Street.

New York, Tuesday, January 4, 1994

Final viewing of Mama at Cooke's—only family were there.

Mass was the regular 11:30 daily mass at Blessed Sacrament,
and many neighborhood people were present. I liked that. The
soprano assisting the service had a fine professional voice. Father
Robert O'Connor, alone on the altar, read the traditional short
service and commented well on life and death. Our non-Catholic
friends admired him.

It was windy and cold under a sombre sky, but Calvary
Cemetery under snow looked beautifully antique, and was
curiously comforting. We took everybody at graveside for a two
o'clock lunch at the Water's Edge in Long Island City. They were
the Robert O'Connors, and Elyse, David, and Leigh with her
friend Tom; Jim O'Connor; the Peter Chandlers [my niece
Deirdre, daughter of my brother Hugh, and her husband], who
drove down from Boston with their two new adopted babies
from Paraguay; the Hugh O'Connors with Sean Carroll; Matt
O'Connor [Deirdre's brother], who flew in from LA last night;
Herbie Holmes, Larry Stern [close friend and business manager],
Lionel Larner, Paul Blitzblau [close friend and widely known
designer-contractor]; Jerry and Anne Stiller; Robert Brown; Teresa Monterosa; Tom Sabatello [for years our driver and my
mother's driver in New York]; and some Irish-American gent of
about sixty who knew my mother from somewhere, and caught a
ride to the cemetery with Herbie, Jerry and Anne (Herbie's car).
He then of course had to be taken to lunch. A classic *schnorrer*.
Every funeral and post-obsequial gathering has one of these.

Larry Stern surprised me, and I was touched to see him. I had no idea he would make the trip in from the Coast.

New York, Wednesday, January 5, 1994

I stayed in all day except for a couple of outings with Emma. On the first of these I met my pal Walter [a homeless man who frequented the Park] from Oklahoma, who offered me a gulp of his Cuervo Gold tequila. I refused. Walter likes me. I have twice given him twenties and he has given me a pair of heavy woolen socks. Today I went back to the apartment and got him a sleeping bag I had promised him, one that Nancy bought a few years ago for one of the kids—David, I think. It was never used—pristine in its green duffel bag. I brought it down and gave it to him at the entrance to the Park, as he wouldn't cross CPW and meet me at the entrance to 75. Embarrassed, I suppose. I made him hide his tequila in one of the plastic bags he was carrying. "Don't let people see that. Many of them are all too glad to be able to call you a drunken bum." Walter, about a third of the way into his trip to Blotto, shrugged and smiled and said "A drunken bum is what I am." Mama would have had a great laugh over that one. I'm afraid he'll have the bag taken from him. I'm afraid he may sell it or trade it for booze. But I can't worry. When he asked me what he could do for me, I told him to ask The Lord to do me a special favor—help someone I love very much. "If *you* ask, Walter, I bet the Lord will do it." Walter thought about it. "If he helps him, will you tell me?" I said I surely will.

Bob came by to show me Mama's will, which he had got from the lawyer. His kids will get the income from the Putnam Fund when Jim dies. Deirdre and Matt can expect well over 100 Gs each. Nancy and I are left nothing; this was our wish. Hugh will get what Mama called "just a token" of her great affection for him—5 Gs. She reveals by implication that she and I talked this over, and were in agreement. It's true. Seeing her signature on the will made me cry. I hadn't cried up to then. She had signed her name in the small beautiful hand I remembered so well. How often she had written Elise P. O'Connor for me!—for the thousands of things I needed, or thought I needed, over a lifetime.

15

· · · · · · ·

And now in the year 1994 it was December again, and Nancy told me that we had an invitation to spend Christmas with other friends in another town. We needed it. There is hardly a town so different from the rest of the world as Rome, yet Rome is still the world, a most comforting corner of it. We accepted the invitation. I got a piece of very loving and entirely useless advice: "Leave your troubles behind you and have fun over there." But the pith of trouble is thought, and thought will not be left.

New York, Tuesday, December 20, 1994
NEW YORK TO ROME

Blues before departure. Why? I don't know. Always happens. The feeling should be elation—beautiful trip starting. But what is normal for the world eludes me. Conclusion? I have a "problem."

All serene getting away. We dropped Emma at a doggy hotel.

Nance did not overpack. We got to Kennedy moderately early for the flight. *Tutto va bene!*

On board the plane, I thought N. would buy out the tax-free gift store. *Now at last we have too much to carry!* Back to normal.

Watched a movie without listening. Do it all the time now— my habit.

Rome, Wednesday, December 21, 1994

Landed at Fiumicino at 8.45 A.M., went swiftly through customs and immigration, I in a wheelchair [legs haven't been good since veins were removed in 1989 and used in cardiac repair], and then waited 40 minutes for our driver. We gave up, took another car and got swindled—$140 from there to Via Sabotino. I was too weary to argue; if I had maintained that the *tariffa* should have been $70, the *autista* would have held up a thumb and forefinger to say there were two of us.

Rested all day. Sydne and Roberto have been in Naples— drove back in the afternoon and we all sat down to a fine dinner made by Lisa [Sydne's youngest sister]: *pasta alla salsa tomate, insalate delle tomate e formaggio, prosciutto, vino, biscotti, cafe, grappa.*

Much talk and into bed by 1 A.M.

Sydne Rome the actress[1] and her husband, Dr Roberto Bernabei, who think of us as their American family, welcomed us to their apartment in Via Sabotino, and we began a week of pre-Christmas visits and parties, with a number of old friends, both Romans and resident Americans. We dined with Father Sean Foley, pastor of the American church in Rome, Santa Susanna. It was through the Paulist priests of that church that we found and adopted Hugh in 1962.

---

[1] An American, close friend, who built her career in Europe.

I Think I'm Outta Here

Rome, Thursday, December 22, 1994

Fog—mist falling, then a few dashes of thin sweet rain. N and I with driver Maurizio went to the Piazza di Spagna; he could go no further into old Rome because of traffic restrictions. I stood beside the *fontana* and recalled being there with Hugh, aged six: an *americano* stared at him and said "You look like an American kid—what're you doin' here." Hugh stared back and said pleasantly "I was born here."

Walked from there to Gucci, Bulgari, Ferragamo, Missoni, Bottega Veneta. No important purchase anywhere, but this is merely reconnaissance: serious forays will occur later.

Back to Via S. Slept for three hours. Why so sleepy? I don't know.

Sydne's party began at 9 P.M.—guests arriving—fifteen altogether, including Laura Ungaro, Sydne's sister-in-law, wife of the designer, and her daughter Cosima, four.

Compliments from people who had seen Sydne in "Who Was Geli Bendl?", a *Heat* episode that I wrote for her and brought her to Georgia to star in. Hugh had got a great kick out of acting in the episode with Sydne, whom he has loved from childhood days. When I was asked at the party if "Geli Bendl" hadn't been an important TV hit in the States ("Surely it must have been!"), I had to confess "I'm afraid nobody really noticed it." The series was widely loved and watched, but as it was no longer a Hollywood but a wholly Atlanta production, it had no importance in Hollywood. What I mean is, "the industry" was no longer watching it.

Nancy and I went out Christmas shopping, and our boy was constantly, above all, in our thoughts. And Sydne, who had known Hugh from the time he was seven, wanted to hear about him, and talk and cry about him—sad, like everyone who loves an addict, to be unable to advise something to do. Who can advise when there is no advice to give? I told Sydne that I had written a new series for CBS entitled *Savannah,* and that I wanted to bring her back to the States to costar in it. I wanted to use some of my *Heat of the Night* cast in it—for instance, Hugh, and I desperately wanted him to "get himself straight."

I needed some help myself, but there is little help available to one who loves the addict—help before a final tragedy occurs, help in learning how to let go of the anxiety of the days, in waiting for the worst. "Let go" is the apt phrase, for it is obviously true that we ourselves invite and cling to our anxieties. Some people are helped by remedial groups like Alanon. Nancy and Angela had already attended Alanon sessions. They had thereby, incidentally, infuriated Hugh—which is typical.

We drove to the Via Veneto for our invariable survey—to see if it was anything like it used to be, and knowing of course that it wouldn't be. "Used to be" was 1961 and 1962 when we were making *Cleopatra,* and the movie business was in immense bloom. The big studio called *Cinecitta* (Movie City) was largely given to the re-creation of Rome of the thirties B.C. But other pictures were being made all over the town, and "the Veneto," as everyone called that teeming thoroughfare, was the place to sit *al fresco* and have a coffee and brandy, and a look at *la dolce vita.* But not now; the avenue was bereft of the gaudy charm of thirty years ago, and when I made the excuse "Well it's winter—" I was reminded by Nancy that winter had not in years past driven glittering posturing youth from that "walk of importance."

Rome, Friday, December 23, 1994

I went with Gigo the photographer to the Spanish Steps to make photos for the Italian TV Guide. *Heat of the Night* is well liked in Italy. Also well liked, *Archie,* or *Archibaldo* here.

8.30 P.M., Roberto took Sydne, Lisa and us to Restaurant Moro, one of the best for food in Rome. N. had *sogliola* and I had simply *fettucine truffato* and a mushroom salad. Perfect. Nancy phoned LA, learned that Hugh went to Atlanta today. Hadwig [Mrs. Stephen Schneck, our personal assistant for nine years] took him to the plane. Angela and Sean have preceded him by a couple of days. Why? Why would he want to stay in LA by himself. On the phone I said to Angela, "He wouldn't be misbehaving, would he?" "You mean some girl?" "Yes. Is it possible?" She replied with a small unamused laugh: "No—no interest in sex, just cocaine."

Rome, Saturday, December 24, 1994

Nancy went out shopping with Sydne and got some things at Armani for a third off. I went nowhere and was content.

I felt vaguely unwell after dinner, which began at about 9 P.M., and so declined to go to midnight mass with everybody. Roberto found my blood pressure okay at 120/80.

Nance stayed in with me and we watched the spectacular midnight mass at St. Peter's. The others went to the artists' church in Piazza del Popolo, Basilica di Santa Maria in Montesanto, where Sydne and Roberto gave the readings.

They went, after mass, to the Bernabeis' apartment in Via Flaminia and exchanged gifts; and Roberto, Sydne and Lisa got back home at 2:30 A.M.

Rome, Sunday, December 25, 1994

We enjoyed Christmas Day dinner at Ettore Bernabei's big apartment in the Via Flaminia. *Tutta la famiglia* and we, and the former premiere of Italy, Amintore Fanfani and his wife. Ettore, Roberto's father and former head of Italian Television (RAI), is now in independent film production. Dinner was a great banquet.

Rome, Wednesday, December 28, 1994
ROME TO LONDON

Loving good-byes to Renato and Sydne, otherwise a bad departure from Fiumicino 3:15 P.M., carrying far too much baggage on board the plane. I used a wheelchair. I could not have done the walking.

Nor could I have walked at Heathrow where we arrived at 5:00 P.M. (time change in London of −1); got a chair again. We were met by a Daimler and driver, Jeff, a rotund and witty cockney, and got to the Connaught by 6.00 P.M.

Dined in the hotel grill from 7.30 to 9.30 P.M. Superb as always.

Tutti americani in the dining room, talking loudly and happily.

London, Thursday, December 29, 1994

Awake at 8:00 A.M., read till 9:30 and ordered breakfast; it came at 10:00 and, though merely prunes, eggs and bangers (sausage), rolls and coffee, was the best breakfast I can remember. How do you make those everyday items superb? This kitchen knows how.

Nance and I rang Sydne in Rome.

The car (Jeff) took us shopping to Harrods and Burberry, then back to the hotel.

Cocktails 5:30 with John Erman, his and Richard Blair's apartment, Eaton Mansions near Sloane Square. Others, Arny and Ann Porath, Joe Hardy.

We later took the Poraths to dinner at Quaglino's, and Nancy spotted Donagh and Ann [Donagh O'Connor, a second cousin of mine from Dublin, a solicitor, and his wife]. I went over and said hello—they came over to us later. They looked well—visiting people somewhere outside of London.

Hotel by 10:30 P.M.

I Think I'm Outta Here

London, Friday, December 30, 1994

Very gray nippy day, but not raining. At Locke's—bought a cap, a hat, a tie, two pairs of braces.

Came back to the hotel, picked up Nance, and we went to the Tate Gallery to the Whistler showing (we were away from the hotel from about 1 P.M. to 4 P.M.). Whistler was far ahead of his time—prefigured the Impressionists by twenty or thirty years—immensely gifted—intellectually/artistically admirable above all modern painters.

We went to Winfield House in Regent's Park at 7 P.M. and had a drink with our ambassador, Admiral Bill Crowe (from Oklahoma), his wife Shirley and a dozen or more American friends. Bill and Shirley are friends of President Clinton's. As chairman of the joint chiefs the admiral backed the president in his reform of sexuality rules in the armed forces. Until 8 P.M. Then we and the Bakers joined the Bakers' friends Susan McCone and Robert Wesely at the Hotel Capital—the hotel owned by David and Margaret Levin of New York—for a big dinner [The Bakers, Patrick and Joan: parents of Claire, from Arkansas like the president, whom they know well].

We got back to the hotel by 12 A.M., and the car took the Bakers home to Winfield House, where they are staying with the ambassador.

London, Saturday, December 31, 1994

I again felt an odd drain of energy like the one in Rome, and declined to go out in the car with Nancy—preferred to stay in and loll around and be ready to make this party tonight. Whether the energy drain is caused physically or merely perceived mentally, I don't know, but the effect—without pain or nausea—is that I don't wish to talk, think, or move.

245

Called Pacific Palisades, left happy new year message on the machine.

N. came home by 6.30 P.M., and we got ready to go to the Residence for the party at 8:30.

London, Saturday, December 31/January 1, 1995

Grand New Year's Eve party. Good dinner, good merry company, all friends of the admiral's and Shirley's for more than twenty-five years. Drank champagne immoderately, got back to the hotel by taxi at about 1:45 A.M.

It seemed a quiet New Year's Eve for a city like London—I suppose because our routes of travel went through quiet quarters of the city. They may have been whoopin' it up in Trafalgar Square.

London, Sunday, January 1, 1995

4:15 P.M. mass at Church of the Immaculate Conception in Farm Street, a five-minute walk from the hotel. Damp evening but not cold. Priest on the altar reminded me of Trevor Howard. His homily was about the "difficulties" (favorite exegetical word) in considering faith and science side by side. A little abstruse. Why, I cannot tell. As a believer in God I have no misgiving about accepting Darwin and the scientific account of life on this planet. I believe that God, in his immeasurable power and unknowable purpose, is the maker of the mind, the master of science, the manager of all phenomena, the designer of all evolution. I suppose it is impossible for men to conceive such power, and impossible for many men to accept through faith the existence of such power, because it consigns man's own awesome power to a secondary status. But how then can God inspire both science and the Bible, which we cannot reconcile? The answer is that God can inspire and reconcile anything. We walked a circuitous way back, just to see a little more of Mayfair. Our mood was glum; we had heard from Angela by phone that Hugh had returned by himself to LA right after Christmas.

At 7 P.M. we used our car to pick up five of Bill Crowe's guests at Winfield House; we brought them to a Chinese restaurant, Fan Ching, then sent Jeff back in the car to Winfield to pick up and transport another load. We did the same things in reverse at the end of the evening. Again we were the admiral's guests—we and most of the joyful crowd who were at the New Year's Eve party. The evening was different for us, because of anxiety about home. I was dull. I must have seemed ill; somebody asked me if I was feeling all right.

Nance lost her purse somewhere. *Thought* she had lost it. She found it finally in our rooms. She is even more distraught than I, and distracted—thoughts of home never leave her.

London, Monday, January 2, 1995

I went nowhere except downstairs to lunch with Nance and Josie [Josie McAvin, an Oscar-winning set decorator, was stage manager of our tour to the Edinburgh Festival of 1951, and has been a close friend since then]. Excellent.

The two ladies went shopping at Harrod's.

Another dinner party at the Residence went on till midnight.

London, Tuesday, January 3, 1995

Car brought us out to the village of Uley in Gloucestershire (in the Cotswolds) to visit the Gordons, Ian and Chris, two-and-a-half-hour drive from London. Arrived for lunch.

Stayed in gabbing—weather too wet for walking the grounds. Napped.

Dinner guests: Lucy and Fiona, wives of Ben and Guy Sang-ster, the latter sons of Chrissy's by a first marriage; Duff and Phyllida Harte-Davis, neighbors, authors.

Bed by midnight after much pleasant chatting. The daughters-in-law are very attractive, smart girls.

Uley, Wednesday, January 4, 1995

Ian drove us to Oxford, an hour or so through Tetbury and Dursley and other picturesque villages of the Cotswolds (Cott's Hills). Lots of sheep farming on the moors.

Ian showed us Oxford city and a couple of the colleges; we entered Trinity, once his.

Lunch at a very good little place, and then Jeff came out from London in the car and met us and drove us back to London by 5 P.M.

We met Liam and Tessa at the Haymarket Theatre, a lovely old house reminiscent of The Gaiety Dublin in its best days [Liam and Tessa Gannon, father and daughter, whom we have known since Dublin days, 1951. Liam and I were acting colleagues at the Gate Theatre]. The play was *Arcadia* by Tom Stoppard—in its eighth month, well reviewed and apparently popular, and to me unengaging—a walk-out really—but we stuck it to the end, three long hours later.

Supper at Langan's at 11 P.M.

London, Thursday, January 5, 1995

Lunch guests of Gloria MacGowran's at Langan's: we, Tara MacGowran, Michael Adams, Alexander Marquess of Bath and a girl named Mariella; Mike Dyer, Bobby Hesketh, and of course Gloria—nine in all [Gloria and Tara MacGowran are the widow and daughter of the actor Jack, another old friend and colleague of mine from Dublin days]. I left earlier, feeling poorly—sent the car back for Nance.

We met Liam and Tessa at Wyndham's Theatre to see *Three Tall Women*. Albee in this entertaining play doesn't have anything to say of societal concern—no view of things—but his characters seem familiar to us—amusing and touching. Unlike Williams, who said that his own characters were bizarre species, Albee invents people we all recognize.

Back to the Connaught Grill, the four of us, for supper.

Car (Jeff) brought the Gannons home; we got to bed by 1:30 A.M.

London, Saturday, January 7, 1995

Hugh rang me 6 P.M. London time, 9 A.M. LA time. We were happy to talk to him, and he sounded quite all right, but I was sure he went wrong when he got back home from Atlanta some time between Christmas and the New Year. There was something suspect about his returning alone to LA—anger between him and Angela that can only have been about drugs.

We had Admiral Crowe and Shirley to dinner here at the Connaught. I broached the question of using the armed forces in the international drug war. The admiral said it made sense in principle, however . . .

Sunday, January 8, 1995
LONDON TO NEW YORK

Left hotel at 8:30 A.M. for Concorde departure 10:30 (5:30 A.M. NY, to arrive before 9 A.M. NY).

Picture of Lord Bath in *The Times*. His five-million-dollar Titian was heisted from his home while he was lunching with the bunch of us at Langan's Thursday. I pointed out to Jeff, our driver, that he and I absented ourselves early from that lunch. Have the coppers thought of that? And here I was, the next day, hopping on a fast plane! "But it's all right, Jeff" I said. "I'm sure they won't detain you long."

I used a wheelchair again. Legs are hurting. It's not the aircraft but the terminals that try my nerves—not the flying but the leaving and arriving. We were a few minutes late getting away at Heathrow. The flight took 3 hr. 15 min., and we arrived at the terminal at Kennedy at 9:15 A.M. NY.

We retrieved Emma *en route* home (Tommy met us), and found her lively and terribly sentimental (cried all the way home in the car), but very thin—hadn't been eating well. She immediately ate very well at the apartment, and enjoyed—and needed—a quick march in the Park.

Nancy talked to Hugh in LA; she said he didn't sound good.

We went (car, Luigi) to mass at St. Paul's at 5:15 P.M., and then to dinner at Patsy's.

New York, Monday, January 9, 1995

Jim died early this morning. A male nurse on night duty with him called Bob at about 6:00 A.M. The nursing service let us know at about 11 A.M., and Nance went over to the apartment to meet Teresa. Bob called, told me he had already made all funeral arrangements for Wednesday, including a mass at Blessed Sacrament at 10:00 A.M., but did not wish to announce the death in the papers—did not want to have to call people and impose obsequies upon them. I told him he was right to do it quickly. I don't know whether he is or not, but I have no opinion worth an argument. Emotionally I feel flat, which is odd. But I have known—everybody knew—that Jim was going this month, and we all, like him, were hoping he would. He has been living in

misery and asked his doctor about "a shot." The doctor regret-
fully refused.

Other than walking Emma, I didn't go anywhere.

Talked to Lionel. He had finally reached Sinitsky, who
admitted apologetically that he had not yet read *Savannah,* and
assured Lionel that I am very important to CBS. I said to Lionel
"That's very nice of Larry Sinitsky, but the truth is, I am of no
importance whatever to CBS. Neither is Larry, neither is his
boss Peter Tortorici." [CBS top executives, soon afterward
dumped by CBS.]

Phoned Hugh about Jim's death. He regretted it—seemed
sober but distracted. Voice toneless, controlled. I thought it's like
a fantastic piece of sci-fi fiction, in which a strange being inhabits
the person of someone you love.

New York, Wednesday, January 11, 1995

A small, cold funeral for Jim. He would not have minded. It
wasn't much better than burial on a battlefield, which, however,
I think he would have preferred. Bob ordered the plainest
possible box. No wake. No announcements. Nance would have
done something different, but she has been too ill to move or
think. So at 10:00 A.M. about 20 people gathered at Blessed
Sacrament in 71st Street. A dozen or so came from The Esplanade. Everybody liked him at The Esplanade. I said a few
words—could have said a few more and made them better. Bob,
Marie, Elyse and David attended. They drove to Calvary in their
own car. Nancy couldn't be there—very sick in bed. Teresa and
Father O'Connor and I went out in a town car. Gloomy, freezing
cold day. We said the prayer—just the seven of us—and left
before the coffin was lowered. No tears. Nothing at all. I can't
figure myself out: I loved him, and should have paid more
attention to him, and didn't; and I should have cried for him, and
didn't. We all just went home.

Jim, I think, got the last place left in the O'Connor plot. Where will the rest of us go? Only at graveside do we ever wonder about it. As for me—wherever I shall last be seen on this earth, find a nearby spot.

I stayed in the rest of the day. Napped. I sleep a lot probably to get away from things.

New York, Thursday, January 12, 1995

Meeting at 10:30 A.M. with Jonathan Segal at Knopf was pleasant but not promising. I think he preferred talking about himself to talking about me (like my pal Walter Anderson at *Parade* magazine), but I enjoyed it that way. I left the 80 pages I prepared for him and came home (car—Tommy).

Call from Victor Navasky. He invited me to join him and Doctorow for lunch. I declined with thanks—wanted to remain here with Nance.

New York, Monday, January 16, 1995

Angela has left Aderno again—staying at the beach, or at the home of a friend, pending Hugh's next move.

New York, Thursday, January 19, 1995

Angela called twice—to tell me where she was (with friends) and again to tell me that Hugh had checked into Brotman at 10:00 A.M., PCT.

Lionel called to say Sinitsky and Tortorici had nixed *Savannah*. I'm sorry about it. But not surprised. The idea and the material are new. "New" confuses them. "New" confuses everybody in television.

I Think I'm Outta Here

Saturday, January 21, 1995
NEW YORK TO LOS ANGELES

Packed.

Flight 89 United late leaving, left at 6:15 P.M. EST, arrived LAX at 8:30 P.M. PCT. Okay flight, but poor food. Watched but did not listen to Stallone movie about explosions and so forth. It is the new Dadaism, in film.

Home to Tilden and into a new bed (redecorated bedroom) by 11:30 P.M. House has been repainted and looks beautiful.

Malibu, Sunday, January 22, 1995

Slept well. Visit from Angela, Sean and Little Nancy at 12:30 P.M. [Nancy Fonseca, 15, daughter of the family who live with us and manage things at Malibu; she was brought home as a new infant and named after my Nancy.] The boy is exceedingly attractive in every way. He'll be two May 18. We all ate a large Mexican lunch prepared by Angelina [Fonseca, Little Nancy's mother]. Hugh is in Brotman. Everybody's hoping.

16

•••••••

I encouraged Nancy to make a trip to Missoula. She doesn't like to be away from here, and from Hugh, at times like this.

Brentwood, Tuesday, January 24, 1995
NANCE LA TO MISSOULA

All up at 5:00 A.M. Hadwig stayed the night here and drove Nancy to LAX at about 6:00 A.M.

Malibu, Wednesday, January 25, 1995

Up at 6:00 A.M. All-night rain still pelting down.

Angela and Sean here for a couple of hours. He's a precious item.

Returned Segal's call at Knopf. He seems respectful of my

writing. He said that he knew there was "a book in there" (pages I had shown him), and would like to help me develop it before putting it in front of the publisher.

Talked to Nance in Missoula. She's anxious to see how the Smithsonian people have mounted the Miller Show. [Fred Miller was the most artistic of the turn-of-the-century western photographers. Portrayed those years of the Crow Indians' social history. He was Nancy's grandfather, and she was curator of a remarkable touring show.]

Hugh called me from Brotman—brief pleasant chat. I don't know why I am so relieved that he is there. Very few addicts are permanently turned around in these places. The usual thing after a patient's sign-out is a few days of sobriety and then a relapse. But he's there—not "using" as I write. Big comfort. A false comfort—every bit as false as a drug high.

Malibu, Sunday, January 29, 1995

Caught a few minutes of DeMille's *Samson and Delilah* on the old movies channel. What a fantastic display of illiteracy, tastelessness, and shrewd commercial instinct.

Talked to Nance in Missoula at 10 A.M. She was having a very good time—especially happy about the way the Smithsonian people have mounted the Miller Show.

To Aderno Way [Angela and Hugh's Pacific Palisades House] to visit the Hugh O'Cs—stayed for dinner of burgers, dogs and corn on the cob. Had not seen Hugh since last September 4th at Malibu. He looked good—was quite sober, was angry with his situation, but not really angry enough with himself. He should be. Too bad he isn't. But he hated going back to Brotman after his 8-hour leave.

Emma was with me and enjoyed a visit with brother Bruno.

I Think I'm Outta Here

Malibu, Monday, January 30, 1995

Call from Garrett about Hugh: he just wanted to know how he was [Dr Garrett O'Connor, my cousin]. What could I say? I said "Hugh is bad, Garry. I'm afraid he's going to walk out of Brotman and binge again."

Nancy—met by car and driver—got home at about 7 P.M.

On TV: Cochran, one of O.J.'s lawyers, unruly in a quiet crafty way, but not interesting—boring. Another of the six or seven defense lawyers, F. Lee Bailey—well spoken but windy. Marcia Clark the prosecutor very well spoken, but bad tempered, easily angered. The judge, Ito, very smart, trying hard to avoid error, but making himself irritating. But so what? They're all doing the best they can—doing their jobs. Easy for me to judge them flippantly.

Malibu, Friday, February 3, 1995

The script Peter Rothberg [from *The Nation*] sent me (10 A.M.) was all wrong for what I want to do. I wrote another—simply a 60-second commercial, and faxed it to their office. Talked to Victor Navasky (in Cambridge, Mass.) about it. He's trying to get advice from the Harvard Business School on putting *The Nation*, for the first time ever, on a profit-making basis.

Malibu, Monday, February 6, 1995

In all day working—and got a little done on *Nash NY*—except for an hour, 4:30 P.M. to 5, when I drove over to Pico to record my commercial for *The Nation* [*Nash NY* is the outline of a novel in my computer].

Earlier: call from Shana Alexander.

Angela and Sean were here. Angela left him for a while to run some errands.

N. and I dined at home on *coq au vin.* We've got to discontinue such foolishness if we're ever going to change our shapes.

Malibu, Tuesday, February 7, 1995

Nance away at 10 A.M. to baby-sit Sean again for a while. She and I stayed in and ate here (201) by ourselves.

Malibu, Friday, February 10, 1995

To Boranni (James) to get the Maserati's wire wheels balanced; back to Foogert to replace the new right front Goodyear with another new one. Then to the body man at Tennessee for an estimate on the damage I did the other day. Old Maser is tough to drive but fun— he's stiff—requires use. It's Hugh's car, born like himself in Italy, same age. Told him about these repairs, etc. Not evidently interested.

Brentwood, Saturday, February 11, 1995

Nance took the Zinners to view the new Getty MOCA museum (under construction) on the Brentwood heights.

I stayed home alternately working and wasting time.

We went to dinner at Carol Rossen's place, met her friend Fred Haines. The Browns were also guests, and so was Piper Laurie. Lots of spirited chat on "the trial," [O. J. Simpson] other chat about *Ulysses*, a screenplay of which Fred Haines wrote (for Strick), which became an inferior film.

Home by about 12:40 A.M.

Brentwood, Monday, February 13, 1995

To Sam with the Maser. Diagnosis: require radio–disc player, three speakers.

To a mechanic to service a/c.

To Dina Merrill's (Ted Hartley) for dinner party for Lynn Redgrave. Among the guests: the Davidsons, Roddy Mac, Craig Stevens and Frances Bergen, David Warner and Sheila, Charlton Heston and Lydia, Michael (radio) and Alanna Jackson. I determined to sit at table with Heston to hear him expound, but he wouldn't. Just chat, at which he's not at all unpalatable.

Brentwood, Tuesday, February 14, 1995

Sean was here—left by his mom—all day, to about 9 P.M. Angela had a lot to do.

Hugh got leave to meet her for lunch, and he met here at 201. He looked solid and strong but his dress was poor. Sean smiled broadly when he saw him. Hugh still assertive, confident, but I doubt whether his actual self-esteem has improved. His clothing compares with the people he has always sought out: inadequate, below par, third rate. He can leave Brotman tomorrow evening.

Brentwood, Wednesday, February 15, 1995

Left the Maserati at Four Oaks Garage, 7th and Colorado, 10:30 A.M.

Home all day.

Dinner at home, we two.

Hugh ended his sojourn in Brotman this evening.

Brentwood, Thursday, February 16, 1995

Home all day, and slept too much.

Got some work done on *Nash* in the afternoon.

Talked to Hugh on the phone. I offered to let him drive either the BMW wagon or the Jag coupe as an alternative to buying an expensive car for himself (he has only the TR-6). He declined the offer, but said he would accept the BMW as a gift which he would then sell—and buy a car he liked better.

FedExed the Laurences to let Serena know that Jan Glaser liked her tape very much.

Ordered in Italian stuff for dinner for the two of us.

Brentwood, Friday, February 17, 1995

Stayed home, both of us and Hadwig, putting closets and storage spaces in order.

Jay Nakimura here to set up Tandberg reel-to-reel. And later Hugh arrived to use it to transfer some old master 7.5s to metal 3.75 cassettes. He's looking very well.

I got in a little work on *Nash NY*.

We joined Denise Nicholas and Clarence Williams (his treat) for dinner at a restaurant called Georgia on Melrose. Southern style, very nice crowd, well mixed—excellent traditional cooking, well run, most attractive. Home with Denise for dessert.

Left at 11:15 P.M., home by 11:45.

Malibu, Sunday, February 19, 1995

Hugh out of Brotman for the day—gave a brunch here at the Redwood. [House next door to our Moroccan house, which I bought to keep a rock group from buying it. Hugh and Angela often used it.]

Buzz [Burgess Meredith] visiting us, was very clear and witty in conversation, as always, but gets distracted by his thoughts and wanders away. He has a stomach problem and goes into Santa Monica Hospital tomorrow morning for tests.

Nice to see Hugh with his friends: Kevin, Susan and kids

Oliver, Sean, Nicholas and Kalina; and the couple from the Palisades, Rhonda and Theo Sojurn, and their little boy Miles. Angela brought our Sean over to see us a couple of times. The other kids came over too.

Gene O'Hara and his friend Becky and her little kid Devon were here. Gene came to look at the Silver Shadow. [Gene O'Hara is chief engineer at our car restoration garage.]

Hugh had lots of extra beef and brought it over for us. We used it to give Gene and his friend and the child some dinner at about 7:00 P.M.

Malibu, Monday, February 20, 1995

Up at 8 A.M. Beautiful day, 3rd in a row, clear and bright with a high around 80 degrees. N. to the Valley to look at John and JoAnn's house.

Telephone system here at 30826 partially out, and the same is so of the doors of our garage.

We baby-sat Sean from 6:30 to 10 P.M., and he and I read many books together. Ange took Little Nancy to dinner and a movie at Cross Creek. Hugh went into town for therapy meetings tonight and tomorrow.

Malibu, Wednesday, March 1, 1995

Angela came in the afternoon and picked up Little Nancy to baby-sit Sean at Aderno [Angela and Hugh's Pacific Palisades house]. They go to a therapy session this evening.

Got in some writing at the Redwood [my home office — working on *Patricios*, a story about the Irish soldiers who formed Mexico's first foreign legion].

We went to mass at Our Lady of Malibu at 7:30 P.M. Received ashes. I never enter this church without remembering my boy's marriage to Angela here — all the hope and happiness.

Brentwood, Saturday, March 4, 1995

We took Angela and Hugh to dinner at the restaurant Georgia. We dined in a bitter atmosphere. No loud words, but many harsh words between our kids, and nobody had a good time. Some very sad silly stuff: for instance, Nancy and I didn't order drinks; we really didn't want them, but Hugh got furious—said we were abstaining because of him, treating him like a child. He insisted that we order drinks for ourselves. We did as he wished. When the drinks came, he said "Screw this!" and ordered a drink for himself. Nobody said a word. Too bad; it was supposed to be celebratory—Angela's birthday. It was miserable.

Brentwood, Tuesday, March 7, 1995

Angela left her house with Sean—came over here at about 6 P.M. Hugh is back on cocaine and she won't remain in the house with him. What a pity. Angela seems at the end of her endurance— furious because Hugh took Sean with him on a coke run to his pusher's apartment. He went in the Jaguar, which wasn't equipped with a child's safety seat. Hugh had been off the coke for 45 days, and then . . . This resumption is undoubtedly the work of his pusher's calling him.

Brentwood, Wednesday, March 8, 1995

Angela and the baby still here. No change evidently at Aderno Drive.

Brentwood, Thursday, March 9, 1995

Lunch at Zinners for the Ian Gordons. [Peter Zinner is a leading film editor, his wife Crista is a sculptor; they are old friends.] Met Sydne Bernard, a prominent art dealer.

Stopped by Hugh's to see him. He looked lousy—coked up, unshaved, shabby in an Eric Clapton T-shirt. Sad. Sad. Heart-breaking.

Brentwood, Saturday, March 11, 1995

Hugh stays home at Aderno smoking coke and drinking. Angela stays here at Tilden with us.

Garry was here from 11:30 A.M. to 4:30 P.M. coaching us on how to make a complete break with Hugh, that being the only way, he says, to force him to a cure—or rather to cure himself. This is the "tough love" tactic. We all nod, and we know we don't want to shut the door on him absolutely. I finally had to say that I could not refuse to talk to him or see him. I know Garry was disappointed by my attitude. He should be. He's put in a lot of time on this case. He's the expert, and he's highly expert. But I can't cut my kid off. I can't. Not strong enough. Joe was here later, stayed with us through dinner, though he had a later dinner date with a pal, then went out to Broad Beach with his new puppy—staying at our place for the weekend.

We're all depressed here.

Brentwood, Sunday, March 12, 1995

Angela went to Aderno during the day, when Hugh was away in the Valley visiting a friend, and packed a lot of stuff for an extended leave-taking. She told him today she was going to effect a legal separation.

Nance and I looked after Sean for a few hours. No problem—he's a very sunny little chappy and easy to manage—very bright and most interesting to talk to and teach and observe.

N. and I went to mass at 5:30 P.M. at St. Martin of Tours in Brentwood.

Brentwood, Monday, March 13, 1995

N. took Angelina, who came in from the beach with Joe, to the clinic where the cashier—memorably sympathetic and concerned—demanded of Nancy and got, up front, $4,000 for an operation on Angelina's ears at St. Vincent's Hospital downtown.

Claire and I worked on organizing the Tilden office, and also a bit on *Patricios.*

Sean was here all day too.

Hugh still at home feeding his cocaine hallucinations. He watches television and thinks he sees Angela on the screen with other men—calls us constantly on the phone to tell us. The phone calls are a dozen a day, at least, sometimes coming late at night. This is the third or fourth time during the past year that he has coked himself out of reality like this.

Angela took Sean to dinner at some favorite little place of theirs.

N. and I were taken to Remi's restaurant in Santa Monica by Ian and Chrissy Gordon. Home by 11:20 P.M.

Nance walked into the house and picked up another nut call from Hugh.

Brentwood, Tuesday, March 14, 1995

Meeting here (201) with Larry Stern. Nancy and I signed applications for remittance of all my pension funds, SAG, AFTRA, DGA, WGA. I don't feel like working any more. We also discussed a change in the wording of the will: the trustees' authority to withhold payment to Hugh at 40 of his total inheritance, and to substitute a system of small regular payments.

Did a little office arranging and a very little script editing. We drove over to the Wingreens in Studio City [Jason Wingreen, an old colleague of mine, played Archie Bunker's friend and bartender], and they brought us in their car to dinner at the Athenaeum Club on the California Institute of Technology campus in Pasadena. Good dinner in every way, in fine surroundings. Most enjoyable evening. We were back "over the hill," via Coldwater, by 11 P.M. Got sad passing Jimmy Cagney's driveway.

Brentwood, Friday, March 17, 1995

Always in years gone by a big embarrassing blast on this night at our restaurant. Attended only two of them, each time to my regret. But it's all over now. Only time an earthquake did anybody any good when it got me out of there. Total loss on that joint two and a half million.

Barbara Koessler arrived at LAX. [A longtime close friend of Nancy's from Missoula, Montana]. N. met her and took her immediately to see Armando Giuliano, the breast cancer specialist at the John Wayne Cancer Institute. Giuliano told her she did not require a mastectomy. He was one of Hugh's doctors when Hugh had the surgery and radiation for Hodgkin's.

Two sober phone calls from Hugh—very contrite. What do they mean?

I took Angela, Barbara, Nance to dinner at the Bel-Air 9 P.M. to 11 P.M.

Brentwood, Saturday, March 18, 1995

Hugh came here (201) for a family talk—a loving conciliatory talk, he hoped. He left angry. He didn't get what he wanted, i.e., Angela's agreement to return home. She told him that she must

265

see him not only sober, but in a promising frame of mind. He left here, went to Barrington [where his pusher lived], as I predicted he would, bought cocaine and returned here. He would not then leave, and from about 7 P.M. till the following morning roamed the house with staring eyes, gripped by hallucinations of men nearby outside, and men entering the house to see Angela. [I earlier described this night, and the morning of the 19th.]

Brentwood, Monday, March 20, 1995

No change. Hugh is home alone inducing big mood swings with cocaine and booze and putting himself beyond the reach of any rational appeal.

Angela is looking for a rental house—wants to get away from him.

Brentwood, Tuesday, March 21, 1995

Talked to Don Crutchfield, requested him to fax me all notes he had made on Harry Perzigian.

Went to see Lt David Miller, LAPD, head of narcotics for West LA, at Butler Avenue, and gave him all the information I had obtained from Don. I simply had to take this action no matter how unpromising it might be.

Tried to work but could not concentrate. Hugh still making his crazy phone calls, about five an hour, all day.

Brentwood, Wednesday, March 22, 1995

Sent Claire to buy some attachments for a tape recorder to permit recording of Hugh's cocaine-insane phone calls, day and night, in order to have some evidence that he ought to be committed. But I couldn't work out the connections on this Merlin phone system we have. When Hugh next called, I told him I was going to tape him. I made believe I had taped him all day, and this seemed to made him speak more carefully—no blue language, that is—but no less crazily than before. He charges Angela with infidelity to keep the talk on her, and on us, in order to keep it off himself. But is that tactic too rational for him? Because he really is not rational. I calmly insist on talking to him only about himself and cocaine, nothing else—cocaine and what it is doing to him—and he loses no time in hanging up with a curse. Ten minutes later he is ringing our lines again. We all take turns talking to him. His mother is the most patient with him, but Angela is very patient with him too; how she suffers it all I don't know, but of course she loves him.

I like to tell myself and others that I can concentrate on my work in any kind of an uproar, and it's true—I can. But this madness overwhelms me. I'm getting very little of anything done. These are punishing days.

Brentwood, Thursday, March 23, 1995

During the day and on into the night I had an attack of nausea which drained me of all fluids—continual vomiting and evacuating for which I took both Lomotil and Imodium. A parallel discomfort, due to the loss of fluids, was a cramping of the legs for which I took quinine.

Brentwood, Friday, March 24, 1995

Phone calls from Hugh—very sober-sounding. James [mechanic at our car place] helped him retrieve his car from in front of our house, where it has been parked for four days.

I spent the day trying to recover some wellness.

I put the dogs in the Maserati and headed for Malibu at about 2:30 P.M.

Nance brought Sean out in the Land Cruiser. We all, except Angela, had a light dinner here, though I wasn't ready to eat anything.

Little Nancy took Sean next door and watched him till his mother got in at about 11 P.M. Angela had been to dinner and a movie with a friend, Mindy.

Malibu, Saturday, March 25, 1995

Beautiful weather. Angela watching the baby. He had a fever. Angela dispelled any illusion that Hugh might have been sober for a night and a day. She knew he was drinking.

We all started for 5 P.M. mass in Malibu but got turned back in front of a landslide on the Pacific Coast Highway.

Back home, Angela and Nancy went to work on Sean, whose fever had shot up—medicating him and cooling him down by sponging—and by 10:30 had knocked a couple of degrees off his fever.

Angela got another phone call from Hugh in which he fired off some of the mean accusations typical of his boozy mode.

Malibu, Sunday, March 26, 1995

Couldn't leave the house. Up three or four times during the night very ill.

Claire came out here with Luke [Claire's son]. Sean, standing alongside the other baby, was told to kiss his cheek, and instantly did so. Luke accepted quite casually.

We all stayed home for dinner, which was a pick-the-fridge type.

We spoke to Hugh at home at about 9 P.M. He renewed his

demand that Angela and Sean come home, and blamed me for letting them stay with me, keeping him and his family apart. He wasn't loud and crazy, but his mind was fuzzy. We pray for him. Nancy is frequently in tears over him these days—hoping he'll fight free of this, that we all won't lose him in it.

Malibu, Monday, March 27, 1995

I phoned Denise Nicholas and begged off her party tonight. Reason—physically and mentally depressed to sogginess.

Claire came out at about 2 P.M., badly delayed by the latest deluge of dirt that hit the PC Highway near Chautauqua. I let her go at 4 P.M. in order to be on time picking up Luke.

Angela, caught in town, couldn't get back here to Broad Beach till 7:30. She talked to Hugh by phone and found him quite gone again on cocaine. I can't think of a comment to make—can't summon words to compose a reaction.

Nance made a nice chicken dinner for us. She watched the Oscar thing; I did not, though at a distance from the TV set I could hear silly fragments of it.

Malibu, Tuesday, March 28, 1995

Hugh killed himself at home at about 4 P.M.

EPILOGUE

....

"**W**hat brought you to acting?"

The question had been often asked, and I repeated on this occasion an answer I had often given, something about realizing romantic fantasies; interviewers seemed to like it, stale as it was. But this interviewer snapped shut his steno pad and said "Well, let's do something better with our morning, shall we?"

I turned to him in surprise. I deserved the snide rejoinder. I had not even been looking at him. It was a perfect spring morning and we were on the terrace of the Carlton Hotel in Cannes, and the vista of boulevard and boats and sea was too distracting.

"It's not that I mind reporting twaddle" he said with a sour little smile; "the readers love it, silly darlings, but I was told you were the kind of person who might want to give me something fresh."

"Ah—" I said, staring at him now, "well I wonder what else—"

I felt chastened. I had come late to the interview and must have seemed rudely uncaring. I said "Maybe you could think of something fresh for me," trying to be quite sincere, but he popped to his feet looking like an irritated little English thrush and retorted "Maybe you could think of something yourself. Ring me up when you do." And off he went leaving me with two coffees and too many petits pains.

Later on Nancy advised "Next time you're asked what brought you to it, just recall your favorite Jimmy Durante line 'Everybody wants to get into the act!' "

Nancy could always think of apt lines I should have remembered. I wondered whether the thrush would have sat still for that one. Most people do feel the urge to entertain, sing a song at the parlor piano, tell a joke at the office, play in a skit at the club. When we evoke merriment around us, we enjoy deep satisfaction. But then in responding to this urge to entertain, some of us discover that we want to do little else; we are compelled to try to wring a living out of performing. In brief, professional acting is a harmless compulsion gone haywire.

I have heard show business characterized as a refuge for childlike persons in flight from all things harsh and real. "Actors are children!" was the benign judgment of the old movie tycoons when they were contemplating something malignant. Actors themselves own to neurosis: "I guess you gotta be weird to go into our business," gurgles a starlet on one of those late night desk-and-sofa shows.

May I recall two pertinent incidents from the long-ago, when I had no idea of acting for a living, but when I began to suspect that I was a neurotic. "Neurosis" is a term of dysfunction, and it is appropriate. I recall incidents of my past from key lines like "Do you know who you are?" and "What brought you to acting?" There are many key lines; here is one:

"You're not proud you're Irish?"

I Think I'm Outta Here

That key line, a very angry question, was shot at me by a fellow with orange hair and little pale eyes. He had mentioned that he was a stevedore, and he was a formidable specimen, but something told me he was yellow under his pink skin. Still, I should have enthusiastically replied that, like him, I was indeed proud I was Irish. I should have bought drinks and offered a toast to our shared pedigree. But I did not.

I said "Why should I be proud? My derivation has nothing to do with me. Know what I mean?"

This of course was a mistake, bad not only for its immediate consequences but for its underlying assumption that the light of logic is welcomed by any man, provided he is not a moron. It took me years to realize that nearly everyone in the world rejects the light of logic, and detests the bringer of the light, unless it happens to flatter the receiver. I am not talking about our familiar reluctance to face truth. What is truth but a mere point of view uttered with passion and dismissed with a laugh? But logic is no joke; it is a coolly threatening process of establishing bleak certainties by eliminating cozy illusions. The logician is fated to get the Bronx cheer, or even (if he is not cautious and swift) to get mobbed.

But this was before my time of realization: it was 1943, a year of war. The locale was Hoboken, New Jersey. My ship, a freighter, was lying at a Hudson River pier; it had offered a card game, idle conversation, books or simple solitude; but I, being nineteen and energetic at night, had opted for livelier pleasures ashore, which I imagined could be found at a bar named Kelly's. I met there a girl who said she was "pure Estonian." Her father, she told me, seemed pleased that the Russians were beating back the Germans, but her mother wanted Hitler to win. The girl was confused. She said she didn't like going to bars, but what was she to do? She hated the quarreling at home. She was afraid of her mother. (So was I, on hearsay alone.) Naturally she was lonely, she said. This promising turn of conversation was interrupted by the Celt described above, who was on my right at the bar. He leaned in and asked whether he had not seen my Irish face before, somewhere or other. I heard those familiar warning voices in my head. I rejected their advice. I wasn't going to leave a fervently lonely Estonian girl. To the question of whether or not this red-headed mug had ever seen my Irish face before, I said probably not. He proceeded unencouraged to expatiate on racial distinctiveness, the ubiquitous Irish face, the Irish character, and finally Irish pride. My response, which I have already recalled, made him glare ominously, yet on I went: "I hate pride, but if I were going to be proud of anything it would have to be something I'd done myself. Anything else makes no sense. And race pride is kind of stupid, I think. You do see what I mean."

He shook his head as though sadly puzzled. With a smile and shrug he turned away, apparently at a loss to say more, but he suddenly whirled back and walloped me on the jaw, knocking me off my barstool. My brain, though conjuring stars and pinwheels, began instantly to calculate how I might slither across the floor to safety, because I was certain I was going to get an awful kicking. The Estonian belle could not save me and no one else would wish to (I have mentioned that the saloon was Kelly's), but to my surprise I was not kicked. When I raised my face from the tiles I saw why: the pink man was moving quickly toward the front door. I got up and lurched after him. Unfriendly drinkers left their stools and grabbed me by the neck and arms, but I managed to gain the street where I spied Danny Boy rounding a corner at a fast clip. Chase was useless. My only hope of vengeance was to tempt him back, and so with all the breath I had left I roared something vile at him (shame prevents my repeating it) about what he could do to himself and for good measure to all the Irish wherever they were.

It failed to bring him back. I roared the imprecation again. He was out of earshot. But a passerby at close range, hearing me very clearly and seeing me all but pinioned between two grapplers, stepped right over and walloped me on the jaw once again. That was the finisher. I went down and out. A cop drove up, got out of his car, revived me and hauled me to my feet. From the doorway of Kelly's my Baltic beauty lightheartedly but most sincerely advised me to go to bed somewhere. She herself was staying on, she said, the company being merry and the evening young. The passerby, standing near her, yelled "My mother came from Ireland, you louse!" The cop helped me to his car and gave me a lift to the pier. Now that was Hoboken. Let me go on to another key line in another time and place.

Ten years later, when I was living in Ireland, I was at a party in Dublin and found myself in front of a slightly unsteady fellow, a native of the town, and he was snarling "You Yanks bombed the poor Greeks!" (the key line). I should have assumed a rueful expression and said "Tragic—we will always regret that." But no.

"You seem to be confused" I said, looking straight into the unfocused eyes of the *amadan*.[1] "You may be thinking of the Rumanians: you see there were strategic oilfields around Ploesti—" He cut me off with a sound like the snort of a bullock. He wasn't having any Ploesti, and he drew back to have a bash at me. Fortunately he was boiled and also of mushy physique, easy to subdue by merely holding both his wrists. But again I did not reckon with an interloper and one was at hand, a wiry imp of a man who in a flash went directly for my right index finger, grasped it and broke it—and of course fled.

At St. Vincent's Hospital in St. Stephen's Green the young resident who reorganized my finger in splints was an acquaintance of mine, and when I told him what had happened he said "Wasting words again, eh? Ah, poor old chap! You remind me of Leopold Bloom[2] going round the town risking mad dogs and mayhem explaining things nobody wants explained."

---

[1] Irish for a simple big gom.
[2] Central character in Joyce's *Ulysses.*

"Am I like that?" I said. I had to laugh thinking of feckless Bloom in Barney Kiernan's public house explaining to unwilling listeners the phenomenon of an erection in a hanged man. To this day I laugh at myself whenever a glance along the bookshelf happens to touch *Ulysses*. All the same, to this day I can still press a pencil with that assaulted finger and induce a shock up to the elbow. The wages of pedantry is pain.

I pause here a moment to mollify the sensitive Irish reader who may be chafing at such reminiscences. I have no wish to throw a baleful light upon "our own kind." My Irishness had nothing to do with my foolishness. I, in those days, was a provocateur. I could have provoked violence at a Trappist abbey. I was for years a chronic and infuriating argufier, though contentiousness was not a family trait. We had plenty of argument within doors, but all agreed that the guiding rule of life outside was tact. I was the only deviate. I remember a moment at the dining room table—I was in my teens—when my grandfather bawled at me "Goddamit don't be always straightening people out! Let them think whatever bloody rot makes them feel good and say nothing!" The matter is now out of memory but I can still hear a chorus of three or four at the table yelling "Yes!" in unison. And I recall my mother advising me later, softly and sympathetically, "If you want to educate people, be a teacher and get paid for it." Eventually, as I have related, I did become a teacher, briefly.

What was it about me anyway? Did I have a true conscientious wish to improve my fellow man? Who besides me would see it: "It's just that you've always had a big mouth," a friend of boyhood once told me.[3] No doubt; but clearly the big mouth was the consequence of something else.

The comparison with Bloom went to the core of the thing.

---

[3]Gerald Briggs of Forest Hills.

The big mouth was the consequence of a neurotic notion that I ought to straighten people out, and (worse still) that people everywhere were anxious for me to do so. Consequently, like poor Bloom, I lived in a swirl of hostility, but I was luckier than Bloom. I found a way to jump out of it. I escaped into the theatre, and there my neurotic notions never produced enmity, at least never to the point of assault; there, in fact, my neurosis was welcomed as kindred. I shall never forget my first professional play rehearsal at The Gaiety Theatre, Dublin, in the spring of 1951—the immediate cordiality of my new friends the actors: they greeted me like an intimate. Now after all these years I am still unfailingly comforted, encouraged and elated in the company of actors. There is something about the work these dear neurotics do, investigating every kind of human character, that develops in them an extraordinary tolerance, forgiveness and good humor. I commend their company even to normal folk.

So then it was danger that drove me to the safety of the theatre. It was neuroticism that caused the danger. What caused the neuroticism, I shall probably never know. Have I changed with the passing years? No. I do talk less because the sound of my voice saying over and over the things I said years ago embarrasses and depresses me. Why do I say the same things over and over? Because I have never changed my opinions about anything.

Thus the interview begun on the terrace overlooking the Croisette comes finally to a finish. The irritable little thrush is probably still working in London, and if he reads all this he has at last a thoughtful answer to his question. Though I see now that the "fresh angle" has still eluded me. There's nothing really fresh about neurosis.